JOURNAL FOR THE STUDY OF THE NEW TESTAMENT
SUPPLEMENT SERIES
16

Executive Editor, Supplement Series
David Hill

Publishing Editor
David E Orton

JSOT Press
Sheffield

MATTHEW'S COMMUNITY

the
evidence of
his special sayings
material

Stephenson H. Brooks

Journal for the Study of the New Testament
Supplement Series 16

Copyright © 1987 Sheffield Academic Press

Published by JSOT Press
JSOT Press is an imprint of
Sheffield Academic Press Ltd
The University of Sheffield
343 Fulwood Road
Sheffield S10 3BP
England

Typeset by Sheffield Academic Press
and
printed in Great Britain
by Billing & Sons Ltd
Worcester

British Library Cataloguing in Publication Data

Brooks, Stephenson H.
    Matthew's community : the evidence of
    his special sayings material.— (Journal
    for the study of the New Testament
    supplement series; 16).
    1. Bible. N.T. Matthew—Commentaries
    I. Title   II. Series
    226'.206   BS3575.3

    ISBN 1-85075-117-X
    ISBN 1-85075-108-0 Pbk

CONTENTS

ACKNOWLEDGMENTS

The following work is a revision of a Columbia University/Union Theological Seminary dissertation entitled 'The History of the Matthean Community as Reflected in the M Sayings Traditions' (1985). Those who contributed to its completion and revision are numerous, and the following is only a partial list: Raymond E. Brown, J. Louis Martyn, John P. Meier, Wayne Proudfoot, Robert Sommerville, Marion L. Soards, Thomas P. Dozemann, Sharon Humphries Brooks, Michael Gervasio, The Religion Departments of Columbia University and Hamilton College, the Biblical Field of Union Theological Seminary, and especially the students of Hamilton College, through whose eyes I have seen the text of Matthew in a new light.

A special word of thanks is due to the Administration and Board of Trustees of Hamilton College, who contributed significant financial support to the completion of this book.

My thanks is also due to David Hill, editor of the series, for acceptance of my work into the *JSNT* Supplement Series, to the staff of JSOT Press for their careful production of the book, and to David J.A. Clines for proofreading the Greek throughout.

For Oscar and Sarah, who, instead of Mother Goose, read to me from the big green Bible Story Book, thereby giving me both my vocation and avocation.

Chapter 1

INTRODUCTION

1. *The Special Matthean Sayings*

a. *The Problem*
In Matt 23.1-3 we read:

> Then Jesus spoke to the crowds and his disciples saying, 'The
> scribes and the Pharisees sit upon the chair of Moses. Therefore, *do
> and keep whatever they say to you*, but do not do according to their
> works; for *they speak*, yet they do not act...'

In Matthew's text, Jesus affirms the right and authority of the
officials of Judaism to interpret Torah. He warns both the crowds
and the disciples, however, not to practice the example of these
leaders.

Later in the chapter (v. 16), without any indication of a shift in
scene, we read:

> Woe to you, blind guides, *the ones saying*, 'Whoever swears by the
> temple, it is nothing; but whoever swears by the gold of the temple,
> is obligated...'

In this saying, the leaders of Judaism are attacked, not for what they
do, but for what they *say* (cf. *legontes* in v. 16 with *legousin* in v. 3). In
Matt 23.1-3, Jesus affirms both the right of the Jewish leaders to
interpret Torah and the accuracy of their interpretation; then in Matt
23.16-22, he explicitly denies their interpretation.

How would the readers of Matthew's Gospel understand these two
contradictory statements? Would the readers see themselves as under
the teaching authority of certain leaders of a Jewish synagogue
(vv. 1-3) or would they deny the teaching authority of the Jewish
synagogue leadership (vv. 16-22)? Or do both statements belong to
the 'past' of the earthly ministry of Jesus and thus no longer describe
the relationship of the readers to Jewish synagogue authorities?

Verses 1-3 and 16-22 contain statements that imply various and even contrary relationships to Jewish authorities sanctioned by reference to sayings of Jesus. What relationship did Matthew advocate for his readers?

Not only are Matt 23.1-3, 16-22 unique in the Synoptics specifically and in the NT generally, but a large portion of Matt 23 is unparalleled in the Synoptics. Sayings similar to those found in Matt 23 also occur in Matt 5.17–6.18 and Matt 10. These sayings, like those in Matt 23, are also unparalleled and suggest the possibility of various relationships between Matthew's community and Judaism. Unparalleled sayings are also found in Matt 5.5, 7-10, 14-16; 7.6, 15-16a; 11.28-30; 12.34-37; 16.17-19; 18.16-19; 19.10-12.

b. *Theories about the Unparalleled Material in Matthew*

B.H. Streeter, T.W. Manson, and G.D. Kilpatrick investigate the unparalleled material in Matthew (which they designate M) from a source-critical vantage.[1] Chart 1 (C. 1) summarizes the results of the work by Streeter, Manson, and Kilpatrick.[2]

Streeter postulates an M source as part of a 'four source solution' to the Synoptic problem. Within his theory, M plays a subsidiary role to discussions of Proto-Luke and Q.[3] Streeter begins his analysis with the assumption of an oral tradition with its origins in the Jerusalem community prior to the flight to Pella (67-70 CE). He also suggests the existence of a Greek written source associated with Peter and preserved at Antioch. As a result of these assumptions, Streeter defines M as all discourse material peculiar to Matthew, including all Q material different enough from Luke that it necessitates a Qmt hypohesis.[4] Streeter's method derives M by subtracting Mark and Q from the discourses. Based on his observations of conflation of Mark with Q, and L (presumably through Proto-Luke) with Mark, Streeter postulates by analogy that wherever parallel passages of Matthew and Luke show marked division, editorial modification by Matthew is less likely than conflation of Q with a parallel source.

Streeter describes the resulting source as Jewish in character, located in Jerusalem, and associated with the viewpoint of James. In this regard, Streeter asserts:

> It cannot be too emphatically insisted that this element in Matthew reflects, not primitive Jewish Christianity, but a later Judaistic

reaction against the Petro-Pauline liberalism in the matter of the Gentile mission and the observance of the Law.[5]

In Streeter's reconstruction M has parallels to Mark, Q, and L; and includes both parables and discourse. While Streeter states that M may be either a single or several sources, he tends to discuss M as if it were a single source.

Manson investigates the peculiar Matthean sayings as part of his larger project of the exegesis of the Jesus sayings. His works are dominated by a concern for the recovery of authentic Jesus material, and this concern colors his evaluation of M. Manson's description of M is less explicit than Streeter's, but his discussion of M shows that he shares Streeter's definition, 'subtraction method', and theory of conflation of M with other sources, particularly Q.

For Manson, M: (1) reflects a community that is already in some sense a school; (2) shows an animus toward the scribes and Pharisees that did not come from Jesus; (3) contains technical terms parallel to Rabbinic literature; and (4) closely connects with John the Baptist traditions. By describing the community of M as a school, Manson suggests a specific life setting for M. In his second and third observations, he notes a significant contradiction in the content of M, which requires explanation:

> And here we may note the curious fact that this document, which of all our sources, shows by far the greatest respect for the Law (Mt V. 17, 19f) and even for oral tradition (Mt XXIII. 1f), at the same time displays by far the greatest animus against the scribes and Pharisees.[6]

As we note above, Matt 23.1-3 and 23.16 display precisely this type of disjunction.

Manson suggests that M should be dated between 65 and 70 CE (based on Matt 5.23-24; 5.17-20) and that it comes from the Jewish Christian community in Jerusalem. According to Manson, the contents of M should be treated cautiously, more so than Mark or Q, because Jesus' teaching has undergone 'adulteration' from Judaism.[7]

Kilpatrick's is the latest and most complete treatment of M. He gives four types of evidence that lead him to the reconstruction of M as a source: (1) orderly form and structure; (2) an editorial style observable in Q and non-Q materials that indicates Matthew's redaction; (3) evidence of conflation and other forms of editing; (4)

stereotyped explanation of several parables. In working out his method Kilpatrick relies primarily, like Streeter and Manson, on the 'subtraction method'. After a careful analysis of Matt 5-6, he employs what may be called a 'rule of plausibility':

> Once the theory of a third source has been admitted to be the most probable explanation of some features of the Sermon, we can with more confidence assume its existence in other contexts where an independent proof would be much more difficult to supply.[8]

Kilpatrick considers no hypothesis other than a written source to explain what he perceives as an underlying pattern in the Sermon on the Mount. He then proceeds on the assumption of a written M to isolate other traditional material throughout Matthew. His resulting summarizing description of the source M as fragmentary with no coherent structure, theme or ideology suggests, against his own assumption, that the hypothesis of a single source underlying the unparalleled material in Matthew is unnecessary. The case for a written M is not demonstrated by Kilpatrick's work; and this negative conclusion calls into question his results in specific verses.

Certain limitations particularly with regard to the presuppositions that govern these studies help to guide a new approach to the M material. Reliance on a theory of the geographical distribution of early Christianity along with a presupposition of sources associated with these locales to account for pre-Gospel tradition imposes preconceptions developed primarily from documents outside the Gospels themselves. For example, is it the case that the M material represents a re-Judaizing of the dominical sayings, or are the so-called Jewish elements in M actually representative of an earlier or original stage of the transmission of the sayings? The new approach undertaken here begins with a separation of pre-Matthean from Matthean material and then proceeds to a hypothesis to account for the isolated material and its inclusion in the First Gospel. In what follows, we will outline such an approach before proceeding to a critical analysis of the M material.

These source-critical theories about the unparalleled material in Matthew, while limited with regard to their presuppositions and methods, encounter within the material itself the question of the relationship of the bearers or originators of this material to Judaism. How is it that this material preserves both a clear Jewish character and an opposition to Jewish leaders? These studies all attempt to account for these problems by referring the material to a single level of pre-Matthean tradition.

On the basis of these surveys of problems in the text of Matthew and critical theories about the unparalleled sayings in Matthew, we may explore the following thesis: An investigation of the unparalleled sayings in Matthew holds promise for understanding the history of the relationship between Matthew's community and Judaism.

c. *Identification and Isolation of M Sayings*
Source-critical theories have proven unsatisfactory in their attempt to explain the *unparalleled sayings in Matthew* as deriving from a written source, M. Without presupposing any particular source theory for this material, we observe that the sayings found only in Matthew may be accounted for in two ways: (a) these sayings may be 'redactional' in the sense of belonging to the material originated by Matthew as editor and author of the Gospel; (b) these sayings may come from pre-Matthean material. A single saying as it is attested by the present text of Matthew may include elements of both (a) and (b). Therefore, we may be able to separate the Matthean elements of a particular saying from its pre-Matthean form. Let us expand our remarks on these two ways of accounting for the sayings in Matthew.

(a) In this study, which deals with the separation of Matthean from pre-Matthean material, the term 'redactional' will be used to refer to several types of unparalleled material.[9] 'Redactional' may indicate what Matthew, the author of the text, added when he retouched a conceptual unit that existed prior to his own writing in either oral or written form. The term may also refer to complete conceptual units that Matthew constructed out of traditional ideas; in other words he may have taken the germ of an idea, which he then developed in his own way. Finally, the term 'redactional' may cover complete conceptual units that Matthew created independently. Any saying in Matthew that is unparalleled by the other Synoptics may be in part or totally redactional.

(b) There are unparalleled sayings in Matthew that were taken by Matthew from a tradition or traditions available only to him among the Evangelists. Complete sayings may have been taken and left unaltered or sayings may have been edited in order to fit the literary and ideological context of Matthew. All complete unparalleled sayings that can be demonstrated not to be from Matthew as well as sayings that can be critically recovered as pre-Matthean by the removal of redactional elements will be referred to as 'M' sayings in the present study. For the purposes of this study, the term *traditional* will refer to any pre-Matthean material, whether oral or written. It may be possible to recover and group together individual traditional sayings that exhibit a common ideology and *life setting* and, therefore, represent a single tradition. The present work restricts the use of the term 'tradition' to a specific set of ideas adhered to by a specific community at a specific time and place. If there are demonstrable social and historical connections between individual traditions, it may be possible to align traditions chronologically into a 'history of traditions'. Finally, such a history of traditions implies a history of the person or persons who preserved the traditions over time, i.e. a community history. *Source* will refer exclusively to a written document. A source may represent a single tradition and/or incorporate multiple traditions. For example the Gospel of Mark is regarded by many critics as a source for the Gospel of Matthew. Studies in Mark also show the probability that Mark employed traditions in the composition of his Gospel. Indications of editorial connection and peculiarities of a written style distinct from the author of the Gospel may indicate a source.[10]

As a sub-category of this second option, we should pause to consider the theory advanced by some critics who work both in Matthew and in Q that certain of these sayings are derived by Matthew from a source designated Qmt. This recension of Q is regarded as being available to Matthew as part of the tradition of his community. Such a hypothesis will be considered in this study as an explanation for an M saying only when significant continuity can be shown in style, vocabulary, and content between a doubly attested saying (Matthew and Luke) and a singly attested saying (Matthew), although even then other solutions are possible, e.g. Matthew creating a saying in imitation of Q. We will assign singly attested passages to Q if they cohere stylistically and theologically with the rest of Q, if they are found in Q contexts, and if adequate arguments can be advanced for the omission of the passages by one of the Evangelists. The hypothesis of a Qmt does not serve as a beginning point for investigating the unparalleled sayings in Matthew.[11]

This study presupposes that a single author, whom for convenience we will designate as Matthew, is responsible for the present text of the First Gospel. *Several criteria will be used for separating M sayings from the work of Matthew.* First, a comparison of Mark and Luke with Matthew will help. Second, internal tensions (aporias), as detected through formal or conceptual inconsistencies, indicate the possible reworking of material by Matthew even where parallels are unavailable for comparison. Third, the style and vocabulary of Matthew, determined through comparisons of Matthew with Mark and Luke, will be used to distinguish sayings that differ from Matthew's usual style and word usage. Stylistically incongruent sayings will be held as potentially from M. Fourth, the content of the sayings will be compared with indications of Matthew's ideology expressed both in the immediate context and elsewhere in the Gospel. Discrepancies in ideology may indicate the presence of pre-Matthean sayings. Only upon a confluence of factors derived from the application of these criteria will a saying be designated M. All M sayings isolated by this method will be both unparalleled and traditional.[12] Let us consider some of these criteria in more detail.

The Use of Parallels as the First Step in Isolating M Sayings
Three types of sayings become apparent when the Synoptics are compared. Some sayings occur in all three Gospels; some occur in two of the Gospels; some are attested in only one Gospel. This basic observation has led to multiple hypotheses about the relationships, literary or oral, among the Synoptic Gospels; hypotheses which we may survey briefly. Literarily, Mark appears to be the middle term between Matthew and Luke, and dominant opinion in current scholarship is that both Matthew and Luke knew a document similar to our Mark.[13] The present study relies on this hypothesis, while recognizing the possibility of oral or written developments of Mark's text within Matthew's community prior to his writing.

The second class of material in Matthew (i.e. doubly attested material) is paralleled in Luke. Majority scholarly opinion hypothesizes that this material (mostly sayings) comes from a tradition used both by Matthew and Luke, designated Q. The hypothesis of a written Q would account for the precise verbal agreement between many parallel passages in Matthew and Luke. Evidence of precise verbal agreement, however, is meager in enough passages to raise the possibility that portions of Q were in oral form. Whether or to what degree Q was oral or written is not of major consequence for the method employed in the present study.[14] (Nevertheless, obvious complexities in the relationship of the Synoptics will be noted within each passage discussed.)

The following investigation of Matt 5-6; 10; 23 will show that an exclusive appeal to literary sources to solve the problem of Synoptic relationships does not account for the evidence in the text of the First Gospel.[15] The form of Q, as well as of Mark, available to Matthew may have been elaborated prior to Matthew's composition under the influence of oral traditions. A full discussion of that issue, however,[16] would require, not only the isolation and analysis of M sayings, but also an exploration of their relationship to both Mark and Q,[17] and so lies beyond the confines of this study.

The Use of Style as a Means of Distinguishing Redactional from Traditional Material

Once parallels have helped to isolate sayings that are peculiar to the First Gospel, our next path is to determine whether those sayings are traditional (and therefore possibly from M) or redactional. For isolating tradition from redaction, the method employed here will rely on observing aporias or disjunctions in the text. Aporias may be formal (i.e. detectable in the grammar of the sentence) or conceptual (i.e. detectable in the flow of thought from one sentence to the next). In either case, *a disjunction in the text that would not be expected from an author who is composing freely* will distinguish sayings that merit further investigation. Obviously such a criterion occurs to the modern critic who is interested in the investigation of the Gospels for purposes of historical reconstruction. The ancient reader or even the Evangelists themselves may not have perceived or been interested in what appear as disjunctions to us.

The style criterion for separating tradition from redaction allows two distinctions. First, it is *hypothetically* possible to separate tradition from redaction by determining the characteristic grammatical and syntactical constructions used by Matthew as compared with Mark and Luke. In *practice*, the effectiveness of such statistical observations has been limited, because studies of style have confined their observations to categories that are insufficiently nuanced to discriminate tradition from redaction.[18] Comparison is needed between Matthew's styles in paralleled and unparalleled material. Even the most scrupulous stylistic comparison leaves open the probability that Matthew's traditions influenced his own style and/or were adapted to that style.

A second type of stylistic observation is more fruitful. Some patterns or parallelisms discerned within the text of the First Gospel appear to be disrupted by Matthew's editorial hand.[19]

The Use of Vocabulary as a Criterion for Isolating M Sayings

As with style, statistical approaches to vocabulary can be misleading. The comparison of vocabulary statistics requires the observation of at least three categories of word usage: (1) usage derived from known traditions (Mark, Q); (2) usage added to known traditions; (3) usage in unparalleled material. Words added to a known tradition are most likely redactional. Category 3 requires careful survey to determine whether the words are redactional or traditional. Patterns of word usage, rather than discrete observations, form the strongest foundation for analysis.

Within an analysis of vocabulary, sensitivity must be shown not only to individual words, but to phrases that denote significant concepts. For example, the phrase 'Kingdom of Heaven' characterizes Matthew's Gospel. Obviously, when we distinguish Matthean vocabulary, the separate words 'kingdom' and 'heaven' would not carry the same significance as the entire phrase. The criterion of vocabulary supports other criteria and helps to analyze aporiae.

The Use of Content as a Criterion for Isolating M Sayings

Two questions best illustrate the employment of this criterion. Is the content of the saying disjunctive with the emphases of its immediate literary context? Is it at odds with the author's emphases observable in the composition of the Gospel as a whole?

To insure as critical an isolation of M as possible, *only complete sayings* that can be established as both unparalleled and traditional will be designated M. The method necessarily emphasizes somewhat one-sidedly the discontinuity and uniqueness of the sayings designated M. Matthew probably incorporates tradition into his Gospel that cannot be critically distinguished from his own style or interests, but our desire to be as certain as possible forces us to consider only what can be distinguished. Consequently, no claim will be made that the M sayings delimited here embody the full extent of special traditional sayings available to Matthew.

2. *The Use of the M Sayings*
to Reconstruct the Matthean Community and its History

a. *Other Areas of New Testament Research*

Although the method employed in this study seeks to develop a
hypothesis about the history of the Matthean community primarily
from evidence derived from the M sayings, any attempt at reconstruct-
ing the history of the Matthean community is affected by conceptions
about types of Christian communities in the first century.

W. Bauer's work in *Orthodoxy and Heresy in Earliest Christianity*
set the stage for new approaches to the development of early
Christianity. Bauer's attempt to show that in the first two Christian
centuries so-called 'heresies' did not constitute the secondary
manifestation of early Christianity in many areas, but rather the
original, has been both modified and challenged.[20] Although Bauer's
work does not apply directly to this study, his thesis continues to
influence many of the scholars discussed here. Subsequent studies by
H. Koester, G. Strecker, and H.J. Schoeps extend Bauer's insights
and point out that the development of early Christianity was not a
straight line leading from Jerusalem to Rome, but was characterized
instead by many centers of Jewish/Gentile Christianity, each with its
own traditions and practices.[21] In short, these studies forbid the
convenient assumption of a simple development of early Christianity
from Jewish/Palestinian to Gentile/Hellenistic churches.

In a recent study of early Christianity at Rome, R.E. Brown
discusses a range of possibilities based less on the ethnic composition
of early Christian groups and more on detectable viewpoints toward
Law and Temple among early Christian missionaries, evidenced in
the NT.[22] He denotes four types that help to define a range of
possibilities. (1) Jewish Christians and their Gentile converts who
practice full observance of the Mosaic Law, including circumcision,
as necessary for salvation. (2) Jewish Christians and their Gentile
converts who do not insist on circumcision as salvific for Gentile
Christians but require them to keep some purity laws. (3) Jewish
Christians and their Gentile converts who require neither circumcision
nor observance of Jewish purity laws regarding food. (4) Jewish
Christians and their Gentile converts who do not insist on
circumcision and Jewish food laws and see no abiding significance in
the cult of the Jerusalem Temple.

J. Louis Martyn in work on the Fourth Gospel suggests a history of
the relationships of a single early Christian group to Jewish

institutions.[23] Martyn finds evidence in John of a group of Christian Jews who attend synagogue with non-Christian Jews in relative peace while carrying on a mission activity. At a later time, this group begins to experience social dislocation due to conflicts developing with other synagogue members and synagogue authorities. Finally, at least part of this group separates from the synagogue, or is expelled, and becomes identifiable as a Jewish Christian community.

The works by Brown and Martyn in other NT literature describe possibilities of early Christian relationships to the institutions of Judaism. Brown points out the crucial concerns of Law and Temple as dividing points between various Christian groups. Martyn explores the relationship between Johannine Christians and the synagogue in their city. The Johannine circle becomes a separate community primarily through self- definition by means of Christology. Whereas at Rome, Brown finds that questions of *orthopraxis* are central in defining the relationships of early Christians to Jewish institutions, Martyn finds that questions of *orthodoxy* dominate the Johannine scene.[24]

b. *Redactional Studies in Matthew*

In redactional studies of Matthew, the issue of the relationship between Matthew's readers and Jewish institutions emerges as a focus of debate. The importance of a careful delineation of traditional and redactional material in the unparalleled sayings is central to a resolution of the problems of the text of Matthew. In three essays, for example, G. Bornkamm presents three different answers to the question of the Matthean community's participation in the Jewish synagogue services.[25] The first of these, 'End-Expectation and Church in Matthew,' proposes that Matthew's community exists within the Jewish synagogue. 'Der Auferstandene und der Irdische' depicts the community as showing signs of significant strain with the synagogue, while still maintaining its position within the synagogue. Finally, in 'Die Binde- und Lösegewalt in der Kirche des Matthäus,' Bornkamm sees the Matthean community as separated from the Jewish synagogue. If we apply Martyn's categories to Bornkamm's work, these positions allow three options for describing the social setting of Matthew and his readers. (1) they are a Christian Jewish group exhibiting no signs of significant dislocation with the Jewish synagogue; (2) they are a Christian Jewish group beginning to find themselves in a situation of ideological estrangement, which is not yet significant enough to warrant separation from the synagogue; (3) they are a Jewish Christian community separated from the primary social institution of Judaism in their city. In the first option, Bornkamm relies on evidence from Matt 5.17-20; 10; 23; 24; in the second, he uses Matt 18.15-20; in the third, Matt 28.16-20. The preponderance of these texts come from unparalled sayings.

Clearly, all three options cannot apply to a single unified group at a single point in its history. The three essays also demonstrate that hypotheses of the relationship between Matthew's community and Judaism depend on analysis of Law, Ecclesiology, and Christology in the First Gospel. Bornkamm's studies, and those that have followed each of his three options, show that a clear delineation of tradition and redaction in the unparalleled sayings is essential to an accurate portrait of Matthew's readers and of the history of Matthew's community.[26]

3. *Procedure for the Study*

Chapters 2, 3, and 4 will isolate the M sayings in Matt 5.17-6.18; 10; 23, respectively. Each chapter will be organized according to thought units made apparent by literary shifts in the text. Within each section of the text, first a translation will be given, followed by an identification of four types of material, always in the same order: (a) verses with parallels in Mark; (b) verses with parallels in Luke; (c) verses likely to come from Matthew; (d) verses with a strong possibility of containing an M saying.

Chapter 5 will accumulate the results from these chapters, describe the material, and establish probable life settings for the sayings or groups of sayings. Use of the preliminary results from Chapter 5 will be an aid in Chapter 6 in recovering other M sayings that may occur throughout the Gospel.[27] Whereas the unparalleled material in Matt 5.17-6.18; 10; 23 occurs in contexts where the use of parallels, style, vocabulary, and content can be employed with relative ease, there are other unparalleled sayings in Matthew in contexts where those criteria are more difficult to utilize. These additional M sayings will also be described and assigned life settings. Chapter 7 will relate the results of the analysis to a hypothesis that suggests a reconstruction of the history of the community and accounts for the tradition(s) recovered.

4. *Conclusions*

In 1959, V. Taylor remarked:

> It is desirable that M should be investigated more closely. This task has been waiting for a generation, and it will always prove difficult, since the sayings are found in Matthew only.[28]

The present study may be seen as the beginning of the systematic inquiry into the unparalleled material in Matthew called for by Taylor a generation ago. It is only a beginning. A complete treatment of the unparalleled material in Matthew would require at least a consideration of the parable material. This inquiry does not involve the parables for three reasons. (1) The unparalleled sayings appear to hold the most explicit material concerning relationships between the Matthean community and Judaism. It is precisely this type of problem, first recognized in Matt 23 that is the driving question of the inquiry. (2) While it is true that parables are formally dominical sayings, recent scholarship on the parable literature has increasingly seen the parable as a special literary form unto itself.[29] Accordingly, a somewhat different method from the one employed here would be necessary for a thorough treatment of the unparalleled parables in Matthew. (3) A complete treatment of the unparalleled parables in Matthew would require an additional study of monograph length. It seemed better in conceptualizing this study to undertake an investigation of the unparalleled Matthean material only one step at a time.[30]

The following study is undertaken primarily as an attempt to understand statements in the text of Matthew that suggest various relationships to Judaism, each of which is sanctioned by reference to the authority of Jesus as the speaker. The study presupposes that an essential ingredient for understanding the First Gospel is an understanding of the social and historical situation of Matthew and his original readers. In an attempt to describe that situation concretely the following thesis is pursued throughout this inquiry. An investigation of the unparalleled sayings in Matthew holds promise for understanding the history of the relationship between Matthew's community and Judaism, and thus holds promise for a better understanding of Matthew's Gospel by the modern reader.

Chapter 2

MATT 5.17–6.18

1. *Matt 5.17-20*

Translation

(17) Do not think that I came to destroy the Law or the prophets! I did not come to destroy but to fulfill. (18) For, amen, I say to you, until heaven and earth pass away not even an iota or a hook will pass away from the Law until everything has happened. (19) Therefore, if anyone abolishes a single one of the least of these commandments and teaches others likewise then he will be called least in the Kingdom of Heaven. But if anyone should do one of the least of these commandments and teach others likewise he will be called great in the Kingdom of Heaven. (20) For, I say to you that unless your righteousness surpasses greatly that of the scribes and Pharisees, you will not enter into the Kingdom of Heaven.

Isolation Leading to M Sayings
Summary: (a) No verses have parallels in Mark; (b) v. 18 has a parallel in Luke; (c) vv. 17, 20 are likely to be from Matthew; (d) v. 19 has a strong possibility of containing an M saying.[1]

(b) Verse 18
Another version of the verse occurs in Luke 16.17 (C. 3). The verbal agreement suggests that both Luke 16.17 and Matt 5.18 depend on the same tradition. Therefore, v. 18 almost certainly comes from Q.[2] The presence in Matthew of the introduction (*amēn legō hymin*, 'amen, I say to you') and conclusion (*heōs an panta genētai*, 'until everything has happened') calls for comment. Outside of 5.18, the two phrases occur together in Matthew only at 24.34, where they appear to be adopted from Mark 13.30 (see also Luke 21.32). Matthew probably provided the introduction and conclusion in 5.18

with the model of Matt 24.34 (Mark 13.30) in mind. Verse 18 comes from Q and, in its present form, has been edited by Matthew.

(c) Verses 17, 20

Verse 17 contains elements of Matthean style. Matthew frequently begins a sentence using *mē* and the second person plural (imperative or subjunctive; 6.19; 7.1; 7.6; 10.26).[3] These sentences are negative command forms. The *mē* and second person plural verb are integral to the syntax of the sentence. On the other hand, the use of *mē* and the second person plural subjunctive (*nomisēte*) followed by *hoti* occurs only in v. 17 and in 10.34-36. This introductory formula is separable from the main clause that follows. Comparison of 10.34-36 with Luke 12.48-51 shows that the original saying was probably found in Q without the introductory formula *mē nomisēte hoti*, 'do not think that'. Similarly, the same introductory formula in v. 17 probably comes from Matthew.

This leaves open the possibility that the remainder of v. 17, 'I came...', was available to Matthew as an M saying. The vocabulary, however, appears to be Matthean. 'The Law or the prophets' designates the entirety of the Hebrew scriptures, which Matthew understands to be the revelation of God's will (Matt 7.12; 11.13; 22.40).[4] The use of *plēroō* 'to fulfill' in formula citations refers to the messianic fulfillment of prophetic promises (1.22; 2.15, 17; 4.14; 8.17; 12.17; 13.35; 26.54, 56).[5]

Notwithstanding these considerations, J.P. Meier suggests that pre-Matthean tradition underlies v. 17 (C. 4). Meier's reasoning includes:

1. Matthew added the *mē nomisēte* to a tradition received in the form of an *ēlthon*-word;
2. *Katalyō* makes perfect sense with *nomos*, but its meaning is unsure with *prophētai*; thus Matthew, whose interest in eschatological fulfillment is demonstrated in his addition (18d), is probably responsible for the inclusion of 'prophets';
3. *Plēroō* was substituted by Matthew for *poieō* (or *phylassō*, *tēreō*) in the original logion.[6]

Meier's argument hinges upon the conceptual tension created by the juxtaposition of the two infinitives and their objects in v. 17. Does the verse as it now stands depart from Matthew's editorial activity both within the pericope and in other passages? As Meier himself shows, the verse fits the redactional interests displayed in Matthew's reworking of v. 18 (the additions are in v. 18a,d). *Ho nomos ē hoi prophētai* is treated in this context as a *single concept* designating the entire revelation of God's will. Further, Matthew's redaction of a Q saying (Luke 16.16a) in Matt 11.13 shows the use of unusual verbs to describe the Law and the prophets (C. 5). Here the verb *prophēteuō* has as its subject 'the prophets and the Law'. The combination of Law with 'to prophesy' does not occur in the Lukan parallel, nor is it attested elsewhere in the LXX or NT. In Matt 11.13, Matthew has identified a limit for the prophetic activity of the old revelation. Matt 5.17 combined with 5.18a,d designates Jesus as the one who eschatologically fulfills the Law and the prophets. The evidence of Matthew's mode of expression in Matt 11.13 reduces the weight of the supposed aporia in 5.17. A clear case for an underlying M saying cannot be demonstrated on the basis of this evidence.[7]

Verse 20 contains little if any indication that a traditional saying underlies Matthew's text. Nothing here distinguishes v. 20 from Matthew's style. The terminology is also typical of Matthew. The phrase, 'to enter into the Kingdom of Heaven', is attested in Matthew at 7.21; 18.3; 19.23-24, as are similar phrases in 7.13; 18.8, 9; 19.17; 21.31; 23.13; 25.21, 23.[8] Matthew also tends to designate the opponents of Jesus as 'Pharisees'. Matthew takes the word from Mark ten times, deleting only two uses in Mark 7.3, 5. In three instances where Mark uses scribes (3.22; 12.28; 13.35), Matthew has Pharisees. In three texts from Q (Matt 3.7 par Luke 3.7; Matt 12.38 par Luke 11.29; Matt 23.13 par Luke 11.52) Matthew has Pharisees, and Luke does not; although Luke, like Matthew, favors the term, using it 27 times. The fact that Matthew and Luke use the term in common only at Matt 23.25 par Luke 11.39 and Matt 23.23 par Luke 11.42 indicates the probability that Q did not contain the same emphasis on the opposition of the Pharisees developed independently by both Matthew and Luke.[9] Matthew uses Pharisees in unparalleled texts at 5.20; 9.34; 15.12; 16.11, 12; 21.45; 23.2, 15; 27.62. In Matthew, there are 26 uses of the word. He tends, by comparison with his known sources, to increase the use of the term Pharisee. While a statistical survey does not rule out the possibility that some of Matthew's independent uses are from pre-Matthean tradition, the lack of other indications of the use of tradition in 5.20 suggests that Matthew is responsible for the term in this use.[10]

Finally, v. 20 acts as an editorial bridge to the material in 5.21-48.[11]
The 'I' saying could be a later addition to a pre-Matthean logion, but
the close association of the verse with Matthew's interests and
editorial activity makes it critically impossible to discern an M saying
in v. 20. The greater probability is that the verse comes from
Matthew himself.[12]

(d) Verse 19
There are several indications that v. 19 is traditional. In a Greek text
two options for the reference of the pronoun exist: *toutōn* may either
have an antecedent (a plural would be expected by the Greek reader)
in the immediately preceding context; or *toutōn* may refer forward.[13] In
the immediately preceding v. 18, no plural antecedent agrees
grammatically with the *toutōn* of v. 19, nor can one be found in v. 17.
The suggestion of some critics has been, therefore, to understand the
entolon touton as a reference to the 'single iota or single hook' of the
Law in v. 18. Such an interpretation, while it does not precisely fit
the grammar of the Greek sentences, recognizes that in Judaism the
Law (*torah*, *nomos*) was made up of many commandments (*miṣvot*,
entolai) and that two concrete metaphors for the Law (iota or hook)
have been used previously. Although such an explanation may apply
for Matthew's understanding of the text, the grammatical problem
engendered by the lack of an antecedent for *toutōn* may be one
indication that Matthew used an earlier tradition.[14]

The verse contains a notably rare word in Matthew, *lyō*. *Lyō*
occurs four times in Matthew. Matt 21.2 is taken over from Mark
11.2 and has the simple meaning 'to untie' (see also Luke 19.30). Of
specific interest are two instances where *lyō* has a meaning similar to
the use in v. 19 (C. 6). All three uses of *lyō* are peculiar to Matthew.[15]
Matt 16.19b and 18.18 are variants of the same legal saying. In these
two verses, *lyō* is best understood to mean 'to loose'. The legal
principle gives the authority on earth to determine what will be true
in the Kingdom of Heaven. In form, 5.19 is also a legal sentence that
enjoins the 'loosing' of commandments at the peril of affecting one's
place in the Kingdom. Since *lyō* appears only in these verses, which
are peculiar to Matthew's Gospel, we have no uses of the term
inserted by Matthew into Markan or Q material with which to
compare them. The presence of the use in only unparalleled sayings
may indicate that here Matthew uses an M saying. When coupled
with the aporia noted in the analysis of *toutōn* this evidence indicates

the probability of an M saying contained in v. 19. In this regard, 'Kingdom of Heaven', also calls for comment. Matthew's preference for the term is indicated by his using it 32 times, as opposed to his using 'Kingdom of God' five times (four times in parallel with Mark or Luke, once independently). The use of Kingdom of Heaven appears to be unique to Matthew in the NT. The term may be due exclusively to Matthew's redaction, or it may be a traditional term taken from the theological vocabulary of his community; its presence in v. 19 does not necessitate the abandonment of the finding that v. 19 probably contains an M saying.[16]

Before v. 19 can be designated M, consideration must be given to the suggestion by several critics that vv. 18 and 19 stood together as a unit in Q or in Qmt.[17] In determining whether vv. 18 and 19 are part of a unit of Q material that came to Matthew already joined, stylistic continuity offers little help, because the Q text cannot be precisely reconstructed by a comparison of Matt 5.18 with Luke 16.17. Grammatical disjunction provides firmer ground. Even in a recon-structed unit comprised by vv. 18 and 19 stripped of redactional elements, there remains the disjunction created by the lack of an antecedent for *toutōn* (C. 7).[18] The disjunction has been explained by the hypothesis that the two verses were joined in a setting where an argument between a Palestinian and Hellenistic community raged. This interpretation began with Bultmann and has been followed by many commentators after him (e.g. Barth, Trilling, and Meier). If the grammatical problem can be explained on the grounds of editorial work on an earlier structure, such a solution is preferable to one that relies on an undemonstrated life setting.[19]

Finally, and most conclusively, the contents of the two logia set them apart. Verse 18b,c supposes the eternal continuation of heaven and earth as witnesses to the eternal validity of the Law. [20] On the other hand, in v. 19 the concept of the Kingdom refers to eschatological judgment and implies that the place of the Law will be different in the end time. The difference in conceptualities between the two verses is most apparent in the absolute demand of v. 18 and the comforting 'curse' of v. 19. The curse of v. 19 assigns place in the Kingdom, not exclusion from it. If vv. 18 and 19 were originally part of the same saying, we would anticipate a more stringent view in v. 19.[21] These considerations, along with the evidence of style, grammar, and content, justify the exclusion of v. 19 from Q. Therefore, Matt 5.19 is a singly attested saying and has met the criteria for inclusion in the M sayings material.

Conclusions
(b) By comparison with Luke 16.17, Matt 5.18b,c belongs to Q.
(c) Style, vocabulary, and consistency with redaction evident in the
Gospel indicate that Matthew wrote vv. 17, 18a,d, 20. (d) Analysis of
an aporia supported by both grammar and content isolates v. 19 as
an M saying.

2. *Matt 5.21-26*

Translation

> *Antithesis 1.* (21) You have heard that it was said to the ancients,
> 'Do not kill, whoever kills is liable to the judgment'. (22) But I say
> to you that everyone who is angry with his brother is liable to the
> judgment; whoever says to his brother '*raka*', is liable to the court;
> whoever says '*fool*', is liable to the Gehenna of fire. (23) If,
> therefore, you are taking your gift up to the altar and if you
> remember that your brother has something against you, (24) leave
> your gift there before the altar and go, first be reconciled to your
> brother, and then when you have come offer your gift. (25) Make
> friends quickly with your opponent while he is with you in the
> road, in order that the opponent may not hand you over to the
> judge and the judge to the officer and you will be cast into prison.
> (26) Amen, I say to you, you will not come out from there until you
> have paid the last quarter of a cent.

Isolation Leading to M Sayings
Summary: (a) No verses have parallels in Mark; (b) vv. 25-26 have a
parallel in Luke; (c) no verses are likely to be from Matthew; (d) vv.
23-24 have a strong possibility of containing an M saying; verses 21-
22 have a strong possibility of containing an M saying.

(b) Verses 25-26
Another version of Matt 5.25-26 is found in Luke 12.58-59 (C. 8).
The agreement in vocabulary and order within the saying indicates
that Q underlies both texts.

(d) Verses 23-24
A similar text occurs in Mark 11.25 (C. 8). A literary relationship is
ruled out by the lack of verbal agreement between the two texts; and
Matt 5.23-24 differs in content from the Markan parallel to such an
extent that it is difficult to reconstruct a common tradition. In

addition to the lack of agreement in vocabulary, the two sayings reflect completely different contexts: the Matthean text supposes knowledge of the temple cult, while the Markan text is set in the worship of the community and contains no reference to temple sacrifice.[22]

A disjunction or seam between vv. 22 and 23 favors the assignment of vv. 23-24 to tradition. Grammatically, the disjunction is noticeable by the shift from the second person plural command (v. 21 *ēkousate*) to the second person singular (v. 23 *prospherēs*) along with the proper pronouns. There is also a shift in scene from court proceedings in vv. 21-22 to a cultic setting over which there is no indication that a court has jurisdiction. The disjunction in both grammar and content is strong evidence that the saying comes from tradition, not free editorial creation, and may therefore be assigned to the M sayings.[23]

Verses 21-22

The seam between v. 22 and v. 23 helped to establish the traditional nature of vv. 23-24. It did not establish, however, whether vv. 21-22 were produced by Matthew himself or belong to the M sayings. Verses 21-22 constitute a unity in style (C. 9). The antithetical formula (*ēkousate hoti errethē . . . egō de legō hymin*) occurs only in Matt 5.21-22, 27-28, 33-34, 38-39, 43-44 in the entire NT, and is therefore stylistically unique.[24]

Verse 21 consists of an introductory formula followed by a direct statement. The first clause of the direct statement comes from the LXX of Exod 20.13 (C. 9).[25] The second clause (*hos . . . krisei*) is without parallel. In form the second clause is a legal rule employing typical LXX style.[26] Verse 22 consists of three clauses that may also be classified as legal rules, and is unified in style with v. 21.[27]

The antithetical formula in vv. 21a and 22a is one stylistic device that ties the two verses together. Furthermore, the relative clauses in 21c, 22c,e,g are constructed in parallel to each other (C. 9). The *pas ho* may be present as a variation on the *hos d'an* in 22c; not as a disruption to the pattern which might be taken to indicate a second editor from the originator. The phrases beginning with *enochos* (21d, 22d,f,h) are also constructed in parallel to each other.

Enochos 'to be liable to' followed by the dative regularly designates the court that tries an offender.[28] In v. 22h the use of the accusative with *eis* is a functional substitute for the dative and should also be understood as designating a court.[29] The sense of the Greek syntax leads to the expectation that *krisis* 'judgment', *synedrion* 'court', and *geenna tou pyros* 'Gehenna of fire' all designate courts.

Krisis occurs in Matthew ten times. One group of uses appears to come from Q, where the formula *en hēmerą kriseōs/en tę krisei* designates the judgment in the coming Day of the Lord (Matt 10.15; 11.22, 24 par Luke 10.12, 14; Matt 12.41, 42 par Luke 11.31). Matt 12.36, although not paralleled in Luke, probably belongs to this group either as Matthew's own adoption of the formula from Q or perhaps as a Q saying not used by Luke. A second use of *krisis* to mean simply 'justice' occurs in Matt 12.18, 20 (a citation of Isa 42.1-4) and in Matt 23.23. The closest parallel in meaning to Matt 5.22h is in Matt 23.33, where the phrase *krisis tou geenna* refers to the eschatological court of Gehenna. This last passage is unparalleled.[30] None of the uses of *krisis* in Matthew can be assigned with confidence to the redactor. Clearly, *krisis* in Matthew usually carries with it an eschatological reference. Further, Matthew usually depends on a source when using *krisis*.

The parallel to *krisis* in the third *enochos* phrase (22f) is *synedrion*. Within Matthew, and also the NT outside of this passage, *synedrion* refers to the Jewish court in Jerusalem, except in Matt 10.17 (par Mark 13.9), where the plural probably refers to local Jewish courts. The use corresponds to *m. Sanh.* 1.6; 4.3, where both the supreme court of 71 and the local courts of 23 are referred to as *sanhedrin* (the Hebrew adaptation of the Greek).[31]

The basic meaning of the Greek word (council) as developed by Philo offers another possibility for the meaning of the term to a first-century audience. He uses the term to designate the resting place of the soul after death; specifically referring to the entrance of God into this council in *Som.* 1.193.[32]

The evidence from Philo is similar in concept to later Jewish *aggadoth* that refer to a heavenly court of 71, organized like the earthly Sanhedrin, although the Jewish texts do not use the term *sanhedrin* for this court.[33] Therefore, it is possible that *synedrion* in v. 22f may refer to a heavenly court. If *krisis* is read in 21d and 22d with an eschatological reference, then the parallelism suggests that the reader would understand *synedrion* to refer to the eschatological court of heaven.

The use of *geenna tou pyros* in v. 22h supports this reading. The grammar and parallelism are consistent with usual references to courts. This understanding is attested by *b. Shabb.* 118a, 27 and *b. B. Bat.* 10a, 37, where the term 'the court of Gehinnom', is used.

Taken together, the evidence for vv. 21-22 allows several conclusions. First, vv. 21-22 are a unity both in style and content. Second, each of the *enochos* phrases are in synonymous parallelism and probably refers in each case to the eschatological court. The vocabulary used to refer to the court is not typical of Matthew's redaction elsewhere. The disjunction between vv. 22 and 23 may therefore be explained as the 'sewing' together of two pieces of M sayings material.

Conclusions
(a) No verses have parallels in Mark. (b) Verses 25-26 (par Luke 12.58-59) come from Q. (d) Based on a comparison with Mark 11.25 and their disjunction from their context in grammar and content, vv. 23-24 may be assigned to the M sayings. Based on an analysis of style, vocabulary, and content, vv. 21-22 may be assigned to the M sayings.

3. *Matt 5.27-32*

Translation

> *Antithesis 2.* (27) You have heard that it was said, 'Do not commit adultery'. (28) But, I say to you that anyone who looks at a woman for the purpose of desire[34] already commits adultery with her in his heart. (29) And if your right eye scandalizes you, pull it out and cast it from you; for it is to your advantage that you should lose one of your members than that your whole body should be cast into Gehenna. (30) And if your right hand scandalizes you, cut it off and cast it from you; for it is to your advantage that you should lose one of your members than that your whole body should go away into Gehenna. (31) And it was said, 'Whoever divorces his wife, let him give her a bill of divorce'. (32) But I say to you that anyone who divorces his wife except on the grounds of incestuous marriage causes her to be an adulteress.[35] And whoever marries a divorcee commits adultery.[36]

Isolation Leading to M Sayings
Summary: (a) Verses 29-32 have a parallel in Mark; (b) v. 32 has a parallel in Luke as well as Mark; (c) v. 31 is likely to be from Matthew; (d) vv. 27-28 have a strong possibility of containing an M saying.

(a) Verses 29-32
Another version of these verses occurs in Matt 18.8-9 par Mark 9.43-48 (C. 10). Matt 18.8-9 appears to depend directly on Mark 9.43-47. Matt 5.29-30 is also dependent on the Markan text, but has been adapted by the redactor to its context.[37] In Matt 18.8-9, a series of three sayings about hand, foot and eye is shortened to two sayings about the hand and foot (18.8 par Mark 9.43, 45) and then the eye (18.9 par Mark 9.47). Matt 5.29-30 appears to be a further development of the same tradition. The order of the sayings has been changed to begin with the eye and then move to the hand. The change may be a means of bringing the sayings into a closer association with 5.28 where, 'the one who *looks* at a woman for the purpose of desire' is described as a transgressor. The text also eliminates the more Semitic *kalon estin se* (Mark)/*soi* (Matt 18.8, 9) in favor of the Greek *symphero* 'it is to your advantage'.[38] Matthew appears to be responsible for vv. 29-30 in their present form. He used the Markan tradition that he reproduced more faithfully in Matt 18.8-9.

(b) Verse 32
There are three texts parallel to v. 32: Matt 19.9; Mark 10.11-12; Luke 16.18 (C. 11). Matt 19.9 depends directly on Mark 10.12, but Matt 5.32 shows evidence of the use of some Q tradition as well as the Markan tradition. In addition, the phrase *parektos . . . moicheuthēnai* is most likely redactional.[39] The verse appears to be formulated from a knowledge of Q and Mark.

(c) Verse 31
Verse 31 is unparalleled, and thus either comes from Matthew or from M. Unlike vv. 21 and 27, where the antithesis appears joined to its following thesis, v. 32 is clearly constructed from traditional material and shows signs of Matthean redaction. Verse 31 departs from the other antitheses in 5.21-48 both by its abbreviated form of the introduction to the antithesis, and its lack of the second person address (*ēkousate hoti*) present in vv. 21, 27, 33, 38, 43. Although this break in style might not alter the basic meaning of the antithetical formula, it suggests to the reader that v. 31 is to be considered somehow differently from the other antitheses.[40]

The break in style between the antithetical formula in v. 31 and that of the other antitheses is made evident by the use of *de* in v. 31.

De is used integral to the antithetical formulas as an adversative that indicates a disjunction from the preceeding sentence (*ēkousate hoti errethē . . . egō de legō hymin*, 'You have heard that it was said . . . but I say to you'). The *de* in v. 31 interrupts the pattern of the formula. Here the *de* occurs at the beginning of the sentence as an editorial link (copulative) between v. 30 and v. 31. This use of *de* especially indicates subordination or a parenthesis.[41]

The use of *palin* in v. 33 confirms this interpretation. *Palin* is regularly used in Matthew to recall a previous sentence or paragraph, and is used occasionally to resume a narrative after an interruption.[42] The use of *palin* with *ēkousate* in v. 33 appears to be an editorial device designed to recall to the reader the series of antitheses begun by vv. 21, 27. Therefore, the abbreviation of the antithetical formula in v. 31 may be used by Matthew to introduce a subpoint to antithesis two.

Finally, unlike vv. 21 and 27, v. 31 does not quote the Decalogue, but alludes instead to Deut 24.1-3.[43] The evidence of Matthean redaction in v. 32, coupled with the indications of scriptural allusion and editorial activity in the abbreviation of the antithetical formula in v. 31, tends to the conclusion that Matthew is responsible for the composition of vv. 31-32a. The translation offered at the beginning of this chapter embodies this interpretation.[44]

(d) Verses 27-28

As was the case with vv. 21-22, vv. 27-28 constitute a stylistic unity. The introduction to the thesis in v. 27 lacks the *tois archaiois* that occurred in v. 21. The deletion does not affect the meaning of the formula, and the parallelism with v. 21 makes it easy for the reader to supply the term. The quotation from Exod 20.13 (*ou moicheuseis*, 'Do not commit adultery', LXX) contains no expansion by means of a conditional sentence as in v. 21. Such an expansion is unnecessary in v. 27, as opposed to v. 21, due to the close association of the LXX text with the following legal rule.

Verse 28 shows similarity in style with v. 22c. It contains the same *pas ho* construction as v. 22c in the protasis. The apodosis, however, is in the aorist. There is no future reference in v. 28, nor is there any designation of punishment or court proceeding as in vv. 21-22.[45]

The use of *pros to* and the infinitive to express purpose is relatively rare in Matthew; it occurs five times, as compared with 33 times for the use of *hina*. In 26.12, the construction comes from Mark 14.8.

The other four uses all come from unparalleled material (5.28; 6.1; 23.5; 13.30). This pattern suggests that the use of *pros to* plus the infinitive comes from traditional material. The vocabulary of vv. 27-28 shows a unique use: the verb *epithymeō* occurs nowhere else in Matthew, and its cognate *epithymia* occurs not at all.

As was the case in vv. 21-22, vv. 27-28 are disjoined in their context from both the preceding verses (25-26) and from the verses that follow (29-30) by the use of the second person plural rather than the second person singular. The content of vv. 27-28 is in conceptual tension with the redactional passage in vv. 31-32. The insertion of the exceptive clause allows a view of divorce in v. 32 more lenient than the view of desire in v. 28. The eschatological stringency of v. 28 corresponds to that of vv. 21-22, but seems to clash with the editor's view in v. 31. Once again, seams resulting from the sewing together of several sayings are evident (in this case Q [25-26] and Mark [29-30] with what is probably an M saying [27-28]).

Conclusions

(a) On the basis of a comparison with Matt 18.8-9 and Mark 9.43-48, vv. 29-30 may be considered Matthean redaction from Markan tradition. (b) Verse 32 shows signs of dependence on both Mark 11.25 and Q (see Luke 12.58-59). (c) Verses 31-32a are the product of Matthew, who used an abbreviated antithetical formula to introduce a subpoint to antithesis two (vv. 27-28). (d) Based on an analysis of style, vocabulary, and content vv. 27-28 may be designated an M saying.

4. *Matt 5.33-37*

Translation

> *Antithesis 3.* (33) Again, you have heard that it was said to the ancients, 'You shall not break your oath, but offer your oath to the Lord'. (34) But I say to you that you are not to swear at all; neither by the heaven, because it is the throne of God; (35) nor by the earth, because it is a footstool for his feet; nor by Jerusalem, because it is the city of the great king; (36) nor may you swear by your head , because you are unable to make a single hair white or black. (37) But let your word be yes, yes, no, no. Beyond this is from the evil one.

Isolation Leading to M Sayings

Summary: (a, b) These verses have no parallels in Mark or Luke; (c) no verses are likely to be from Matthew; (d) vv. 33–37 have a strong possibility of containing an M saying.

(d) Verses 33–37

Verses 33–37 are unparalleled in Mark or Luke. Another version of the verses is found in Jas 5.12 (C. 12). A direct literary relationship between the two passages is doubtful. Jas 5.12 is the shorter of the two forms of the saying; it does not contain elements A,B,C,A',b,c,d. On a form-critical basis, these observations would argue that James has preserved a more primitive form of the saying.[46] Matt 5.34–36 (elements a,c), however, uses the more Semitic form *en* and the dative for an oath, where James 5.12 uses the classical Greek construction of *omnymi* and the accusative.[47] The most probable hypothesis is that the two passages depend on similar tradition, which has developed along independent lines. The core tradition contained at least elements corresponding to B',a,C',D'.

The possibility that the antithetical formula was original to the saying cannot be excluded on the basis of comparison with Jas 5.12.[48] The parallels in extra-canonical literature lack reference to the antithetical formula, although they all show reliance on Matthew's text (C. 13). The first three texts clearly rely on Matt 5.33–37. All three attribute the saying to Jesus, without any direct reference to the antithetical formula. *Ps-Cl. Hom.* 3.55.1 appears to reflect the influence of Matt 5.33 in the introductory line, 'To those who think (as the scriptures teach) that God swears...'. The reference to scripture and the association of God with oath taking may indicate an interpretation of the antithetical formula. Both Justin and *Ps-Cl. Hom.* 3.55.1 reproduce almost verbatim Matt 5.37 except for the *to nai nai, (kai) to ou, ou* phrase. The passage may be a harmonization with James. The absence of the article, however, makes the Matthean text ambiguous and allows interpretation of the passage as an oath itself; in this case, the phrase would be viewed as an effort to clarify the Matthean text. The lack of other elements from James in these texts tends to support this option.[49]

The parallel in Epiphanius may be a harmonization of both James and Matthew. The saying itself is almost a quotation of Jas 5.12. The influence of Matt 5.37 is noticeable in the last line. The introduction in Epiphanius, which assigns the saying to the Gospel, may refer to a gospel harmony.[50]

These four parallels, whose vocabulary shows dependence on the edited text of Matthew (v. 37b in particular),[51] indicate the relative freedom with which the saying on oaths was used in Palestinian and Syrian Christianity in the second to fourth centuries. The freedom of these writers in their use of written passages from the Gospels allows no assertion, based simply on logical deduction from form-critical principles, that the antithetical formula was not part of the original saying. The parallel in Jas 5.12 suggests only that there is traditional material in Matt 5.33-37; it does not set the boundaries of that tradition. We therefore are in accord with the positions of Dibelius and Strecker, cited above.[52]

There are several indications that Matthew edited v. 37b. In both 5.20 and 5.47, Matthew is probably responsible for the use of *perissyō/perisson*.[53] The use of *to perisson* 'beyond this' in 5.37b may be one indication of Matthean redaction. *Ponēros* 'evil one' occurs more frequently in Matthew than in any other NT work (26 of 78 times). Eight of Matthew's uses are from Q and one from Mark.[54] Of the uses peculiar to Matthew, seven are adjectival (7.17, 18; 9.4; 12.34; 18.32; 20.15; 22.10) and six are nominal (5.37, 39; 6.13; 13.19, 38, 49). The last group is the concern here. In Matt 13.19, Matthew takes over a sentence from Mark 4.13-20 and substitutes *ho ponēros* for *ho satan*, indicating his own understanding of *ho ponēros*. Similar instances in Matt 13.38 (by influence from 13.19) and 6.13 (not present in Luke 11.4) are also most likely redactional. The context of the saying, which opposes Jesus' will ('Do not swear at all') to the will of the 'evil one', argues for the same meaning in 5.37b.

The presence of a corresponding line in Jas 5.12 (see element D) suggests that some tradition might have been before Matthew as he wrote, but a critical reconstruction of the vocabulary is difficult if not impossible.

Verse 36 (C. 12, elements c, d) shows signs of having originated in a different context. The clause is disruptive in both style and content. In contrast with the style of the other three *mēte* clauses (elements a, b), which are each constructed on the pattern of *mēte* plus a noun plus *hoti* plus the verb *estin*, v. 36 is constructed on a different pattern of *mēte* plus a verb plus *hoti* plus two verbs (see C. 12 elements c, d). Further, the first three *mēte* constructions depend grammatically on the clause 'Do not swear at all' (B'), while v. 36 can be grammatically independent.

The disjunction in style is further supported by differences in content. Elements a, b rely on concepts derived from scripture (Isa 66.1; Ps 47.3 LXX) that are substitutes for the name of God. Elements c, d, however, do not have an apparent scriptural basis and contain no explicit reference to oaths taken with God, or the cosmos, as guarantor. The absence of v. 36 in Jas 5.12 tends to support these observations. In addition, v. 36 contains no clearly identifiable redactional style , vocabulary, or interest. It appears that Matthew has sewn together two pieces of tradition. Accordingly, v. 36 may be assigned to the M sayings.

The unity of style and content in vv. 34b–35 has already been used to help isolate v. 36 as an M saying. Matthew's editorial work has also been recovered in v. 37b. The parallel in Jas 5.12 has been used to help indicate possible traditional material in vv. 33–35. These arguments establish a strong probability that vv. 34b–35 are a pre-Matthean unity. The style of the verses is unified throughout, with no observable disjunctions to support a suspicion of further editorial additions. The vocabulary also gives no specific indications of Matthew's activity. Matt 5.34b–35, and some unrecoverable form of v. 37 may be assigned to the M sayings on this basis .

Determining the relationship between the antithetical formula and the pre-Matthean material in vv. 34b–35, 37 is more difficult. Did Matthew construct the antithesis in vv. 33–34a (as in 5.31), or is it part of the original logion (as in vv. 21–22, 27–28)?

There is no disjunction in style between vv. 33–34a and 34b to indicate an aporia caused by the joining of separate levels of transmission. The thesis of v. 33 contains what appears to be a scriptural reference, *ouk epiorkēseis* 'you shall not break your oath', followed by an expansion, *apodōseis de tǫ kyriǫ tous horkous sou,* 'but offer your oath to the Lord'. A similar pattern was evident in v. 21. The scriptural quotation is in the same style as the references to the Decalogue in vv. 21, 27 (C. 14). The precise wording does not occur in the LXX. Comparing *ou pseudomartyrēseis* with *ouk epiorkēseis* eases the difficulty. While *epiorkeō* does not occur in the Decalogue of the LXX, its meaning in secular Greek is well established as either 'to bear false witness', or 'to swear falsely'. Therefore, it is synonymous with *pseudomartyrēseis*.[55] The quotation in v. 33 may be either an alternative translation of the MT or simply a different reading of a Greek Bible manuscript no longer available to us.[56] In view of the use of the LXX in vv. 21 and 27, the latter option seems more probable. The expansion (*apodōseis . . . sou*) is similar to Ps

49.14 LXX. The changes in form (*apodos* [LXX] to *apodōseis*, and *tas euchas* [LXX] to *tous horkous*) may be an adaptation of Ps 49.14 to the style of the quotation in v. 33a, as well as a means of bridging to the material in vv. 34b-35, 37.

Since (a) there is no discernable disjunction between vv. 33-34a and 34b-35, 37 (the latter having been assigned to M sayings); (b) the means, of constructing the antithesis in vv. 33-34a is similar to the process in vv. 21, 27 (which have been shown to be unified with their following logia); (c) no clear Matthean redaction (except *palin*) can be discerned; then vv. 33-35, 37 may be assigned to the M sayings.

Conclusions
(d) Based on analysis of vocabulary and comparison with Jas 5.12, v. 37b is the work of Matthew, who relied on an underlying saying no longer critically recoverable. Based on comparison with parallels in James, Justin, *Pseudo-Clementine Homilies*, and Epiphanius in addition to an analysis of style, vocabulary, and content, vv. 33-35, 37a,b may be assigned to the M sayings. Based on analysis of disjunction in style and content, v. 36 is an M saying originally independent of vv. 33-35, 37 and was probably brought to its present context by Matthew.

5. *Matt 5.38–42*

Translation

> *Antithesis 4*. (38) You have heard that it was said, 'An eye for an eye and a tooth for a tooth'. (39) But I say to you that you are not to resist the evil one. But whoever strikes you on the right cheek, turn also the other to him. (40) And to the one who wants to sue you even to take your underwear, allow him also your coat. (41) And whoever requires one mile, go with him two. (42) To the one who asks of you, give, and do not turn away from the one wishing to borrow from you.

Isolation Leading to M Sayings
Summary: (a) No verses have parallels in Mark; (b) vv. 39b-42 have a parallel in Luke; (c) vv. 38-39a are likely to be from Matthew; (d) no verses have a strong possibility of containing an M saying.

(b) Verses 39b-42
Another version of Matt 5.39b-42 occurs in Luke 6.29-30 (C. 15); therefore, the verses may be assigned to Q.

(c) Verses 38-39a

Verses 38-39a contain a complete antithetical formula and may be understood as a free-standing logion. The logion is stylistically unified. Verse 38 consists of a scriptural quotation taken from Exod 21.24 (identical to Lev 29.20; Deut 19.21) *opthalmon anti opthalmou, odonta anti odontos*, 'an eye for an eye and a tooth for a tooth'. Unlike the quotations in Antitheses 1, 2, 3 (vv. 21, 27, 33), the quotation in v. 38 does not come from the Decalogue. Verse 39a uses *poneros* in much the same manner as another use, peculiar to Matthew, in 13.49. Most likely 13.49, which is part of the allegorizing interpretation of the Parable of the Seine Net in 13.47-48, comes from Matthew.[57] The stylistic unity of v. 38 with 39a, along with the observations concerning scriptural quotation and redactional activity in 39a, allows little possibility for critically discerning an M saying here. Matthew may well have composed the antithetical formula of vv. 38-39a in imitation of the M sayings in vv. 21-22, 27-28, 33-37 and connected it with the Q material of 39b-42. In the absence of compelling evidence to the contrary, this seems the most likely explanation of the text.

Conclusions

(b) Based on comparison with Luke 6.29-30, vv. 39b-42 are from Q.
(c) Based on an analysis of style and vocabulary, as well as on comparison with previously isolated M sayings, vv. 38-39a are from Matthew. Matt 5.38-42 contains no M sayings.

6. *Matt 5.43-48*

Translation

> *Antithesis 5.* (43) You have heard that it was said, 'Love your neighbor and hate your enemy'. (44) But I say to you, love your enemies and pray for those who persecute you. (45) Thus you will be sons of your father who is in heaven, because he makes his sun rise over the evil and the good and he rains upon the righteous and the unrighteous. (46) For if you love those who love you, what benefit do you derive? Do not even the tax collectors do the same? (48) Be, therefore, yourselves perfectly loving, as your heavenly father is perfectly loving.

Isolation Leading to M Sayings

Summary: (a) No verses have parallels in Mark; (b) vv. 44-48 have a parallel in Luke; (c) v. 43 is likely to be from Matthew; (d) no verses have a strong possibility of containing an M saying.

(b) Verses 44-48
Another version of Matt 5.44-48 is found in Luke 6.27-28, 35b, 32-33, 36 (C. 16). The agreement in vocabulary and order is sufficient to assign vv. 44-48 to Q.

(c) Verse 43
This verse is only the first half of the antithetical formula. It is unified in style with v. 44. Verse 43 was probably constructed as an introduction to the Q material in vv. 44-48.[58]

Conclusions
(b) Based on a comparison with Luke 6.27-28, 35b, 32-33, 36, vv. 44-48 are from Q. (c) Verse 43 was probably constructed as an introduction to the Q material in vv. 44-48.

7. *Matt 6.1-18*

Translation

(1) Watch out that you do not perform your righteousness in front of people in order to be seen by them. But if you do not heed this, you do not have a reward from your father who is in the heavens. (2) Therefore, when you give alms, do not sound a trumpet before you like the hypocrites do in the synagogues and roadways in order that they might receive glory from people. Amen, I say to you, they have their reward. (3) But when you give alms do not let you left (hand) know what your right (hand) does, (4) thus your alms may be in secret and your father who sees in secret will reward you. (5) And when you pray, do not be like the hypocrites who love to pray while standing in the synagogues and on the street corners that they may be seen by people. Amen, I say to you, they have their reward. (6) But when you pray, go into your inner room and when you have closed your door, pray to your father, the one who is in secret, and your father who sees in secret will reward you.

(7) But when you pray do not babble like the Gentiles, for they suppose that by their running off at the mouth that they will be listened to. (8) Therefore, do not be like them, for your father knows the things of which you have need before you ask him.

(9) Therefore, you shall pray like this:

Our father who is in the heavens;
(10) Let your name be made holy;
    Let your kingdom come:
    Let your will be done
        as in heaven also upon the earth;
(11) Our bread for the present, give us today;
(12) And forgive us our debts, as we have also
        forgiven those who have incurred debts against us;
(13) And lead us not into temptation, but
        deliver us from the evil one.

(14) For if you forgive the people their trespasses, your heavenly father will also forgive you. (15) But if you do not forgive people, neither will your father forgive you your trespasses.

(16) And when you fast, do not be downcast like the hypocrites, for they disfigure their faces so that they might be seen by people when they fast. Amen, I say to you, they have their reward. (17) But when you fast, anoint your head and wash your face, (18) so that you might not be seen by people while you are fasting, but rather that you might be seen by your father who is in secret, and your father who sees in secret will reward you.

Isolation Leading to M Sayings
Summary: (a) Verses 14-15 have a parallel in Mark; (b) vv. 9-13 have parallels in Luke; (c) no complete verses are likely to come from Matthew; (d) vv. 1-8, 16 -18 have a strong possibility of containing M sayings.

(a) Verses 14-15
Another version of these verses is found in Mark 11.25b (C. 17). The agreement in vocabulary and word order shows that vv. 14-15 probably come from Mark. The logion has been expanded to include both a positive and a negative statement.[59]

(b) Verses 9-13
Verses 9-13 have a parallel in Luke 11.1-4 (C. 17). On the basis of agreement in vocabulary, style, and content, vv. 9-13 come from Q.[60]

(d) Verses 1-8, 16-18

These remaining verses show a regular style and pattern, which may
be one indication of the use of a unit of sayings available to Matthew
prior to the composition of the Gospel (C. 18).[61] Verses 7-8 appear to
disrupt the pattern present in vv. 2-6, 16-18. There is a shift
unexplained in the narrative from the second person singular in v. 6
to the second person plural in v. 7. The grammatical disjunction is
further supported by a stylistic disjunction.[62] Verses 7-8 depart from
the pattern A,B,a,b,c,A',B',b',c' found in vv. 2-6, 16-18, whose
carefully constructed parallelism is indicated in the diagram.

Departures include:

> A lacks *hotan* plus a finite verb and instead uses a participial form;
> b, c are not present;
> A' is not present
> b' is not present;
> c' lacks a parallel to the *en tǭ kryptǭ* present in the corresponding
> elements in 2-6, 16-18.

The stylistic discontinuity is supported by discontinuity in content.
Unlike vv. 1, 2, 5, 16, vv. 7-8 make no reference to reward (*misthos*).
Verses 7-8 also contain no reference to hypocrites, unlike vv. 2, 5, 16.
The polemic of vv. 7-8 is directed against Gentile religious practice
rather than Jewish synagogue piety as in vv. 2-6, 16-18.[63]

The disjunctions in grammar, supported by analysis of style and
content, establish that vv. 7-8 are removed from their original
context, and that Matthew is probably responsible for their inclusion
within a piece of material in vv. 1-6, 16-18. The lack of redactional
elements and the disjunction mentioned above also indicates that
vv. 7-8 are probably an M saying. Once again, Matthew has sewn
together sayings from different contexts.

Verses 1-6, 16-18

As was shown above, the verses are unified in both style and content.
The pattern of vv. 2-6, 16-18 is apparent. Two key terms that hold
the unit together conceptually appear distinct from Matthew's
language. First, *misthos* 'reward' is attested only where Matthew
takes it from a source (5.12 par Luke 6.23, 35 ; 10.42[41] par Mark
9.41), except for a single occurrence specific to Matthew (Matt 20.8).
The concentration of the term here may indicate an underlying

tradition, since the dominant pattern of use in the rest of the First Gospel is to use this term when depending on a source. Second, and more probative, the appelative for father, *ho blepōn en tǭ kryptǭ (kryphaiǭ)* 'the one who sees in secret' occurs only in 6.4, 6, 16 in the entire NT. Instead, Matthew uses *tǭ en tois ouranois* 'the one who is in the heavens' (13 times) in other passages. On the basis of stylistic and conceptual unity distinct from Matthean editing elsewhere, vv. 2-6, 16-18 may be assigned to the M sayings material.

Verse 1, which functions as an introduction to the M sayings unit in vv. 2-6, 16-18, demands special attention. Three options appear possible: (1) v. 1 is an editorial bridge to the M sayings unit beginning in v. 2; (2) v. 1 is an introduction to the M sayings unit that was already part of the M unit beginning in v. 2; (3) v. 1 contains a pre-Matthean saying with redactional touches.

The grammatical disjunction between v. 1 and the following unit favors to some extent the separation of v. 1 from the unit. The shift from the second person plural to singular (v. 1 *prosechete* to v. 2 *poiēs*) indicates the disjunction. On the other hand, the style in v. 1 includes characteristics distinct from Matthew's style elsewhere in the Gospel. First, *prosechete* 'watch out' is followed by *apo* 'from' plus the noun in every other use in Matthew (7.15, 16.6 [par to Mark 8.15]; 16.11, 12; 10.17); here no *apo* follows. Second, *pros to* plus the infinitive, as was observed above, occurs only in unparalleled material. *Hina* is used more frequently to indicate purpose (33 times as opposed to five times). The *pros to* construction was isolated as part of an M saying in 5.28.

The content of v. 1 links it conceptually with the following unit. The use of reward is introduced in v. 1b and continues in vv. 2-6, 16-18. The most significant term in v. 1, *dikaiosynē*, remains the strongest evidence for assigning v. 1 to the redactor.[64] But it should be analyzed not in isolation but as a conceptual unit whose significance arises from its use with *poieō*. The concept *poiein dikaiosynēn* 'to perform righteousness' is unique within Matthew and occurs only five times in the NT (only in 6.1 in Matthew; 1 John 2.29; 3.7, 10; Rev 22.11). In each occurrence the use refers to human acts toward God. The combination occurs 26 times in the LXX.[65]

In Tannaitic literature, *ṣedaqah* becomes a technical term for almsgiving.[66] Tobit 12.9 may be an early indication of this use of the word since it couples *dikaiosynē* and *eleemosynē* 'almsgiving' (C. 19). The use in 6.1 is similar to the use of Tobit 12.9 and appears to move in the direction of Tannaitic tradition. Taken in context with the following unit, *poiein dikaiosynēn* appears to be an umbrella concept that holds together almsgiving, prayer, and fasting. The use here is unique within Matthew. The use of *dikaiosynē* itself is insufficient to assign v. 1 to the redactor.

The use of *tǭ en tois ouranois* probably comes from the redactor. If v. 1 contains underlying tradition, then comparison with the following unit suggests that the original phrase was *tǭ bleponti en tǭ kryptǭ*.

The three options that were described above can now be reassessed. Given the uniqueness of certain stylistic characteristics and the conceptual unity of v. 1 with the following unit, the M sayings unit in vv. 2-6, 16-18 probably already contained an introduction underlying the final text of v. 1. Matthew himself probably retouched the introduction, and is responsible for the use of *prosechete* (the second person plural) as a means of assimilating 6.1 into the style of the sayings of Jesus in the theses of the antithetical formulas. The designation of God as 'the one who is in the heavens' is most likely Matthew's work as well. These probabilities suggest the following hypothetical reconstruction of the saying underlying v. 1 (C. 20). This confluence of evidence permits the assignment of Matt 6.1-6, 16-18 to the M sayings.

Conclusions
(a) Verses 14-15 are probably a development of Mark 11.25b. (b) By comparison with Luke 11.1-4, vv. 9-13 may be assigned to Q. (d) Based on discontinuity in grammar, style, and content, vv. 7-8 may be assigned to the M sayings. Based on an identifiable pattern broken by Matthew's editing, as well as on their distinct style, vocabulary, and content, vv. 2-6, 16-18 may be assigned to the M sayings. Based on an analysis of style, vocabulary and content, v. 1 represents Matthew's editing of an M saying that introduced the unit in vv. 2-6, 16-18.

Chapter 3

MATTHEW 10

1. *Matt 10.1-16*

Translation

(1) And when he had called his twelve disciples, he gave them power over unclean spirits so that they might cast them out and so that they might heal every disease and every ailment.

(2) And the names of the twelve apostles are as follows: first is Simon, the one called Peter, and Andrew his brother,[1] James the son of Zebedee and John his brother, (3) Philip and Bartholomew, Thomas and Matthew the tax collector, James the son of Alphaeus and Thaddeus, (4) Simon the Canaanite and Judas the Iscariot (the one who betrayed him).

(5) (a) Jesus sent out the twelve after he had instructed them, saying, (b) 'Do not go in the way of the Gentiles and do not enter the city of the Samaritans; (6) but rather go out to the lost sheep of the nation of Israel. (7) And as you go, preach, saying, "The Kingdom of Heaven has drawn near". (8) (a) Heal the sick, raise the dead, cleanse the lepers, cast out the demons. (b) You received for free, give for free. (9) Do not acquire gold nor silver nor copper in your pocket (10) or purse on the road, nor acquire two shirts or shoes or a staff, because the workman is worthy of his food. (11) But whatever city or village you enter, inquire as to who is worthy in it. And remain there until you leave. (12) And as you enter a family, greet them; (13) and if on the one hand the family is receptive then let your peace go out upon them, but if on the other hand the family is not receptive then let your peace return to you. (14) And whoever does not receive you nor listens to your words, then, after you have gone outside of their household or city, shake the dust from your feet. (15) Amen, I say to you, it will be more tolerable for the land of Sodom and Gomorrah in the day of

judgment than for that city. (16) (a) Look, I send you as sheep in the midst of wolves, (b) therefore, be as wise as snakes and gentle as doves.

Isolation Leading to M Sayings
Summary: (a-b) vv. 1-4 have parallels in Mark and Luke; vv. 7-16 have parallels in Mark and Luke; (c) v. 8b is likely to be from Matthew; v. 16b is likely to be from Matthew; (d) vv. 5-6 contain a possible M saying.

(a-b) Verses 1-4
Another version of the verses occurs in Mark 6.7; 3.13-19 (the latter passage has a Lukan parallel in 6.12-16) (C. 21). Matthew apparently relies on Mark here. Variations in the list of disciples and in the introduction (v. 1) probably come from the editor, who may have supplemented Mark with his own tradition. That tradition, however, is not clearly recoverable from the present text.

Verses 7-16
The parallels to these verses in Mark 6.8-13 and Luke 10.4-12 should be considered separately. C. 21 shows a significant overlap of Mark and Q in this passage. Matthew's order diverges noticeably from both Mark and Luke. Nevertheless, when the agreement in vocabulary is taken into account, each complete saying except vv. 8b, 16b is paralleled either in Mark or Luke, or in both. Verses 7-16a may be assigned to Mark and Q, with the recognition that unique elements in the verses may come from Matthew or from the development of the Mark and Q traditions in his community prior to his writing.[2]

(c) Verse 8b
This brief statement is difficult to analyze. Matthew could have included v. 8b from his own knowledge of aphorisms current in his day; he could have created it himself; or he could have found it as an expansion of Q and Mark already present in his own tradition. The saying functions as an effective introduction to the concrete instruction of vv. 9-10. The style, vocabulary, and (most importantly) content are not observably disjunctive from Matthew's editing in this context or elsewhere. Therefore, v. 8b should be assigned to Matthew.[3]

Verse 16b
This saying yields few clues for its determination. It may have
circulated independently from its present context. Bultmann assigns
the saying to the realm of secular wisdom.[4] The style, vocabulary,
and content fail to set the saying apart from the final text of the
Gospel. The comparison with Luke 10.3 (C. 21) suggests that the
saying is an addition to Q. With the same caveats noted to v. 8b, the
verse is best attributed to Matthew.

(d) Verses 5-6[5]
The form of vv. 5-6 consists of two parts: a single logion (5b-6, *eis
hodon . . . Israēl*) is introduced by a phrase (5a) that links the saying
with its context and at the same time attributes the saying to Jesus.[6]
The phrase *toutous tous dōdeka* has as its antecedent the entirety of
vv. 2-4, but particularly the *tōn de dōdeka* of v. 2. The introduction of
v. 5a is partially parallel to Mark 6.7 and Luke 10.1. The final form of
v. 5a is probably due to Matthew's editing of the Markan and/or Q
tradition.

While the style of vv. 5b-6 fits the general pattern of Matthew's
editing, the vocabulary includes phrases that are unusual in either
Matthew or the NT. The only use of *eis hodon ethnōn* in the entire
NT occurs at v. 5b. A second phrase there, *polin Samaritōn*, appears
nowhere else in Matthew's Gospel.[7] A third phrase, *ta probata ta
apolōlota oikou Israēl*,[8] is doubly rare. The phrase may echo the idea
in Jer 50.6 (27.6 LXX; see also Ezek 34.4). *Probata apolōlota* is present
in Jer 27.6 (LXX), but the text from Jeremiah does not refer to the
'house of Israel'. Although the term 'house of Israel' appears
extensively in the LXX, it appears relatively infrequently in the NT.
Matthew has *oikou Israēl* only here and in 15.24.[9] The combination
of these three unique elements in one saying gives evidence for
assigning vv. 5b-6 to the M sayings.

Furthermore, the content of vv. 5b-6 is different from the interests
of Matthew. Matthew develops his own understanding of the mission
to the Gentiles by his redactional placement of 10.18 (par Mark
13.10). At 10.18, Jesus predicts a witness to Gentiles under
conditions of persecution *within the mission of the disciples*.

The occurrence of 'the lost sheep of the nation of Israel' at Matt
15.24 ties the story of the Syro-Phoenician Woman together with the
mission charge in 10.5-6. While the traditional relationship of the

two verses is open to scholarly conjecture,[10] the inclusion of 15.24 within a Markan pericope (Mark 7.24-30) is due to Matthew's composition. The statement of Jesus in 15.24, 'I was sent only to the lost sheep of the nation of Israel', echoes 10.5-6; but the woman's daughter, a non-Israelite, is healed. Matthew indicates to his reader that even *within his ministry* Jesus was willing to go beyond his own limitation of mission to Israel.

Most commentators recognize that Matthew gives his own understanding of a Gentile mission in 28.18-20.[11] The mission to the Gentiles in 28.18-20, however, is not paralleled within the ministry of Jesus or his disciples. It includes 'making disciples', an activity comprised of baptizing and teaching. The mission apparently involves the Gentiles being incorporated into a community. This motif is absent *within the mission of Jesus and his disciples* throughout the rest of the Gospel.[12] Contrasts to the mission to Israel in 10.5-8 are apparent. The mission to Israel is one of preaching; the content is the same as Jesus' own proclamation in Matt 4.17. The acts that are to accompany the disciples' mission are those of Jesus (compare 10.8 with the miracles of chs. 8-9).

In view of Matthew's own interests and the evidence of peculiar vocabulary present in vv. 5b-6, this saying may be designated M.

Conclusions
(a) Comparison with Mark 6.7; 3.13-19 shows that vv. 1-4 are probably from Markan tradition. (b) Based on a comparison with Mark 6.8-13 and Luke 10.4-12, vv. 7-16a (excluding 8b) show evidence of being a conflation of Mark and Q. (c) Verse 8b may be assigned to the redactor. Verse 16b may be assigned to the redactor, while recognizing the possibility that it originally came from a popular aphorism. (d) Based on an analysis that shows their vocabulary and content to be distinct from Matthew's own use and interests, vv. 5b-6 may be assigned to the M sayings.

2. Matt 10.17-25

Translation

(17) Beware of the men! They will turn you over to sanhedrins and they will beat you in their synagogues; (18) and you will be brought on my behalf as a witness to them and to the Gentiles. (19) And when they turn you in, do not be concerned about how you should

speak or what you should say; (20) For you are not those who
speak, but the spirit of your father is the one who speaks through
you.

(21) And brother will turn in brother to be put to death, and father,
son; and children will rebel against parents and they will kill them.
(22) And you will be hated by everyone because of my name; but
the one who sticks it out to the end, that one will be saved. (23) (a)
And when they persecute you in this city, flee into another; (b) for
amen, I say to you, you will not finish the cities of Israel before the
Son of Man comes. (24) A disciple is not above his teacher, nor a
slave above his owner. (25) (a) Enough for the disciple that he
becomes like his teacher and the slave like his owner. (b) If they
have called the head of the house Beelzeboul, how much more the
members of his household.

Isolation Leading to M Sayings
Summary: (a) vv. 17-22 have a parallel in Mark; (b) vv. 24-25a have
a parallel in Luke; (c) v. 25b most likely comes from the editor; (d)
v. 23 contains a possible M saying.

(a) Verses 17-22
Another version of the verses occurs in Mark 13.9-13 (see Luke
21.12-17; 12.11-12). Matthew relies on Mark here (C. 22).[13]

(b) Verses 24-25a
These verses have a parallel in Luke 6.40 (compare John 13.16;
15.20). On the basis of agreement in vocabulary and order, they may
be assigned to Q (C. 22).

(c) Verse 25b
The form of the saying consists of a simple *logion*, which may have
circulated apart from its present context. Its style is not particularly
typical of Matthew: *ei . . . posō mallon* occurs only in Matt 7.11
outside of this passage, where the use depends on Q (Luke 11.13).
The rare occurrence of the style is noteworthy, but inconclusive.

The evidence from vocabulary is also inconclusive. The effect of
the saying depends on the juxtaposition of *oikodespotēs* and *oikiakos*.
Oikodespotēs 'householder' occurs six times in Matthew, once in
Mark, four times in Luke. Matthew does not include the Markan use
(21.18 par Mark 14.4), but does use the word in a Q saying at 24.43
(par Luke 12.39). The remaining uses in 10.25; 13.27, 52; 20.1, 11;

21.33 are unparalleled. All except 10.25; 21.33 are in M parables. At 21.33, Matthew edits Mark 12.1 by including 'householder'. *Oikiakos* occurs in 10.25 and in what is probably a redactional expansion of Q in 10.36 (Luke 12.53; Mic 7.6). The study of vocabulary is inconclusive.

The content of the saying is somewhat disjoined from its immediate context; nevertheless, the reader can easily locate the implied referent. In 9.34, Matthew reproduces Mark 3.22, but deletes 'Beelzeboul'. In 12.22-24, he again reproduces Mark 3.22, this time including Beelzeboul. He uses a Q version of the story as well at 10.27-28 (Luke 11.18b-20). While 10.25b could have arisen prior to Matthew's writing in a context with Markan and Q traditions like that of 12.22-28, its more probable function is as a referent to 9.34 and a preparation for 12.22-28. The verse may not be designated an M saying.

(d) Verse 23[14]

The form of v. 23 consists of two sayings: v. 23a (*hotan . . . heteran*) is a logion that may be classified as either a prophetic-apocalyptic saying, or a legal saying; v. 23b (*amēn . . . anthrōpou*) is a prophetic-apocalyptic saying, and belongs to both the Amen-Words and the Son-of-Man sayings categories.[15] Each saying will be considered separately.

Verse 23a. No stylistic peculiarities set the saying apart from Matthew's usual style.[16] The vocabulary includes the use of *diokō* 'to persecute', which is most likely redactional. In 5.10, 11, 12, the use appears to be from Matthew (cf. the Q tradition [Luke 6.22]), as does the use in Matt 5.44 (Luke 6.27-28). The one unparalleled use outside of 10.23a is in Matt 23.34. Here, the entire concept of persecution from city to city occurs in an expansion of a Q saying (Luke 11.49-51), *kai diōxete apo poleōs eis polin*. The agreement in content between the two verses is most likely due to Matthew's editing.

The saying in v. 23a also fits Matthew's organization of ch. 10. The reference of *polei tautē* 'this city' would formally reach back to v. 15 (*polei ekeinē*).[17] The persecution described in v. 23a includes the conditions envisioned in vv. 16-22. The saying in v. 23a is consistent with Matthew's editing and shows no disjunction with the style or vocabulary common to Matthew.

Verse 23b. As noted above, v. 23b is both an Amen-Word and a Son-of-Man saying. One traditional form of Amen-Words, analyzed by K. Berger, is composed of *amēn legō hymin* plus *ou mē* plus the aorist subjunctive. The more specific style of v. 23b includes a *heōs an* after the *amēn*. Matthew has five uses of the formula. (1) In 5.18, Matthew is responsible for the form, as a comparison with Luke 16.17 shows. (2) In Matt 5.26, Matthew has built upon a Q saying (Luke 12.59) and is responsible for the form. (3) Matt 16.28 depends for the form on Mark 9.1.[18] (4) Matt 24.34 depends on Mark 13.30. (5) Matt 10.23 has no parallel.[19] The stylistic study suggests that the specific form employed in 10.23b could depend on either traditional material or redaction.[20]

In vocabulary, the use of *teleō* stands out. The word regularly occurs as part of an ending to discourse material in Matthew in the phrase *hote etelesen ho Iēsous* 'when Jesus had finished' (7.28; 11.1; 13.53; 19.1; 26.1). Two other uses of the word occur in unparalleled material. At 17.24, the meaning is 'to pay (a tax)'. In 10.23b, the meaning appears to be 'to end' or 'to finish'.[21]

In the clear redactional uses of *teleō*, the action to be finished is specified by a supplementary participle, which may be either implied by the context or supplied explicitly (e.g. the explicit *diatassōn* in 11.1). In 7.28; 13.53; 19.1; 26.1, the reader would understand either *legōn* or *lalōn*. The use in 11.1 follows the Classical Greek construction, which frequently supplies a supplementary participle with the verbs that mean 'to begin, cease, endure, grow weary'.[22] The use tends to drop out in Hellenistic Greek. Matthew's use of *teleō* in the redactional passages is in keeping with the tendencies of Hellenistic Greek. As Matt 11.1 demonstrates, Matthew uses the supplementary participle to specify a completed action.

In v. 23b, it is difficult to determine a participle and prepositional phrase that fit the construction of the saying and that refer to the immediate context. Obviously, the use of *teleō* in v. 23b requires some supplementary action, since 'the cities' makes little sense in the saying as the direct object of 'to finish'. The first preceding verb that may be supplied by the reader is *pheugō* in v. 23a. Thus, for the Greek reader, v. 23b might mean, 'For, amen, I say to you, you will not finish (fleeing [*pheugontas*] into/from [*eis/apo*]) the cities of Israel. . .'. A second option would supply *diōkō*. 'For, amen, I say to you, you will not finish (being persecuted [*diōkomenous*] in/through [*eis/dia*]) the cities of Israel. . .'. The first option supplies the nearest verb without requiring a change of voice. The preposition *eis* may be supplied from v. 23a, although *apo* might fit the sense of the sentence better. The second option effectively concludes the situation described in vv. 16-22. The verb, however, must be shifted to the passive voice. The supplement of *eis* from v. 23a fits the sense of the sentence, perhaps, in a better way than in option one. While both options are possible readings of the text, their roughness, or discontinuity, may indicate the use of a piece of tradition in v. 23b.[23]

In support of this aporia, we find that v. 23b is contrary to Matthew' s redactional interests. Matthew's understanding of mission, outlined above, is in tension with v. 23b. Further, Matt 24.14 (par Mark 13.10) emphasizes Matthew's point of view regarding the end time and its relationship to mission. Matthew rearranges the Markan order, 'And this Gospel of the Kingdom will be preached in the whole world as a witness to all the Gentiles (*tois ethnesin*) and then will come the end (*telos*)'. The final clause, which does not occur in Mark, is probably redactional and voices Matthew's eschatology. Verse 23b is an eschatological saying that anticipates the completion of something (mission or persecution) by the disciples limited to the cities of Israel before the end (the coming of the Son of Man), the verse is in tension with Matthew's own eschatology.[24]

Based on a study of vocabulary, along with a syntactical tension supported by a content analysis that separates this verse from Matthew's redactional interests, v. 23b may be assigned to the M sayings.[25]

Conclusions
(a) By comparison with Mark 13.9-13, vv. 17-22 may be assigned to Markan tradition, with allowances for Matthew's redactional touches. (b) By comparison with Luke 6.40, vv. 24-25a probably come from Q. (c) On the basis of an analysis of style, vocabulary, and content, v. 25b may be assigned to Matthew. On the basis of an analysis of style, vocabulary, and content, v. 23a probably comes from Matthew. (d) On the basis of tensions in vocabulary and syntax, supported by content contrary to Matthew's redactional interests, v. 23b may be assigned to the M sayings.

3. *Matt 10.26-39*

Translation

(26) 'Therefore, do not fear them; for nothing is veiled that will not be unveiled and nothing is hidden that will not be made known. (27) What I say to you in darkness, speak in the light and what you hear in private preach from the roofs of houses. (28) And do not fear the one who kills the body but is unable to take life; rather, fear the one who is able to destroy body and life in Gehenna. (29) Are not two sparrows sold for half a penny? And one of them will not fall upon the ground without the knowledge and consent of your father. (30) But even the hairs of your head are each one numbered. (31) Do not be afraid; you surpass by great value the worth of a sparrow.

(32) 'Therefore, everyone who confesses me before people, I will also confess them before my father, who is in heaven; (33) and whoever denies me before people, I will deny them also before my father, who is in heaven.

(34) 'Do not think that I came to cast peace on the earth; I did not come to cast peace but a sword. (35) For I came to divide man against his father and daughter against her mother and daughter-in-law against her mother-in-law, (36) and his family will be a man's enemies.

(37) 'The one who loves father or mother above me is not worthy of me, and the one who loves son or daughter above me is not worthy of me. (38) And whoever does not take his cross and follow after me is not worthy of me. (39) The one who finds his life will lose it, and the one who loses his life in my behalf will find it.'

Isolation Leading to M Sayings

(b) The entire section has parallels in Luke (C. 23). On the basis of agreement in vocabulary, content, and order, these verses may be assigned to Q.

4. *Matt 10.40-42*

Translation

(40) 'The one who receives you, receives me, and the one who receives me receives the one who sent me. (41) The one who receives a prophet in the name of a prophet will get a prophet's reward, and the one who receives a righteous person in the name of

a righteous person will get a righteous person's reward. (42) And whoever gives a cup of cold water to drink to one of the least of these in the name of a disciple, truly I say to you, he will not lose his reward.'

Isolation Leading to M Sayings
Summary: (a) vv. 40, 42 have parallels in Mark; (c) v. 41 is most likely from Matthew.

(a) Verses 40, 42
These verses have parallels in Mark 9.37, 41 (cf. Matt 18.5; Luke 10.16; John 13.20) (C. 24). Verse 40 depends on Mark 9.37 for the use of *dechomai* 'to receive'. It also carries over from Mark the phrase *dechetai ton aposteilanta me* (receives the one who sent me), which occurs only in Mark 9.37 (par Luke 10.16) in the Synoptic tradition. Matthew appears to take over and expand Mark 9.37b in Matt 10.40. He uses Mark 9.37a in Matt 18.5.

More clearly than v. 40, v. 42 depends on Markan tradition. Here agreement in style, vocabulary, and word order are sufficient to assign v. 42 to the Markan tradition. Matthew is probably responsible for the amen formula, as well as *eis onoma mathētou* 'in the name of a disciple'. The shift from *en* in Mark to *eis* in Matthew is in keeping with the interchangeability of the two prepositions in metaphorical use in Hellenistic Greek. Matthew uses *eis onoma* outside of this passage at 18.20 and 28.19. He uses *en onoma* only when quoting Ps 118.26 at Matt 21.9 and 23.39. He, therefore, may have a stylistic preference for the use of *eis* in construction with *onoma*.[26] From comparison with Mark 9.37, 41, Matt 10.40, 42 show signs of depending on Markan tradition.

(b) Verse 41
The verse fits Matthean style, vocabulary, and content. Stylistically, the participial construction of the relative clauses in v. 41a,b corresponds to Matthew's redaction of Mark in v. 40. The vocabulary continues Matthew's use of *dechomai* in the participles (v. 40), but uses *lambanō* 'to receive', which he prefers to *dechomai*, as the main verb.[27] Finally, the *eis onoma* construction may also be a mark of Matthew's editing.

The verse also bears conceptual similarities to other passages in the Gospel where Matthew's editing appears to be present. In 13.17,

Matthew edits a Q saying (Luke 10.24) to include 'prophets' and 'righteous people', where the latter term was probably absent from Q. Again in 23.34, Matthew adds a reference to the *dikaioi* 'righteous' to a Q saying (Luke 11.47). There is no evidence of an M saying in v. 41.

Conclusions
(a) Based on a comparison with Mark 9.37, 40, vv. 40, 42 are from Markan tradition. (c) Verse 41, although it is unparalleled, probably comes from Matthew.[28]

Chapter 4

MATTHEW 23

1. *Matt 23.1-12*

Translation

(1) Then Jesus spoke to the crowds and to his disciples (2) saying, 'The scribes and the Pharisees sit upon the chair of Moses. (3) Therefore, do and keep whatever they say to you, but do not do according to their works; for they speak, yet they do not act. (4) And they tie up burdens that are heavy and hard to carry[1] and put them on people's shoulders, but they, themselves, do not want to move them with their finger. (5) And they do all of their works in order to be seen by people; for they make their phylacteries broad and they lengthen their tassels, (6) and they love the first couch at the banquets and the first seat in the synagogues (7) and greetings in the market places and to be called "Rabbi" by people. (8) But you, do not be called "Rabbi", for your teacher is one, and you are all brothers. (9) And do not call someone[2] among you "Father" on earth, for your heavenly father is one. (10) Nor be called "Instructors" because your instructor, the Christ, is one. (11) But the greatest among you will be your servant. (12) And whoever exalts himself will be humbled and whoever humbles himself will be exalted.'

Isolation Leading to M Sayings

Summary: (a) vv. 6-7a, 11 have parallels in Mark; (b) vv. 4, 12 have parallels in Luke; (c) vv. 1, 7b most likely come from Matthew; (d) vv. 2-3, 5, 8-10 are possible M sayings.[3]

(a) Verses 6-7a, 11

Mark 12.38-39 contains another version of vv. 6-7a (C. 25). The agreement in vocabulary and content indicates that Matthew relies on Mark here. Luke 11.43 contains another version of these verses in the form of a woe against the Pharisees. Q may also underlie the Matthean text, as evidenced by the agreement in the order here (*prōtokathedrias . . . aspasmous*) between Matthew and Luke against Mark.[4] There is no evidence of an M saying here.

Mark 10.43, which Matthew also uses in Matt 20.26, contains a parallel to v. 11. The agreement in vocabulary and content is sufficient to assign v. 11 to the Markan tradition (cf. also Mark 9.35).

(b) Verses 4, 12
Luke 11.46 contains a parallel to v. 4 (C. 25). While Matthew and Luke do not agree precisely in vocabulary, the agreement in content allows for the assignment of v. 4 to Q.[5] Luke 14.11 (see also 18.14) parallels v. 12 (C. 25). The Matthean and Lukan versions of the tradition are closely parallel in vocabulary and content. Verse 12 may be assigned to Q.

(c) Verses 1, 7b
These verses likely come from Matthew. While v. 1 parallels Mark 12.37 in the sense that both are introductions to the scene for sayings of Jesus, Matthew and Mark do not agree in vocabulary or content. Matt 23.1 and Luke 20.45 both have the disciples and crowds as the audience of Jesus, but the lack of other agreement in the passage speaks against assigning v. 1 to Q. In another editorial introduction, Matt 5.1-2, Matthew includes both the crowds and disciples as Jesus' audience. The presence of parallels and content disjunctive from Matthew's interests are insufficient for assigning v. 1 to any level of the tradition, rather than to redaction.[6]

As noted above, v. 7a depends on Mark 12.38. Verse 7b expands the Markan tradition included in vv. 6-7a, and also introduces the discussion of the use of 'Rabbi' in v. 8. Since Matthew is responsible for the association of the various traditions in vv. 3-7a, he probably composed v. 7b in order to associate the Markan tradition in vv. 6-7a with the material in vv. 8-12.

(d) Verses 2-3, 5, 8-10
These verses contain possible M sayings.

Verses 2-3, 5. Verse 4, which comes from Q, interrupts an observable continuity of style, vocabulary, and content between vv. 3 and 5 (C.

26). The underlined elements in the diagram establish the continuity between vv. 3 and 5. Both sentences begin with *panta* followed by a conjunction (*oun*, *de*) and the third person plural verb. The phrase, *ta erga autōn* 'their works' (used only here in Matthew), ties the two sentences together as well. The verb *eipōsin* 'they say' in v. 3 apposes *poiousin* 'they do' in v. 5. Verse 3b establishes the connection between the two thoughts, 'for they speak, yet they do not act'. The progression in the verbs establishes a synthetic thought development, which is interrupted by v. 4.

Stylistically, Matthew does not usually use *pros to* with the infinitive; the construction occurs only in unparalleled passages, two of which have been designated M sayings (5.28; 6.1). *Pros to theathēnai* 'in order to be seen' occurs only here and in Matt 6.1.

Certain words and concepts are uncharacteristic of Matthew's use. Verse 2 contains the only use of Moses in Matthew independent of Mark. The use of *kathedras* 'seat' is one of two uses in Matthew. The other use at Matt 21.12 depends on Mark 11.15. The concept 'seat of Moses' is unattested elsewhere in the NT.[7]

The terms 'scribes' and 'Pharisees' in v. 2 occur together in Matt 5.20; 12.38; 15.1; 23.13, 14, 15, 23, 25, 27, 29. Matt 5.20 probably comes from Matthew. Matthew adds 'scribes' to his source (Mark 8.11) at Matt 12.38. Matt 15.1 takes over the reference to Pharisees and scribes from Mark 7.1. The entire phrase comes neither from Mark nor Q in the uses in Matt 23. 'Pharisees' comes from Q at v. 22 (Luke 11.42) and v. 25 (Luke 11.39), but 'scribes' is not present in Q. The formula appears to be Matthew's.[8] The saying that underlies vv. 2-3, 5 likely contains a reference to some group of opponents, but the group's specific designation remains uncertain.

The injunction *poiēsate kai tēreite* (*do and keep*) occurs only here in Matthew. Matt 5.19, where *poiēsē kai didaxē* occurs, contains the closest conceptual parallel. Only in 23.3 and 5.19 is *poieō* used with another finite verb linked by *kai* in Matthew. The parallel raises the possibility that 23.3 is of the same type of material as 5.19, which has been designated an M saying. Finally, *phylaktēria* 'phylacteries' occurs only in v. 5 in the entire NT.

The use of *tēreō* 'to keep' here may be compared with Matt 28.20. In the latter text, Jesus instructs his disciples to keep (*tērein*) *his* commandments. In Matt 23.2-3, those who sit on Moses' seat are the arbiters of what disciples are to do and keep. The content of vv. 2-3 is denied by Jesus at 28.20; by the composition of the Gospel, Matthew creates a tension between two traditions about the sayings of Jesus. His redactional perspective comes to the fore, not only in 28.20, but also in 5.21-48; 15.1-20; 16.11-12; 19.3-9, where the Matthean Jesus clearly denies the authority of those in charge of Jewish tradition to interpret the Law.

The concentration of unique vocabulary and of concepts distinct from Matthew's use and perspective makes probable the presence of an M saying in vv. 2-3, 5. On the basis of a disjunction in style and thought development created by the insertion of Q material between vv. 3 and 5, further supported by an analysis of style, vocabulary, and content, vv. 2-3, 5 may be assigned to the M sayings, with the exception of the phrase 'scribes and Pharisees'.

Verses 8-10. These verses display a parallel structure (C. 27). Disruptions to the parallel structure are underlined in the chart. The vocabulary contains words that characterize Matthew's editing. *Adelphos* (brother) occurs 15 times in Matthew outside of v. 8 in reference to people who are not blood relations, but share in a community with Jesus. Of the 15 uses, one depends on Mark, five on Q, five are probably redactional, and four occur in M sayings.[9] The pattern of use allows no firm conclusions, since the term characterizes both Matthew's editing and his traditions.

The phrase *ho patēr ho ouranios*, 'the heavenly father', occurs six times in Matthew outside of v. 9. In three instances, the phrase is a redactional addition to a known tradition (6.14 par Mark 11.25; 6.26, 32 par Luke 12.24, 30). In 5.48, the phrase appears to be part of a redactional summation. The saying in 15.13 that contains the phrase is unparalleled, but is most likely a redactional addition to the Markan tradition (see Mark 7.17). Finally, the use of the phrase in Matt 18.35 is in a redactional addition to a Matthean parable. The use of 'heavenly father' in v. 9 probably comes from Matthew.[10]

The use of *ho Christos* without further modification in v. 10 requires comment. The term occurs nine times in Matthew outside of this passage. The use comes from Mark four times. On four occasions, Matthew uses the term in a saying from a source, although the source does not contain the designation. The term occurs once in an unparalleled verse that is probably redactional. On the basis of these observations of the pattern of use, *ho Christos* probably comes from Matthew in v. 10, although the general availability of the title in early Christian tradition makes assurance difficult on this point.[11]

Verses 8-10 also contain unique words and concepts. Outside of vv. 7b, 8, only Judas, the betrayer, calls Jesus 'Rabbi' in Matthew (26.25, 49). Matthew changes Mark's use of the term to *kyrios* 'Lord' at Matt 17.4 (Mark 9.5) in the mouth of Peter. In Mark 11.21 Peter addresses Jesus as 'Rabbi', while in Matt 21.20 the disciples address him without the employment of a title. In Matt 9.28; 20.33 (par Mark 10.51) Matthew, unlike Mark, does not allow the blind men to address Jesus as *rabbouni*. In 9.28, 29, Matthew makes it clear that the two believe in Jesus. His reworking of Mark suppresses those parts of his tradition that have believers, including disciples, use 'Rabbi' as a title for Jesus.[12]

The term parallel to 'Rabbi' in v. 8, *didaskalos* 'teacher', receives similar treatment in Matthean redaction. Outside of v. 8, non-believers or hostile opponents use the term most often. This type of use depends on Mark three times and comes from Matthew five times.[13] In Matt 10.24-25a (Q), the saying is parabolic and does not designate Jesus explicitly as 'teacher '. In Matt 26.18 (par Mark 14.14), Jesus indirectly identifies himself as the teacher of the disciples. Outside of v. 8, Matthew tends to allow only non-believers or opponents to call Jesus *didaskalos*. In one instance that depends on a source, the title may apply to Jesus. As in the case of 'Rabbi', Matthew appears to suppress Jesus' being called *didaskalos* by believers during his ministry. While *Rabbi* and *didaskalos* occur outside of this passage as a term of direct address to Jesus from others, v. 8 is the single clear instance in the Gospel where Jesus in the indicative speaks of himself as both rabbi and teacher. The employment of these terms in this way is unique to v. 8 within the Gospel.[14]

Finally, *kathēgētēs* 'instructor' in v. 10 occurs nowhere else in the NT. In secular Greek, the meaning is simply 'teacher' (*paidagōgos*).[15] By Matthew's redactional addition of 'the Christ' in v. 10, he indicates that the term means more than teacher in his understanding. In its earlier form v. 10 may have been a synonymous parallel to v. 8.

It is evident by reference to the parallelism of v. 8 (C. 27) that the terms that are most likely redactional are the elements of each saying that break the parallel structure. The words less typical of Matthew's normal use occur within the elements of the sayings that maintain parallel structure. The coincidence of the analysis of vocabulary with the observations on structure suggests that here Matthew reworks a sayings unit already available to him.[16] On the basis of style and vocabulary, vv. 8-10 may be assigned without the obvious redactional elements to the M sayings. By eliminating the redactional elements and by using the simple form of v. 8 as a guide, a hypothetical reconstruction of the underlying saying results (C. 27).

Conclusions
(a) By comparison with Mark 9.38-39, vv. 6-7a, 11 may be assigned to the Markan tradition. (b) By comparison with Luke 11.46 and Luke 14.11 (18.14), vv. 4, 12 come from Q. (c) On the basis of analysis of compositional position, style, vocabulary, and content consistent with redactional interests, vv. 1, 7b come from Matthew. (d) On the basis of analysis of style, vocabulary, and content disjunctive from editorial intent both within the context and in texts elsewhere in the Gospel, vv. 2-3, 5 and vv. 8-10 may be assigned to the M sayings.

2. Matt 23.13-33

Translation

(13) 'Woe to you, scribes and Pharisees, hypocrites, because you slam the door of the Kingdom of Heaven in people's faces; because neither do you enter nor do you allow those who are entering to enter.[17]

(15) 'Woe to you, scribes and Pharisees, hypocrites, because you travel around the sea and land in order to make one proselyte, and when he becomes one you make him twice as much a child of Gehenna as yourselves.

(16) 'Woe to you, blind guides, the ones saying, "Whoever swears by the temple, is obligated". (17) Fools and blind ones, because what is greater, the gold or the temple that makes the gold holy? (18) and, "Whoever swears by the altar, it is nothing; but whoever swears by the gift on it, is obligated". (19) Blind ones, for what is greater, the gift or the altar that makes the gift holy? (20) Therefore, the one who swears by the altar swears by it and by everything on it; (21) and the one who swears by the temple swears by it and by the one who inhabits it; (22) and the one who swears by heaven swears by the throne of God and by the one who sits upon it.

(23) 'Woe to you, scribes and Pharisees, hypocrites, because you tithe dill and anise and cumin and leave aside the more heavy matters of the Law, justice and mercy and faith; but these things you should have done and not neglected those others; (24) Blind

guides, those who strain out the gnat and gulp down a camel.

(25) 'Woe to you, scribes and Pharisees, hypocrites, because you clean the outside of the cup and dish, but inside they are full from robbery and self-indulgence. (26) Blind Pharisee, clean first the inside of the cup in order that the outside of it might also be clean.

(27) 'Woe to you, scribes and Pharisees, hypocrites, because you resemble whitewashed tombs, which outside appear beautiful, but are inside full of dead bones and all uncleanness. (28) Thus, even you appear righteous to people on the outside, but on the inside you are full of hypocrisy and lawlessness.

(29) 'Woe to you, scribes and Pharisees, hypocrites, because you build the tombs of the prophets and decorate the graves of the righteous, (30) and you say, "If we had existed in the days of our fathers, we would not have been participants with them in the blood of the prophets". (31) Thus, you witness against yourselves because you are children of those who killed the prophets. (32) And as for you, fill up the measure of your fathers! (33) Snakes, offspring of vipers, how will you flee from the court of Gehenna?'

Isolation Leading to M Sayings
Summary: (a) no verses have parallels in Mark; (b) vv. 13, 23, 25-26, 27, 29-32 have parallels in Luke; (c) v. 28 most likely comes from Matthew; (d) vv. 15, 16-22, 24, 33 contain possible M sayings.[18]

(b) Verses 13, 23, 25-26, 27, 29-32
Verse 13 has a parallel in Luke 11.52 (C. 28). The verbal agreement and agreement in content show that both passages probably depend on Q. Verse 23 has a parallel in Luke 11.42. Agreement in vocabulary and content shows that both passages depend on Q. Verses 25-26 parallel Luke 11.39-41; Q probably underlies both passages, although a precise reconstruction of Q at this point is difficult. The Matthean version appears to be a more developed form of the Q tradition than the Lukan version. Verse 27 parallels Luke 11.44. Here, Matthew's editing is apparent from the emphasis on the contrast between inside and outside. Luke probably contains a more original form of the tradition.[19] That both sayings are cast as woes favors the assignment of the verse to Q. Verses 29-32 parallel Luke 11.47. With allowance for Matthew's editing, particularly in vv. 30 and 32, vv. 29-32 may be assigned to Q.

The parallels between Matthew and Luke reveal a complex tradition history underlying the woe formulas in Matthew. Q almost

certainly contained sayings in the form of woes in at least four
instances (Matt 23.13, 23, 27, 29 and their parallels in Luke 11.52, 42,
44, 47). The common elements of the formula in Q were (in order):
ouai hymin, hoti 'woe to you, because'. Matt 23.25 contains a woe
with the same underlying formula, but the parallel in Luke 11.39
does not give the verse as a woe. Since Luke introduces his discourse
with v. 39, it appears most likely that Matthew remains consistent
with Q's formulation here, and that Luke has removed the woe
formula in order to introduce his narrative. Matt 23.4, 6 contain
sayings given in Luke as woes (Luke 11.46, 43), but not presented as
woes in Matthew. It remains difficult to establish critically whether
or not Q contains these sayings as woes. By comparison with those
woes that clearly come from Q, the employment of the full formula
ouai hymin grammateis kai Pharisaioi hypokritai, hoti 'woe to you,
scribes and Pharisees, hypocrites, because' comes from Matthew. In
v. 15, the introductory formula of the unparalleled woe may be
Matthean, but the analogy of Matthew's use of Q also raises the
possibility of a traditional woe formula. Verse 16 departs from the
usual Matthean formula, which we will examine below. Probably
Matthew received five woes from Q (23.13, 23, 25, 27, 29). To these
he added two more woes at vv. 15, 16-22.[20]

(c) Verse 28
The verse acts as a summary application of the metaphor in v. 27.
The distinction between outside and inside probably comes from
Matthew's editing of the Q saying in v. 27. While v. 28 could possibly
have circulated independently from its present context, Matthew
more probably wrote v. 28 as a summary of v. 27.[21]

(d) Verses 15, 16-22, 24, 33
These verses contain possible M sayings.

Verse 15. Verse 15 is a Matthean woe formula (*ouai hymin* . . ., *hoti*
and the second plural verb *periagete* 'you travel around'). The style
shows no discontinuity with Matthew's usual use. Evidence of
Matthean redaction in the woe formula and in the style of the saying
does not, however, preclude the possibility of an underlying woe
saying, as the development of the woes taken from Q shows.

The vocabulary contains words and concepts that seldom occur in
both Matthew and the NT. *Prosēlytos* 'proselyte' occurs only here in

the Gospels. Acts 2.11; 6.5; 13.43 are the only other attestations of the word in the NT. In every case, the word refers to those who were first converts to Judaism and then later became Christian.[22]

The concept 'son of Gehenna' also is not typical of Matthew's redactional interest. The word *geenna* comes from Mark at Matt 5.29 (Mark 9.43, 45, 47) and at Matt 18.9 (Mark 9.43, 45, 47). The word comes from Q at 10.28 (Luke 12.5). It has no parallel at Matt 5.22; 23.15; 23.33. In no passage does Matthew add the word to an identifiable source (e.g. Mark, Q). In 23.33, as shown below, there is a suspicion of M material that cannot be further validated because of insufficient evidence. The weight of the evidence suggests that in v. 15 the use of *geenna* does not come from the redactor and most likely comes from the use of an M saying.

With the obvious redactional elements eliminated from v. 15, the saying reads, 'You travel around the sea and land in order to make one proselyte, and when he becomes one, you make him twice as much a child of Gehenna as yourselves'. The form of the saying demands that some group be cast as the opponents. For an answer to the questions whether an M woe underlies Matthew's text here as the Q woes do elsewhere in the chapter, and whether the saying's pre-Matthean form designates such a group, an investigation of vv. 16-22 is required.

Verses 16-22. These verses have a discernable parallel structure (C. 29). A is an introductory woe formula that identifies the opponents as 'blind guides'. B presents their argument on swearing by the temple and its gold. C is a further invective against the opponents, followed by D, a rhetorical question that exposes the false base of their argument. A' (*kai*) recalls the introductory woe in A. The subject of what follows in A' is the *hoi legontes* of A. B' presents a second argument on swearing, this time by the altar and its gift. C' recalls the invective of C by repeating *typhloi*. D' is a rhetorical question that, like D, exposes the false base of the opponents' argument. d' is a positive formulation of the proper interpretation of swearing based on the argument developed through A', B', C', D''. In the same way, d is the positive formulation from the argument developed through A, B, C, D. As the diagram shows, A, B, C, D, d are parallel in syntax to A', B', C', D', d'. The structure runs A, B, C, D, A', B', C', D', d', d. While parallel in structure to d' (v. 22) and d (vv. 20, 21), e (v. 22) does not relate directly to either of the two previous lines of argument. Instead, e seems to be a synthetic expansion related to v. 21, on the basis of the conceptual association established by *tǭ katoikounti* 'the one who dwells' (v. 21) and *tǭ kathēmenǭ* 'the one who sits' (v. 22), both of which are circumlocutions for God. The stylistic unity and careful balance of the verses indicates a probability that at least vv. 16-21, and perhaps v. 22 as well, are an original unity. The synthetic expansion of v. 22 could come either from the original composer of the saying, or from a later commentator. There are no signs of significant disjunctions within the pericope.[23]

The woe formula employed in v. 16 is unique within ch. 23. All other woes are in the form *ouai hymin, grammateis kai Pharisaioi, hypokritai hoti* followed by a verb in the second person plural. In v. 16, the formula is *ouai hymin, hodēgoi typhloi legontes* (woe to you, blind guides, the ones saying). The sayings that follow are in the third person. The style of v. 16, therefore, sets it apart from the style of the other woes in ch. 23, for which Matthew himself appears to be responsible. It is unlikely that vv. 16-22 circulated without a woe formula, because the content of the verses requires the designation of some set of opponents; therefore, no disjunction is apparent between vv. 16a and 16b.

The vocabulary contains concepts that are rare within Matthew. The use of *hodēgoi typhloi* 'blind guides' (v. 16), *mōroi kai typhloi* 'fools and blind ones' (v. 17), and *typhloi* 'blind ones' (v. 19) establishes a continuity of content within the unit and distinguishes the vocabulary of the unit from other Matthean uses. Matthew uses *typhlos* 'blind' either to designate the physically blind (9.27, 28; 11.5; 12.22; 15.30, 31; 20.30; 21.14) or to advance a polemic (15.14; 23.16, 17, 19, 24, 26). The single polemical use outside of ch. 23 (Matt 15.14) introduces a Q saying (Luke 6.39). Both Matt 15.13 and 14 appear to be Matthew's additions to the Markan tradition that underlies Matt 15.1-20 (Mark 7.1-23).[24] The use of 'blind Pharisee' at Matt 23.26 appears redactional, by comparison with Luke 11.40, where the opponents are designated as fools (*aphrones*). The remaining uses in Matt 23 come in unparalleled sayings. The preponderance of use in unparalleled sayings indicates that *typhloi* as a designation for opponents probably originates in M material, and not with Matthew himself. In those cases where Matthew is more clearly responsible for the term, it designates Pharisees specifically (15.14; 23.26). Such use is in keeping with Matthew's treatment of the Pharisees as the enemies of Jesus. In 23.16-22, the woe itself does not name the Pharisees as the opposition, but rather the connection to the Pharisees, obviously important for Matthew, is established only by the placement of vv. 16-22 within the chapter. The evidence suggests that the woe formula in v. 16, because it does not adhere to the other woe formulas in the chapter (which are probably redactional) comes from an underlying M saying.

Finally, the content of vv. 16-22 may be compared with Matt 5.33-37, which has already been designated M. In the Gospels, only these two passages address the issue of swearing. Matt 5.34 explicitly enjoins swearing in any form. The argument in 23.16-22, however, presupposes that there is a proper way to swear. Although the argument in vv. 16-22 attempts to expose the improper casuistry of the opponents, it does not deny the validity of an oath. Matt 5.33-37 shows Jesus as above any real argument; instead, he commands. In contrast, Matt 23.16-22 by its very structure conveys an argument and repudiation of the opponents' position. The dissimilarities between 5.33-37 and 23.16-22 establish a disjunction between the view of swearing in the two pericopes as well as their view of Jesus' role. The two different treatments may well indicate that Matthew uses two different traditions from the M material, one at 5.33-37 and the other at 23.16-22.[25]

In summary, the parallel structure in vv. 16-22 indicates the possibility that Matthew used a block of M material already available to him in the composition of these verses. The concentration of unusual vocabulary makes this possibility more probable. The disjunction between vv. 16-22 and 5.33-37 probably comes from the employment, by Matthew, of two different traditions within M. Verses 16-22 may be assigned to the M sayings.

These results can now be applied to the suspended question from v. 15. The designation of vv. 16-22 as a woe saying from M suggests v. 15 may also come from an M woe saying. This possibility is strengthened by the form and content, which require a group of opponents. The requirement could be met in v. 15 by designating the 'blind guides' from v. 16 as the opponents. These speculations make probable the case that Matthew used two woes from M material to supplement those available to him from Q.

Verses 24, 33. Only at vv. 24 and 33 are final summarizing invectives added to the woes based on Q (C. 28). These two verses have no parallels. Verse 24 is an invective directed against the same set of opponents as in v. 16, 'blind guides' (*hodēgoi typhloi*). The reader of the text must understand, 'You, [so and so], are blind guides'. in order to make the phrase into a sentence. The invective fits uneasily with its immediate context and the metaphor of straining and gulping does not seem to fit the question of tithing.[26] Taken together, these points suggest that v. 24 might originally have stood after v. 22, rather than in its present position, and that it was thus part of an M saying unit.

Verse 33 also requires a context to be understandable. The verse's invective seems to fit its immediately preceding context. The phrase *kriseōs tēs geennēs* 'court of Gehenna', however, raises a suspicion of an M saying in v. 33, since the use of *geennēs* appears to be uncharacteristic of Matthew's redaction in other passages (see above). Verse 33 may depend on an M saying from the same original unit of material that contained vv. 15, 16-22, 24. The evidence, however, is too inconclusive to support adequately the assignment of the verse to the M sayings. Verse 33 is best assigned to Matthew, particularly because no disjunction in context is observable.[27]

Conclusions

(a) No verses were found to depend on Markan tradition. (b) By comparison with Luke 11.52, 42, 39-41, 44, 47, vv. 13, 23, 25-26, 27, 29-32 depend on Q. (c) By analysis of its compositional position and emphases consistent with Matthew's interests, vv. 28, 33 come from Matthew. (d) On the basis of an analysis of style, vocabulary, and content disjunctive from Matthew's editorial interests, vv. 15, 16-22, 24 may be assigned to the M sayings.

3. *Matt 23.34-39*

Translation

(34) 'Because of this, behold, I send to you prophets and wise men and scribes; some of them you killed and crucified and some of them you beat in your synagogues and persecuted from city to city. (35) Thus all the righteous blood shed on the earth from the blood of Abel the righteous to the blood of Zachariah the son of Barachiah, who was killed between the temple and the altar, will come upon you. (36) Amen, I say to you, all these things will come upon this generation. (37) Jerusalem, Jerusalem, she who killed the prophets and stoned those sent to her, how often I have wanted to

gather your children in the same way that a hen gathers her chicks
under her wing, but you did not want it so. (38) Behold, your house
is being left desolate to you. (39) For I say to you, you will not see
me from now on until you say, "Blessed is the one who comes in
the name of the Lord".'

Isolation Leading to M Sayings

The entire section has parallels in Luke 11.49-51; 13.34-35 (C. 30).
On the basis of agreement in vocabulary, order, and content, these
verses may be assigned to Q.

Chapter 5

ANALYSIS OF THE M SAYINGS

1. *Introduction*

Fourteen M sayings were isolated in Chapters 2–4 (C. 2). These sayings were available to Matthew prior to his writing and thus may be designated traditional sayings.[1] In this chapter these traditional sayings will be analyzed in an attempt to identify possible traditions within the fourteen M sayings isolated thus far.

The analysis of Chapter 5 proceeds in three steps. First, clues from syntax and content may imply a common ideology and life setting. Therefore, individual traditional sayings may be grouped as representatives of single traditions. Second, it is possible on the basis of the content and life setting of each saying to determine if certain of the sayings cannot come from the same tradition as others. Third, after completing these two steps of analysis a provisional picture of the traditions available to Matthew as evidenced by the fourteen M sayings will be proposed. Each of these traditions will represent a specific set of ideas adhered to by a specific Christian group. Individual sayings that can neither be grouped with nor clearly excluded from other sayings may evidence other traditions or may be affiliated with M sayings yet to be isolated by the work of ch. 6. Further investigation in ch. 6 and the hypothesis of a history of traditions developed in ch. 7 may make it possible to suggest more specific life settings for some or all of these sayings. This provisional picture of the traditions represented in the M sayings will be used in ch. 6 as an aid in the isolation and analysis of other M sayings. These remaining sayings prove more difficult to isolate and analyze than the previously isolated sayings because they tend to occur as single logia in contexts where extensive editorial activity and/or the lack of a clear use of Mark and Q make critical leverage difficult to obtain.[2]

2. *Evidence of Groups of Sayings*

Sayings nos. 1, 2, 4, 5

Saying no. 1 contains the grammatical difficulty of the appropriate referent for 'these commandments' (*toutōn entolōn*).[3] Previous analysis eliminated redaction as an explanation for *toutōn*, but left open the possibility that the problem was bequeathed to Matthew by tradition. Grammatically, *houtos* may be used to refer forward. The LXX of Deut 1.1 contains precisely this use in reference to the *logoi* of Moses.

These (*houtoi*) are the words, which Moses spoke to all Israel . . .

Significantly, the insertion of Matt 5.20 by Matthew between sayings nos. 1 and 2 (Matt 5.19, 21) would have created the grammatical problem of the reference of *toutōn* present in the text; a problem that did not antedate this editing.

Previous studies in the antithetical form concentrate on the content of each antithesis and its relationship to what is known of Jewish interpretations of the Torah during the NT period. The primary question has been: Which of the antitheses revoke and which deepen or extend the Torah? The Jesus in the antitheses has been portrayed either as a new lawgiver (New Moses) or as the ultimate interpreter of the Law (Supreme Rabbi).[4] This analysis, however, will focus primarily on a second question: What is the meaning of the antithetical formula and what does that formula itself indicate about its life setting?[5]

Each of these sayings is composed of three elements: (1) the thesis, 'You have heard that it was said (to the ancients)'; (2) a scriptural citation or paraphrase; (3) the antithesis, 'But I say to you'.[6] As for the element 'to the ancients' in the thesis (1 above), *tois archaiois* may refer to those who received the written Law on Sinai.[7] The citation of scripture from the LXX, which follows in (2), supports this identification. Written Torah is cited, rather than *halakhah*, a rabbi's opinion.[8]

By its construction, the text has already referred to the scene of the giving of the Law on Sinai. If we return to the Sinai scene as recorded in Exodus, it may be possible to gain some guidance as to what sorts of inferences a first-century audience might have derived from the use of the antithetical formula.[9] In Exod 19.7-9 the relationship between God, Moses, and the people of Israel is specified prior to the giving of the Decalogue.

(7) So Moses came and called the elders of the people, and set before them all these words which God had commanded him. (8) And all the people answered together and said, 'All that God has spoken we will do and we have heard'. And Moses reported the words of the people to God. (9) And God said to Moses, 'Lo, I am coming to you in a thick cloud, that the people may hear when I speak with you, and may also believe you forever'.[10]

In v. 7, 'these words' apparently refers back to the content of Exod 19.3-6 (note the parallel phrase in v.6) in which God recites to Moses the acts of deliverance from Egypt and God's intention of making a covenant with the people Israel. In vv. 7-9 Moses acts as the spokesperson between God and the people. In v. 9, God declares the intention to speak so that the people may overhear the words to Moses. Even in v. 9, the role of Moses as mediator of the Law remains apparent to the reader.

In Exod 20.1, the Decalogue is preceded by, 'And God spoke all these words (*logous toutous*), saying . . . '[11] The text makes clear that the Decalogue is spoken by God; God is the author and creator of the Decalogue. It is clear from the provisions of Exod 19.10-25 that Moses as well as Aaron and the priests are the direct audience of the Decalogue. Exod 20.18-19 indicates that the people of Israel do not hear the commandments directly, but rely on Moses to communicate to them what God has said.

From these texts that concern the giving of the Torah on Sinai we may surmise that the Torah was generally understood as authored, spoken, by God. Moses appears as the primary communicator of God's Torah. Presumably, Aaron and the priests act as further confirmation of the accuracy of his mediation. At no point in the Exodus text does Moses speak any words other than what God has told him to speak; he is never represented as the author or originator of the Torah. Moses speaks only as an intermediary.

If the antithetical formula is constructed so as to recall the scene at Sinai, then the implication of Jesus' claim 'But, I say to you' is that he is the author and originator of what follows; the point is pressed upon the hearer by the use of the *de* in an adversative sense. Unlike the Exodus texts, there is no indication of a consultation between Jesus and God; no theophany occurs. Jesus as the speaker places his own present active indicative 'I say' (*legō*) in direct contrast to the passive 'it was said' (*errethē*). If, on the basis of this evidence, we suppose that the understood subject of *errethē* is Moses, then 'the ancient generation' refers to the people Israel. If the understood subject is God, then 'the ancient generation' may more specifically refer to Moses along with Aaron and the priests.[12]

For the first hearers or readers of the antithetical formula,[13] the two rather nuanced exegetical options for reading *errethē* may have been of little consequence with regard to the view of Jesus implied in the employment of the antithetical formula. In either understanding Jesus does not function like Moses; he is not simply a mediator with no independent voice of his own. Jesus, who employs the antithetical formula, is the authoritative presenter and author of commandments. He stands as it were with God as giver of Law; therefore he is not under the Law as given by God through Moses but is free to modify or abrogate the words of God as recorded in Torah.[14]

Saying no. 1 also corresponds ideologically with sayings nos. 2, 4, 5 in employing a similar concept of eschatological judgment. Saying no. 1 (Matt 5.19) may be classed form-critically as a 'sentence of holy law'.[15] Saying no. 1 indicates that the abolishing of the commandments of Jesus results in the assignment of the lowest place in the Kingdom of Heaven, while the keeping of the commandments results in a high place in the Kingdom. We might expect a less 'comforting' curse. The curious aspect of this type of curse in saying no. 1 is that exclusion from the Kingdom based on failure to observe the commandments is not put forth as an option. Saying no. 2 (Matt 5.22) in its second sentence states that anger with the brother, or the use of derogatory names, results in judgment before the final eschatological court.[16] It should be noted that saying no. 2 does not specify what the verdict will be and therefore does not explicitly go beyond saying no. 1. It coheres with saying no. 1 in that it assigns judgment for the abrogation of commandments to no human court but to the eschatological court; it is a sentence of holy law. If sayings nos. 1 and 2 occurred together with sayings nos. 4 and 5 in a pre-Matthean tradition, then they provide an understanding of eschatological sanction for the words of Jesus recorded in sayings 4 and 5 even though these latter two sayings contain no explicit eschatological sanction.

We have found evidence, then, that saying no. 1 is best understood as the introduction to sayings nos. 2, 4, and 5. The problem of the referent for 'these commandments' is solved by understanding the *toutōn* as referring forward to the commandments of Jesus in sayings nos. 2, 4, and 5. Further support for this conclusion comes from the ideological implications derived from the content of the sayings. Saying no. 1 as well as sayings 2, 4, and 5 bring to the mind of the hearer the scene of the giving of Torah on Sinai. The content of saying no. 1, which assigns a place in the Kingdom of Heaven on the basis of the keeping of these commandments of Jesus, indicates that Jesus' commandments have an eschatological sanction. Saying no. 2 also indicates this view. Hence, the tradition preserved in sayings 1, 2, 4, 5 probably reflects a Christian group who regards Jesus as the quintessential eschatological giver of commandments.

Two aspects of this tradition suggest that the Christians who adhered to these sayings were not part of a first-century Jewish community. First, Jesus' use of the antithetical formula is unparalleled by any other Jewish religious figure mentioned in the Jewish documents of the period. Nor can we discern any expectation attached to a messianic figure in Judaism that would anticipate such behavior.[17] It is doubtful that such a viewpoint as expressed in these sayings would be acceptable to a Jewish community in the first century dominated by Jews who did not believe in Jesus as the Messiah. Second, the direct abrogation of oath taking in saying no. 5 probably sets the Christian group outside of most first-century Jewish communities. Both the rabbis and the Qumran community prescribe the taking of oaths as a religious duty under certain circumstances.[18]

Saying no. 3

The community rule stated in saying no. 3 gives specific information about the social setting of the community that preserved or created it. By its content, no. 3 depicts a group who worship in the temple, or know about such temple worship and value such worship positively. It remains impossible to determine whether or not the saying comes from the period before or after the fall of the temple, since other Jewish sources as well as New Testament documents written after 70 still speak of the temple at times in the present tense.[19]

Saying no. 6

This community rule is a logion which could have circulated independently. The saying was earlier shown to interrupt the pattern of saying no. 5. On this basis its inclusion within saying no. 5 is probably best attributed to Matthew. It is unlikely to be from the same tradition as saying no. 5. The brevity and content of the saying simply offer little foothold for critically approaching its life setting.

The saying is somewhat similar to rabbinic traditions that castigate the frivolous taking of oaths.[20]

Sayings nos. 7 and 11

H.D. Betz contends that the sayings which compose saying no. 7 were collected by, and are representative of, a single community.[21] The sayings define appropriate religious behavior for almsgiving, prayer, and fasting. Bultmann designates these sayings as rules of Christian piety, which he thinks are used to define the piety of the Christian community over against Judaism.[22]

A description of hypocritical opponents in saying no. 7 offers a clue to the social setting for the community that adheres to this rule. The *hypokritai* are those who do their righteousness in order to be seen by other humans (*pros to theathēnai*). The activities assigned to them are almsgiving, prayer, and fasting, which parallel the known activities of regular Jewish piety in the NT period.[23] The hypocrites of saying no. 7 appear most likely to be synagogue-attending Jews.

Saying no. 7 identifies the mistake of these hypocrites as performance of pious acts for reward from other humans, rather than from God. In contradistinction to this mistake, the saying invokes the Father who sees and rewards in secret (*ho patēr sou ho blepōn en tǭ kryptǭ apodōsei soi*). This designation of God occurs nowhere else in the NT and is rare, if not unique, in Jewish documents of the period.

The element contained in the third division of the saying raises special difficulties. The command to wash the face and anoint the head directly contradicts the prescriptions for observing public fasts, as they are specified for the ninth of Ab and the Day of Atonement. The prescriptions for fasting in saying no. 7 may place the group who adhere to them beyond the conventional Judaic practice of the period and thereby bring them into conflict with members of a Jewish synagogue that observed such practice.[24] On the other hand, however, such a perspective might still have been tolerable within a Jewish synagogue, especially if the prescription was understood to refer to weekly fasting, rather than to the yearly fast on the Day of Atonement. A reference to weekly fasting would best conform to the rest of the saying; for the other two acts, almsgiving and prayer, were definitely weekly. In such a case no Jewish religious scruple would have been violated, especially if these acts were kept private as called for in the saying.

The probability that the group indicated by saying no. 7 was part of a synagogue dominated by non-Christian Jews is enhanced by the association of saying no. 7 with no. 11. In both sayings the phrase *pros to theathēnai* 'in order to be seen' designates the motivation for the acts of the opposing group. In identifying the opponents in saying no. 11, the designation of those seated 'upon Moses' seat' clearly indicates the leaders of a synagogue. The command in the second sentence affirms the leaders' position as proper teachers of religious behavior based upon their line of interpretative authority traced to Moses: 'Therefore do and keep whatever they say to you'. But the action of the leaders is castigated, 'for they speak, yet they do not act'. The apparent polemic in saying no. 11 is like that of no. 7. It appears to be an intramural argument and the specific charge is that those castigated perform acts of piety in order to be seen by others.

The connection of vocabulary and content between sayings nos. 7 and 11 allows us to hypothesize that these two sayings come from the same tradition. The group who adhere to and preserve this tradition accept the authority of certain leaders of a synagogue and also criticize the public displays of piety of the leaders and other members of the community. The dispute indicated by this tradition is best understood as an intramural dispute between certain Christian members of a synagogue community and other members of the community. Sayings of Jesus that define proper religious behavior are being used in the dispute; it is even possible that they are the initiators of the dispute. The two sayings appear to be instruction to a Christian group within a synagogue community. The synagogue is probably led by non-Christian Jews.

Saying no. 8
Saying no. 8 creates particular difficulties for interpretation.[25] As was noted when saying no. 8 was isolated as M, it interrupts the pattern of saying no. 7.[26] The most plausible way to account for this interruption is that saying no. 8 was placed here by someone other than the originator of saying no. 7, perhaps Matthew himself. The negative conclusion that sayings nos. 7 and 8 come from different traditions suggests that saying no. 8 probably comes from a life setting different from no. 7.

The content of saying no. 8 indicates that the Christians who promulgate or adhere to the saying fear the incursion of Gentile religious practices into their group. Such a warning would be particularly apt if the group was admitting Gentile converts. The Christian group would then primarily be composed of Jews who now also consider themselves Christian. The saying may have been used to instruct new Gentile converts and to wean them away from their previous religious practices.

Sayings nos. 9 and 10

In content, saying no. 9 limits the mission of the community to Israel and forbids an active mission to Gentiles and Samaritans. The saying does not explain the limitation.

A supplementary participle is necessary to complete the action of the verb *teleō* in saying no. 10; therefore the saying did not occur as a single isolated logion in the tradition prior to Matthew's editing, since it requires a context to be understandable. Saying no. 9 supplies the context necessary to make saying no. 10 understandable. Placed together, the two sayings result in a unit.

> Do not go in the way of the Gentiles and do not enter the city of the Samaritans; but rather go out to the lost sheep of the nation of Israel. For amen, I say to you, you will not finish the cities of Israel before the Son of Man comes.

The reconstruction clarifies the grammar by suggesting that the reader supply the supplementary participle *poreumenoi*, as well as a preposition *pros*, for the verbal action indicated by *teleō*: 'For, amen, I say to you, you will not finish (going to) the cities of Israel until the Son of Man comes'. The reference to 'the *city* of the Samaritans' and 'the *cities* of Israel' shows a further affinity.

Attaching saying no. 10 to saying no. 9 reveals a rationale for limiting the mission to Israel: the parousia will occur during the mission. Such a limitation surely belongs to the first generation of Christianity in Palestine, because within Palestine one could speak of 'cities of Israel' and within the first generation early Christian missionaries could visit all of these cities. Furthermore, within Palestine the geographical designation of the 'city of the Samaritans' makes the clearest sense in reference to Samaria, itself. This interpretation suggests that the tradition represented in sayings nos. 9 and 10 comes from a Christian group involved in a mission to Jews within Palestine, who conversely do not engage in an active mission to Gentiles and Samaritans.

Saying no. 12
Saying no. 12 deals with the titles and offices of a community. In the saying Jesus denies to his followers the use of at least one title of respect current in Judaism and probably used in at least some synagogues in the first century—Rabbi. The second sentence may also refer to the use of the title 'Father' in reference to certain Jewish teachers.[27] The community that adheres to or produces saying no. 12 does not accept the titles which designate specific Jewish leaders. It may have used or formulated this saying in direct antithesis to titles used in a first-century synagogue.

The saying implies certain theological and christological views among the group that promulgated or preserved this tradition prior to Matthew. God is seen as the only father, and in context, the authority for the group's organization and life. Jesus is seen as the only teacher. The group probably refuse, on this basis, to recognize any other authority as teacher or interpreter.

These aspects of the life setting implied by the content of saying no. 12 indicate that the Christians who adhere to saying no. 12 probably do not affiliate themselves with a synagogue dominated by non-Christian Jews. They may formulate their own organization in awareness of and in antithesis to the organization of a particular synagogue. As we saw, the group that adhere to sayings 1, 2, 4, and 5 see themselves in antithesis to Jewish adherence to the Mosaic Torah followers of Jesus, the single teacher, as the giver of the eschatological commandments. The group that adhere to saying no. 12 formulate their leadership in antithesis to the claims probably made by certain Jewish teachers. The similarity in ideology and life setting allows us to hypothesize that sayings nos. 1, 2, 4, 5 and 12 come from the same tradition. The hypothesis may be further tested in ch. 6, if other M sayings of a similar ideology and life setting are isolated.[28]

Sayings nos. 13, 14
Previously, we have argued that these sayings occurred together in pre-Matthean material.[29] Form-critically, sayings nos. 13 and 14 are Woe Oracles. (Saying no. 14 also contains a legal argument and is therefore a mixed form.) The Woe form requires opponents; in both sayings, these appear as 'blind guides' (*hodēgoi typhloi*), and so are leaders. Saying no. 13 gives the further information that these guides advocate proselytizing of Gentiles. The reference may fit the activities of either Jewish or Christian groups in the first century.[30]

Saying no. 13 denounces these proselytizing activities on the basis that the Gentile becomes worse than the guides themselves. Apparently the 'blind guides' err in some way on their terms of admission of the Gentile into their community. Further, the saying also assigns these 'blind guides' to the same realm of judgment and death as their proselyte—the saying implies that the guides are themselves sons of Gehenna. Perhaps there is concern for the eschatological destiny of the Gentile on the part of the group reflected in saying no. 13. Those who adhere to saying no. 13 may know of what they consider to be an appropriate mission to Gentiles on different terms from that of the 'blind guides', but whether or not they themselves practiced it is unclear; they are simply opposed to the mission engaged in by the 'blind guides'.

Saying no. 14 provides further information about these blind guides: they improperly interpret the taking of oaths. Besides the form of a 'woe' the saying takes the form of a legal debate.[31] The rebuttals implicitly presuppose the propriety of oath taking, with the temple, its cult, and God as guarantors of the oath. Probably, then, the saying comes from a Christian group who values the Jewish temple and cult as significant to their religious practice, whether or not the temple is still in existence. In this regard the life setting of saying 14 is similar to saying no. 3 discussed above, and these sayings may represent the same tradition. The group that preserved or created saying no. 14 argue with the leadership on their own terms. The importance and acceptability of swearing remains unchallenged; only the halakhic interpretation of the proper way to swear is attacked. The group engage in their own interpretation based upon a saying of Jesus, and reject the authority of certain leaders who offer a different interpretation. Whether the 'blind guides' envisioned by sayings nos. 13 and 14 are Jewish leaders or other Christians cannot be critically determined simply by reference to the content of these two sayings. The use of the word 'Gentile' as well as the importance of the temple and its cult in these two sayings indicates the probability that the dispute is among those who share a common Jewish heritage.[32]

Conclusions

By an analysis of syntactical clues as well as indications of similar ideology we have suggested that prior to Matthew's writing certain of the M sayings were already associated in traditions available to

Matthew. Certain relatively probable associations between sayings have been suggested:

Sayings 1, 2, 4, 5
Sayings 7, 11
Sayings 9, 10
Sayings 13, 14

Other more hypothetical associations based on ideology and life setting have also been suggested.

Saying 12 affiliated with 1, 2, 4, 5
Saying 3 affiliated with 13, 14

3. *Evidence of Mutually Exclusive Traditions*

From the evidence of the M sayings we may further attempt to clarify the traditions available to Matthew by looking at the ideologies and life settings to see if any of the sayings thus far derived are indicative of traditions so diverse as to preclude direct association prior to Matthew's use of them.

Saying no. 12 compared with saying no. 11
Saying no. 12 denies the titles of certain synagogue leaders. By organizing itself under the exclusive leadership of God as Father and Jesus as the *teacher* and *instructor*, the community refuses to recognize the authority of those synagogue leaders implied by the titles 'Father' and 'Rabbi'. On the other hand, saying no. 11 affirms the teaching authority of certain synagogue rulers. The two sayings appear to represent significantly different ideologies and life settings. We may hypothesize that saying no. 12 comes from a tradition different from that of saying no. 11 and, by extension, from no. 7.

Saying no. 5 compared with saying no. 14
A comparison of sayings nos. 2, 4, and 5 with nos. 13 and 14 reveals that sayings nos. 5 and 14 treat similar content on oath taking in two completely different ways. In no. 5, Jesus forbids swearing in any form; in no. 14, the criticism of specific oaths presupposes a proper way of swearing. The contrast in treatments appears vividly in the structures of the sayings. In no. 5, the command is absolute; no legal argumentation is engaged in; and no opponents are named as an identifiable group. In no. 14, a group of opponents (blind guides) are

explicitly engaged and defeated in a legal argument.[33] The full comparison of content between sayings nos. 5 and 14 indicates that they probably belong to mutually exclusive traditions; therefore, sayings nos. 1, 2, 4 and 5 come from a different tradition than that of nos. 13 and 14.

Saying no. 11 compared with sayings nos. 13 and 14
In saying no. 11 the authority of certain synagogue leaders is affirmed as binding in the teaching and interpretation of rules for religious behavior. By contrast the 'blind guides' named in sayings 13 and 14 offer an erroneous interpretation and are implicitly not to be followed. The position of the group in relationship to certain leaders in saying no. 11 is significantly different from the position of the group that adheres to sayings nos. 13 and 14. Saying no. 11 and by extension no. 7 probably come from a different tradition from the tradition represented by nos. 13 and 14.

4. *A Provisional Picture of Traditions in the M Sayings*

The analysis of ch. 5 suggests a picture of at least three distinct traditions that are represented in the 14 M sayings isolated in Chapters 2–4.

> Sayings nos. 1, 2, 4, 5 and possibly 12
> Sayings nos. 7, 11
> Sayings nos. 13, 14 and possibly 3

In addition sayings nos. 9 and 10 were probably found together as a unit prior to Matthew's editing, but we cannot exclude them from or associate them with any of the above traditions. There is no indication of a mission stance in the tradition represented by sayings nos. 1, 2, 4, 5 and 12, nor of a clear date. Information about mission or date or geographical locale is also missing from sayings nos. 7, 11. Saying no. 13 does contain a reference to a Gentile mission, and we suspect that the argument with the authorities in no. 13 involves the terms of admission of Gentiles into a community. But is the opposition in saying no. 13 to the Gentile mission of the 'blind guides' on the basis of a limitation of the Christian mission to Palestinian Jews as specified in nos. 9-10? Critical certainty is impossible at this point, and rather than relating sayings 9-10 to any of the three traditions we have isolated, we will for the moment regard them as independent.

Similarly, the information derived from the content of sayings nos. 6 and 8 makes it difficult to associate them clearly with other M sayings at the traditional level. It is probable that no. 6 does not come from the same tradition as no. 5, as we noted above. Whether saying no. 6 may be associated with either sayings nos. 7, 11 or nos. 13, 14 cannot be critically determined. It is suggestive that no. 6 treats the same subject, oath taking, as no. 14 and with a similar seriousness. Saying no. 8 treats the problem of the reception of Gentiles into an early Christian group. Above we found it unlikely that saying no. 8 comes from the same tradition as no. 7, the saying in which it is embedded in Matthew's text. It is probable, however, since saying no. 8 directly discusses the problem of Gentile converts, that it is unlikely to come from a Christian group that does not proselytize in some way. Thus it probably does not come from the same tradition as sayings nos. 9, 10. At this point it may neither be excluded from nor associated with any of the other M traditions.

The provisional picture of traditions in the M sayings and of the ideologies and life settings in each of the M sayings previously isolated provides a further aid in isolating and analyzing the remaining M sayings in our next chapter. In turn, the results of Chapter 6 may further modify the picture presented here.

Chapter 6

ISOLATION OF FURTHER M SAYINGS

In addition to the complete M sayings that occur in large blocks in narrative contexts, other unparalleled sayings in Matthew may contain M sayings material. A survey of the text of Matthew, compared to Mark and Luke, yields eight sayings that may contain M sayings (doublets are listed together).

1. Matt 5.5, 7-10
2. Matt 5.14, 16[1]
3. Matt 7.6
4. Matt 7.15
5. Matt 11.28-30
6. Matt 12.34, 36-37
7. Matt 18.16-19; 16.17-19
8. Matt 19.10-12

For each of these sayings, this study will: (a) offer a translation; (b) analyze the style, vocabulary, and content in an effort to derive evidence for assignment either to Matthew or to M; (c) when an M saying is isolated, suggest a life setting including possible connections with other M sayings.

The accumulated results and analysis of M in Chapter 5 will aid in the isolation of further M sayings. Style, vocabulary, and particularly content that are more continuous with the previously isolated M sayings than with Matthew's own interests will help to distinguish other probable M sayings.

1. *Matt 5.5, 7-10*

a. *Translation*

(5) Blessed are the humble, for they shall inherit the earth.[2] (7) Blessed are those who do mercy, for they shall receive mercy. (8)

Blessed are the pure in heart, for they shall see God. (9) Blessed are
the peacemakers, for they shall be called God's children. (10)
Blessed are those who are persecuted in behalf of righteousness, for
theirs is the Kingdom of Heaven.

b. *Analysis*
Verse 5

The style of v. 5 is identical to the beatitudes derived from Q in vv. 3,
4, 6 (Luke 6.20-21). Whether the style is imitated by Matthew or an
earlier tradent cannot be critically determined; therefore, unless
elements of vocabulary and content can be shown to be disjunctive
from those typical of Matthew's, the style must be presumed
redactional.

Verse 5 contains two rare terms: *prays* 'humble' and *klēronomeō*
'inherit'. *Prays* occurs only twice in Matthew outside of this passage.
One use is a citation of Zech 9.9 at Matt 21.5, which interprets Jesus'
entry into Jerusalem. The citation probably comes from Matthew,
although a traditional association of the prophecy in Zechariah with
the entry into Jerusalem cannot be ruled out. The second use is more
noteworthy. At Matt 11.29, in an unparalleled saying, Jesus refers to
himself as 'humble, lowly in heart'.

Klēronomeō also occurs twice outside of v. 5. Matthew adds the
term to his sources at 19.29 (Mark 10.30; Luke 18.30) and uses the
term again at 25.34 in an unparalleled narrative. The phrase reads
'inherit eternal life' in 19.29 and 'inherit the Kingdom' at 25.34. All
three uses appear to be consistent with Matthew's own understanding
of eschatological judgment. The evidence of M sayings in v. 5 is
inconclusive. No observable disjunction in vocabulary or content sets
the verse apart from Matthew's usual concerns. No clear evidence
shows the verse as more typical of M than of Matthew's redaction.
Therefore, v. 5 cannot be assigned to M.

Verse 7

Neither style nor vocabulary set v. 7 apart from Matthew's usual
use. *Eleeō* 'to do mercy' occurs six times in Matthew outside of this
passage. Three of these occurrences depend on Mark; two are added
to a Markan pericope by Matthew; and one occurs in an M parable.[3]
Matthew's use of the cognate *eleos* indicates the likelihood that the
vocabulary of v. 7 is Matthew's. At 9.13, Matthew adds a citation
formula from Hos 6.6 (repeated at 12.7). At 23.23, Matthew's version

of the Q saying (Luke 11.42) uses *eleos* as one of the three weightier matters of the Law which the scribes and Pharisees ignore. The performance of mercy in the ministry of Jesus is contrasted with the failure of the scribes and Pharisees to show mercy (9.13; 12.7; 23.23). The use of *eleeō* in 5.7 seems consistent with Matthew's own redactional use of the term. Although v. 7 is unparalleled, it cannot be assigned to M.

Verse 8
As in v. 7, the style in v. 8 contains no observable disjunction with redaction. The phrase *katharoi tę̄ kardią* 'pure in heart' is unique within the NT, and probably depends on Ps 24.4 (23.4 LXX). It would, therefore, be available to Matthew or to a previous tradent in his community. The word *kardia* is used 15 times in Matt (Mark 11; Luke 22; John 7). The closest conceptual use to Matt 5.8 comes in an unparalleled saying at Matt 11.29, where Jesus describes himself as *tapeinos tę̄ kardią* 'lowly in heart'. The use of 'heart' here is also consistent with the uses in 15.18-19 (par Luke 7.21); 18.35 (in an unparalleled parable); and 24.28 (par Luke 12.45). The distribution of the word in both Markan and Q traditions as well as the possibility of redactional uses elsewhere, hampers the certainty of any conclusion about v. 8. The verse, therefore, cannot be assigned to M.

Verse 9
Stylistically consistent with its surrounding context, v. 9 shows no peculiarities that set it apart from Matthew's usual use. In its vocabulary, *eirēnopoios* is a *hapax logomenon* in the NT (the verb occurs in Col 1.20). *Huioi theou* is used here and in three other passages that are likely to be redactional (Matt 5.45 compared with Luke 6.35; see also Matt 8.12; Matt 13.38). The presence of a *hapax* is suggestive but not conclusive. The presence of 'children of God' is most likely redactional. The verse cannot be critically assigned to the M sayings material.

Verse 10
Verse 10 also appears to be redactional. The style of v. 10 is consistent with both the beatitudes derived from Q (vv. 3, 4, 6) and the unparalleled beatitudes (vv. 7, 8, 9). Specific Matthean vocabulary occurs in the verse. *Eneken dikaiosynēs* is close to the use in Matt 6.33, where Matthew adds *dikaiosynē* to a Q logion (Luke 12.31). By

its context in the beatitudes, as well as by the reference to persecution, the use apparently indicates that the righteousness for which the believer is persecuted belongs to the Kingdom (i.e. to God). The use is different from the single occurrence in an M saying previously isolated (Matt 6.1, saying no. 7), where righteousness refers to the acts of almsgiving, prayer, and fasting, i.e., to human acts toward God. The redactional addition of *righteousness* to Q in 5.6 also indicates Matthew's own perspective. Matt 5.6, 10; 6.33 are the primary indicators of Matthew's own understanding of *dikaiosynē*.[4]

Diōkō 'to persecute' characterizes Matthew's vocabulary. In 5.11, 12 the term is added to a Q logion (see Luke 14.34-35). At 5.44, Matthew again uses the term where Q likely did not have it (see Luke 6.28). The term is redactional at 10.23a. In Matt 23.24, the word is probably added to Q by the redactor. The style, vocabulary, and content of 5.10 all point to redaction.[5]

2. *Matt 5.14, 16*

a. *Translation*

> (14a) You are the light of the world. (14b) A city set upon a hill is not able to be hidden. (16) Thus let your light so shine before people that they might see your good works and glorify your father, the one who is in the heavens.

b. *Analysis*

Verses 14, 16 consist of three sayings. Verse 14a probably comes from Matthew. While unparalleled, it is stylistically identical to v. 13, which Matthew appears to have composed as an introduction to a saying derived from Q (see Luke 14.34-35). No observable disjunction from Matthew's usual use appears in the vocabulary or content. There is no clear indication of an M saying here.

Verse 16 has no observable discontinuity in style from Matthew's usual use. Further, distinctive Matthean vocabulary occurs in the verse in the phrase *ton patera hymōn ton en tois ouranois* (your father, the one who is in the heavens). Other vocabulary and content display insufficient distinction from Matthew's normal use to give evidence of an identifiable traditional saying underlying the verse.

Verse 14b is a possible M saying. It has a parallel in *Gosp. Thom.* 32-33a.

(32) Jesus said, 'A city being built on a high mountain and fortified cannot fall, nor can it be hidden'.

(33a) Jesus said, 'Preach from your housetops that which you will hear in your ear [(and) in the other ear]. (33b) For no one lights a lamp and puts it under a bushel, nor does he put it in a hidden place, but rather he sets it on a lampstand so that everyone who enters and leaves will see its light.[6]

On the form-critical principle that expansions of detail, particularly adjectival expansions, are secondary,[7] *Gosp. Thom.* 32 may be a later form of a traditional saying preserved also in Matt 5.14b. The subsequent saying in *Gosp. Thom.* 33a is similar to the Q saying preserved in Matt 10.27 and Luke 12.3. *Gosp. Thom.* 33b is also similar to, and perhaps later than, the Q tradition underlying Matt 5.15, Luke 8.16; 11.33. *Gosp. Thom.* 33b is perhaps closest to the form of Q preserved in Luke, but that may be due to Matthew's more extensive rewriting of Q than Luke in this instance. The presence of a traditional saying in *Gosp. Thom.* 32, which parallels Matt 5.14b in a context formed by Q sayings, suggests the likelihood that v. 14b also comes from Q. The parallels in *Gospel of Thomas* at least raise sufficient doubt to prevent the assignment of v. 14b to M.

3. *Matt 7.6*

a. *Translation*

(6a) Do not give the holy to dogs, (b) neither cast your pearls before swine, (c) lest they trample them with their feet (d) and afterwards turn to attack you.

b. *Analysis*

Verse 6 lacks a smooth connection with its surrounding context either in Matt 7.1-5 or 7.7-12.[8] A catchword connection may be established by the use of *didōmi* in both vv. 6 and 7. Based on these observations, we note that an aporia of content occurs at v. 6.

The observation of the aporia is further supported by source criticism. The entire section (Matt 6.19–7.28) appears to be based on Q material arranged according to Matthew's own outline. Matt 7.1-5 parallels Luke 6.37-42, while 7.7-12 has a parallel in Luke 11.9-13. Here, v. 6 must come either from Matthew or from the M sayings material.

The style of v. 6 fits well the command style of the entire section. Matt 6.19, 25, 34; 7.1 all use the negative command form of *mē* plus the second plural subjunctive. The vocabulary in v. 6a contains words that are probably non-Matthean. *Kyōn* 'dog' occurs only here in Matthew. The variant and perhaps diminutive form *kynarion* occurs in Matt 15.24, 26, which Matthew takes from Mark 7.27, 28. *To hagion* 'holy things' is rare in the Gospels, occurring only here and in Luke 1.35. *Margaritas* 'pearl' is found outside of this passage only in Matt 13.45, 46 in the Gospels. There, the word probably depends on underlying tradition.[9] *Choiros* 'pig' is used only here in the metaphorical sense. Elsewhere, the literal meaning is employed by Matthew in dependence on Markan tradition (Matt 8.30, 31, 32 par Mark 5.11-16; Luke 8.32-33). The concentration of unusual vocabulary in v. 6a, b indicates strong evidence for an underlying M saying.

Verse 6c, d, on the other hand, contains vocabulary that more closely conforms to Matthew's usual interest. *Katapateō* 'to trample' occurs only here and at 5.13b, which parallels Mark 9.49-50; its addition here appears redactional. *Strephō* 'to turn' occurs five times outside of this passage and appears redactional in every use.

The form of v. 6 can be classified as a logion/exhortation. A core logion may be identified in vv. 6a, b.[10] The ensuing clause introduced by *mēpote* (lest) could be an expansion. The final clause (v. 6c, d) contains the highest concentration of redactional terminology.

Two sayings similar to v. 6 occur in *Gosp. Thom.* 73.

> Do not give what is holy to dogs, lest they throw them on the dung heap. Do not throw the pearls to swine, lest they grind it to bits.

The presence of the two sayings in *Gosp. Thom.* 73 suggests the probability that the traditional saying underlying Matt 7.6 contained a form of the clause introduced by *mēpote*. Although uncertain, the evidence inclines toward the finding that some traditional clause underlies v. 6c, d. The redactional elements in this clause are not definite enough to verify Matthew's responsibility for the expansion of a simpler form from his tradition. The parallel with *Gosp. Thom.* 73 is too weak for us to postulate (as above for Matt 5 .14) that the saying originally stood in Q.

The meaning of the text in its present Matthean context is obscure. Within rabbinic texts, 'dogs' were frequently used as an unkind metaphor for the Gentile world, and 'pigs' frequently symbolized Rome.[11] This basic reference would imply an anti-Gentile polemic that certainly falls outside Matthew's redactional interest. Within its redactional context, the saying may be taken to mean a general injunction not to give holy things to the unworthy.[12] The content of the saying is similar to that of saying no. 8, where certain Gentile religious practices are castigated.

An aporia supported by analysis of vocabulary and content provides the evidence that Matt 7.6 probably contains an M saying. Saying no. 8 and this saying, which we shall list as no. 15, may be related at a pre-Matthean level of tradition.

c. *Life Setting*

The saying fits best a life setting in a community that employs a polemic against certain impious Gentiles. Saying no. 8 is the only other M saying that implies a derogatory perspective against certain Gentiles in regard to religious practice. While saying no. 15 does not directly concern religious practice, surely practice, ideology, and artifacts are encompassed by the reference to 'pearls' and 'holy things'. Both sayings fit well a life setting in which Gentile converts are being educated away from their former religious practices. Saying no. 15 would function in such a context, we may suggest, to warn against the sharing of religiously significant ideas or items with non-Christian Gentiles. We may hypothesize that sayings nos. 8 and 15 represent the same tradition based upon these indications of a similar ideology and life setting.

4. *Matt 7.15-16a*

a. *Translation*

> (15) Look out for false prophets, those who come to you in sheep's clothing, but they are hungry wolves on the inside, (16a) by their fruits you will know them.

b. *Analysis*

These verses fit well with their following context. A new paragraph begins at v. 15, and vv. 16b-20 join easily with the syntax and content of vv. 15-16a.

Source criticism shows that vv. 16b-20 probably come from Q (see Luke 6.43-45; also compare Matt 12.33). The smoothness of the joining of the saying in vv. 15-16a to what follows indicates that either Matthew or a previous tradent builds up the pericope out of a Q saying probably preserved in its earlier form in Luke 6.43-45.

An analysis of style and vocabulary reveals no traditional material. The use of *prosechete apo* 'beware of' appears to be the usual Matthean style (see Matt 10.17; 16.6, 11). *Pseudoprophētai* 'false prophets' are a special concern of Matthew, as indicated by his redactional addition of the term to Markan tradition at Matt 24.11 (compare Mark 13.9-22). The content of vv. 15-16a is consistent with Matthew's own interest in warning his readers against false prophets. No such interest arises in any of the previously isolated M sayings traditions.

In conclusion, since Matt 7.15-16a shows no disjunction in style, vocabulary, or content from Matthew's usual use or interests, and since it cannot be related to previously isolated M traditions, these verses most likely come from Matthew.[13]

5. Matt 11.28-30

a. *Translation*

(28) Come to me all those who labor and are burdened and I will give you rest. (29) Take my yoke upon you and learn from me, because I am humble and lowly in heart, and you will find rest for yourselves. (30) For my yoke is easy and my burden is light.

b. *Analysis*

Syntactical disjunctions point to vv. 28-30 as an independent unit. An inexplicable shift occurs from Jesus' prayer to the Father (vv. 25-27) in the third person to a second person command form addressed to an audience specified only as 'those who labor'. An editorial shift of scene and ensuing narrative separates Matt 12.1-8 from vv. 28-30.

A review of the composition of the entirety of ch. 11 also helps isolate vv. 28-30 for consideration as possible M sayings material. Matt 11.1 constitutes a redactional introduction to a new narrative section. Verses 2-27 all have parallels in Luke and are probably from Q.[14] The gathering together of material from what appear to be different contexts in Q is best attributed to redaction; Matthew appears to have composed chapter 11 primarily from Q material organized for his own purposes. Verses 28-30 stand out in this context because they are unparalleled. Their disjunction syntactically from the Q material that immediately precedes them indicates the probability of either Matthew's own redaction or M sayings.

The style of the saying in vv. 28-30 is clearly from Matthew, who seems to prefer the use of *deute* 'come'. He uses the construction six times to Mark's three times (Luke, 0; John, 2; Revelation, 1). The word appears to be redactional at 22.4 (compare Luke 14.17); 25.34; 28.6. The structure of the verses shows a unity that cannot be broken into independent sayings (C. 31). Elements A, B, A', B', in addition to being syntactically parallel, indicate a promise in A, A' of a reward that will come in the immediate future. Elements C, C' identify the nature of the speaker, i.e. who Jesus is. Form-critically, the entirety of vv. 28-30 may be identified as a wisdom saying. The lack of any clear indication that the future tenses refer to an eschatological reward separates this form from a prophetic/apocalyptic saying.

In addition to *deute*, the vocabulary contains several words that occur frequently in Matthew. Matthew has *airō* 'to take' 18 times (Mark, 20; Luke, 20; John, 24) predominantly in verses dependent on Mark. The use here is conceptually closest to Matt 16.24 (par Mark 8.34), where the disciples are instructed to take up their cross. But the word shows no clear pattern of use and is not distinctively Matthean. Matthew uses *manthanō* 'to teach' three times. One use, Matt 24.32, depends on Mark 13.28. At Matt 9.13 the word is added to Mark 2.17 and introduces a quotation from Micah. Once again, mere infrequency of the use does not allow firm conclusions, because the word is not peculiarly Matthean. *Prays*, however, has a good claim to be redactional; the term was found to be probably redactional at 5.5. Further, the word occurs in a citation passage at 21.5. The choice of Zechariah for the quote seems best attributable to Matthew.

The evidence of words not easily attributed to Matthew is compounded by a high concentration of words that are clearly not Matthean. The following occur only here in Matthew: *kopiaō* 'to labor', *phortizō* 'to burden', *zygon* 'yoke', *tapeinos* 'humble', *chrēstos* 'light', *elaphros* 'light'. A high concentration of uncharacteristic vocabulary may be an indication of the use of tradition by Matthew.[15]

The tradition that underlies Matt 11.28-30 may be from Sir 51.23, 26, 27, where the ideas of labor, yoke, and finding rest also occur. Commentators have also suggested that Matthew alludes here to Jer 6.16.[16] Clearly vv. 28-30 are a re-formulation of a wisdom tradition. The question is whether this reformulation was accomplished first by Matthew or by someone in the pre-Matthean traditions.

The content identifies Jesus here and at 11.19 (see 23.34-37) as a figure similar to that of Wisdom, which is also encountered in Jewish wisdom literature. While Jesus is treated similarly to Wisdom, Matthew does not make an explicit identification of Jesus as Wisdom anywhere in the text of the First Gospel. Nor does Matthew's Gospel contain clear mythic motifs of the descent of Wisdom and its incarnation, such as the ones that have been suggested for Johannine Christology. K. Stendahl, primarily on the basis of this passage, argues that the 'school of Matthew' seems to have studied wisdom-type texts and applied them to Jesus. He finds, however, only two allusions to wisdom literature in Matthew, at 27.43 (Ps 22.9; Wis 2.10-20) and at 11.28-30. Stendahl thinks, nevertheless, that earlier tradents in Matthew's community are responsible for the wisdom interest in Matthew's text.[17]

E. Schweizer, M.J. Suggs, Koester, Meier, F. Christ all have found that sapiental themes occur throughout the composition of Matthew 11 and 12.[18] Bultmann suggests that 11.28-30 depends upon pre-Matthean Christian tradition. Barth, in disagreement with Bultmann, argues that 11.28-30 is Matthew's construction.[19] He observes that, while 11.28-30 does depend on tradition, that tradition is available to Matthew himself, as well as to any previous tradent. Further, 11.28-30 serves Matthew's purpose of showing Jesus as humble. Barth finds redactional expressions of the idea in 3.14-15; 8.17; 12.14-15; and most notably in the citation formula of Zech 9.9 at 21.4. Humility is demanded of the disciples at 5.5; 18.1-10; 19.13-15; 20.20-28; 23.8-12. In Matthew's text, only Matt 11.28-30 identifies the humility of Jesus with the humility of the disciples. Hence, Barth sees 11.28-30 as essential to the overall Christology of Matthew and argues that it cannot be separated from Matthean redaction.

Barth's argument, coupled with the compositional and thematic integrity of chs. 11 and 12, leads to the conclusion that vv. 28-30 fit Matthew's redactional interests. The high concentration of *hapax logomena* may be best accounted for, not by the hypothesis of underlying M tradition, but by Matthew's own understanding of wisdom motifs and his possible allusion to texts in Sirach and Jeremiah. We may add to this consideration the negative, albeit potentially incomplete evidence, that none of the other M sayings previously isolated shows signs of influence from a Wisdom-like Christology. Ockham's Razor is useful in this case: with no clear interest in a Wisdom-like Christology in other M traditions, and with an organized redactional interest in attributing wisdom-like characteristics to Jesus, vv. 28-30 probably come from Matthew.[20]

6. *Matt 12.34, 36-37*

a. *Translation*

> (34) Brood of vipers, how are you able to speak good things, when you are evil? For from the fullness of the heart the mouth speaks. (36) And I say to you, in the day of judgment people will render account for every careless word which they have spoken. (37) For out of your words you will be judged, and out of your words you will be condemned.

b. *Analysis*

Verse 35 has a parallel in Luke 6.45, and therefore will not be considered as a possible M saying. It may, however, have been inserted into a unit of sayings that originated prior to Matthew's authorship. Verse 36 joins uneasily with v. 34. Emphasis shifts from evil words to careless words. Further, the second sentence of v. 34 is completely ignored in v. 37. Matthew may have added v. 34b as a bridge to the Q saying that underlies v. 35. The idea of fullness of the heart accords well with the treasure out of which a person brings forth. The editorial strain in connecting the two ideas, however, remains apparent.

Verse 34a probably comes from Matthew. The term *gennēmata echidnōn* 'brood of vipers' requires a group of opponents in order to be understood. The saying itself depends on the context of Matthew's narrative, particularly the controversy story in Matt 12.22-30, which provides the narrative setting for the following sayings. Matthew, as opposed to Mark 3.22, characteristically designates the Pharisees as Jesus' opponents; and the Pharisees would fit as the opponents envisioned here. Matthew uses the phrase three times in his Gospel. The style in all three sayings that contain *gennēmata echidnōn* is the same: the phrase is followed immediately by a rhetorical question. In the other two uses at 3.7 and 23.33, the ensuing question explicitly mentions the eschatological judgment ('coming wrath', 'court of Gehenna'). Here, the indication of judgment is established by the placement of vv. 36, 37 after the rhetorical question. Further, Matthew apparently takes the term *gennēmata echidnōn* from Q at Matt 3.7 (par Luke 3:7); and he uses it in his own construction of 23.33. The compositional evidence seems to indicate that Matthew took a form of prophetic/minatory saying from Q and used it to his own purposes in these three contexts. Thus v. 34 probably comes from Matthew.

Verse 36 is in the form of a prophetic saying introduced by the phrase *lego de hymin* 'and I say to you'. Such sayings occur at every level of the traditions used by Matthew, including the redactional. The saying that follows is in the third person singular, which distinguishes it from v. 34. Certain vocabulary and concepts in v. 36 also set it apart from Matthew's usual use. Matthew uses the word *rhēma* 'word' only four times. At 4.4, the use depends on Deut 8.3 (LXX), at 18.16 on Deut 19.15 (LXX), and at 26.75 on Mark 14.75. Matthew himself seems to prefer the use of *logos* (34 times) to *rhēma*. The use of *apodidōmi* with a following accusative, giving the meaning 'to render (something, someone)' or 'to give account of', occurs only here and in Matt 5.33, an M saying. Elsewhere *apodidōmi* is used absolutely, a usage seemingly preferred by Matthew. Even within this last category, however, there are M sayings (6.4, 6, 18) and unparalleled material that may be traditional in parables (Matt 18.25, 26, 28, 29, 30, 34; 20.8). Thus, twelve uses of *apodidōmi* occur in unparalleled material; one use depends on Mark 12.17 at Matt 22.21; one use is probably from Q (5.26 par Luke 12.59); and only two uses can be considered clearly redactional, at Matt 16.27 (see Mark 8.38) and 27.58 (see Mark 15.46). *Apodidōmi* is not characteristic of Matthew's vocabulary.

Conceptually as well, v. 36 does not fit the usual redactional interests of Matthew. Only in vv. 36-37 in the entire Gospel does Matthew express the idea that what you say is determinative for your place in the final judgment. Matthew's own perspective may be seen in 16.27, 'For the Son of Man is to come with his angels in the glory of his Father, and then he will give to each according to what he has done.' The closest conceptual tie to vv. 36-37 occurs in Matt 5.22 (M saying no. 2, see also saying no. 1), where what one says to one's bother can jeopardize the individual before the eschatological court. On the basis of vocabulary and content unlike Matthew's usual use and more closely associated with an M tradition, v. 36 probably depends on an M saying.

Verse 37 also contains a probable M saying. In addition to the content arguments stated above, elements in vocabulary support this probability. The use of the verb *dikaioō* occurs only in a saying taken from Q at Matt 11.19 (Luke 7.35) outside this passage. Verse 37 takes the form of a community rule or legal sentence and is akin to the 'sentence of holy law' form, which implicitly refers to the future eschatological judgment.[21] The implication becomes explicit if v. 37 is assigned with v. 36 to a sayings unit that pre-dates Matthew's editing. We must deal with two contrary pieces of evidence, however, before assigning v. 37 to the same unit as v. 36. First, *gar* 'for', the only syntactical tie linking v. 37 to v. 36, is frequently used by Matthew to join two disparate pieces of tradition or a piece of tradition and one of redaction. Second, by its introductory phrase (*legō de hymin*), v. 36 addresses a plural audience, whereas v. 37 addresses the second person singular (*sou*). If the introductory I-word was added to v. 36 by Matthew, then the apparent disagreement in syntax and the possible conceptual disjunction in vv. 36-37 are easily removed. Since the conceptual continuity between vv. 36-37 is strong, and the discontinuity from Matthew's conceptuality is equally strong, Matthew's editorial modification of a received saying is the most logical option. Verses 36-37 contain an M saying which we shall list as no. 16.

c. *Life Setting*

The absence of a clear social indicator hampers the determination of a precise life setting for the saying. The content of the saying shows a line of reasoning somewhat similar to that of both rabbinic texts and the Dead Sea Scrolls.[22] The content and mode of reasoning, however, in saying no. 16 may be aligned with saying no. 2. In saying no. 2, a legal rule condemns the calling of one's brother *raka*, or *mōre* 'fool', and assigns the judgment of that brother to the eschatological court. Saying no. 2 and saying no. 16 both emphasize what one says as having direct condemnation in the eschatological court. The similarity in content suggests a similarity in life setting. Saying no. 16 may represent the same tradition as nos. 1, 2, 4, 5, and possibly 12. It probably represents a legal rule that is adhered to by a Christian group who formulate their Christology and organization in direct antithesis to specific Jewish ideology of the period.[23]

7. *Matt 18.15-20 (16.19)*

a. *Translation*

(15) And if your brother sins, correct him between you and him alone. If he listens to you, you have gained your brother. (16) But if

he does not listen take with you one or two others, in order that every word might be established by the evidence of two or three. (17) But if he disobeys them, then to the church; and if he disobeys the church let him be to you like a Gentile and tax collector. (18) Amen, I say to you, whatever you bind upon the earth will be bound in heaven, and whatever you loose upon the earth, will be loosed in heaven. (19) Again (amen) I say to you that if two of you should agree about any matter upon the earth, which they should ask, it will be done for them by my father, the one who is in the heavens. (20) For where two or three are gathered in my name, there I am in their midst.

b. *Analysis*

Matt 18.15-20 falls into three separate literary units. Each is marked off by aporias that may indicate the use of traditional material in all or some of the units. The three units are: vv. 15-17; v. 18; vv. 19-20.

Verses 15-17 constitute a syntactical unit, which is evidenced by the fact that vv. 16-17 require v. 15 to provide an intelligible context; and their thought progression follows logically upon the saying in v. 15.[24]

Verse 18 is disjoined from vv. 15-17 first by the introductory formula *amēn de legō hymin*. The shift to the second person plural (*hymin*) in v. 18 from the second person singular (*soi*) in vv. 15-17 may indicate the use of different material by Matthew. Further, the content of v. 18 has no necessary connection to vv. 15-17 and could have stood as an independent logion.

Verses 19-20 are disjoined in content from v. 18. They have no necessary connection to the saying on binding and loosing. The emphatic use of the (*amēn*) *legō hymin* formula may once again indicate the editorial merging of different traditions. Matthew's characteristic use of *gar* (for) occurs again as a connecting particle that joins disparate pieces of tradition. Initially, there is no reason to disjoin v. 19 from v. 20; their content appears coherent. But the possibility remains that the two verses were originally independent logia. Each unit of sayings within 18.15-20 will be analyzed independently for possible M sayings.

Verses 15-17

Verse 15 has a parallel in Luke 17.3. Luke contains the simpler form of the saying and may therefore preserve Q better in this instance. Matthew's version of the verse has undergone editorial expansion, particularly in the phrases *elegxon auton metaxy sou kai autou monou. ean sou akousę ekerdēsas ton adelphon sou* 'correct him between you and him alone. If he listens to you, you have gained your brother'. Verses 16 and 17 directly depend upon these elements. Verse 16, in its first clause (particularly *mē akousę*), requires the latter part of v. 15 to be understandable. Also the progression of first taking one or two others, and then (v. 17) going to the church, presupposes that the conditions in v. 15 have already been met. In its present form, v. 15 probably comes from the same level of tradition as vv. 16-17.

Verse 16 includes an allusion to Deut 19.15 in its LXX form.[25] A similar allusion occurs in 2 Cor 13.1; Paul neither quotes the injunction as from scripture nor as a word of the Lord. Rather, he assumes that the injunction requiring two or three witnesses is common knowledge among the Corinthians. Furthermore, the injunction is used there, as here in Matthew, without direct reference to legal proceedings in the court of the community. In 1 Tim 5.19, the saying has taken on a legal standing with reference only to the officials of the church. The author of 1 Timothy attributes the saying to the authority of Paul. The use of Deut 19.15 in these various contexts in early Christian tradition indicates that this norm for community behavior was probably the property of a large cross-section of early Christianity, perhaps derived from Judaism. The use of Deut 19.15 does not seem to have reached the same level of legal status anywhere in the NT as that given to it by the rabbis.[26] Its inclusion here may come from Matthew or from a previous tradent. Barth argues that the scriptural allusion in v. 16b is due to Matthew's editing of a preexistent unit in vv. 15-16a, 17.[27] Nevertheless, the allusion fits well the progression established in vv. 15-16a. The reference to 'one or two' in v. 16a coheres with the two or three in v. 16b: if the original brother (v. 15) is counted, then the total number of complainants fits the two or three of the allusion in v. 16b. Barth's evidence that Matthew is inclined to use scripture provides insufficient ground for assigning v. 16b to Matthew. Contrary to Barth's position, W. Thompson suggests that v. 16b is a pre-Matthean addition on the grounds that Matthew prefers to refer to scripture by the introductory phrase *hina plērōthen to rhēthen*.[28] We find his solution untenable for two reasons. First, the full formula referred to by Thompson occurs only in citation formulas, and it is not clear that each of these formulas comes from Matthew.[29] Second, the indications from the use of the principle in Paul and 1 Timothy show the likelihood that the principle was known, not as scripture, but as accepted practice in disparate Christian communities. Therefore, the author of the saying would not regard the saying as scripture (similar to the manner in which Paul employs the saying). The allusion to Deut 19.15 in v. 16b is not clearly disjunctive from its context, and, contrary to the views of both Barth and Thompson, v. 16b should be considered as part of the same level of tradition as vv. 15-16a, 17. We must look at other evidence to determine whether these verses are traditional or from Matthew.

The vocabulary contains both characteristic and uncharacteristic elements. *Kerdainō* 'to gain' occurs fairly frequently in Matthew, with an impersonal object signifying material gain (Matt 16.26 par Mark 8.36; Luke 9.25; Matt 25.16, 17; 20.22). Only here does the word occur in Matthew with a personal object (see 1 Cor 9.19-22). The use is unusual, but not so clearly uncharacteristic that it compels the assignment of its use to pre-Matthean tradition. *Elegchō* 'to correct' is a *hapax legomenon* in Matthew (cf. Luke 3.19; John 3.20; 8.46; 16.8).

In v. 16, the use of *paralambanō* 'to take with' is a clear preference in Matthew's vocabulary (Matt, 16 times; Mark, 6; Luke, 6; John, 3; Acts, 6). The use of the verb followed by *meta* (with), designating the person or thing one takes, occurs only in Matt 12.45 (par Luke 11.26), a Q saying. This refined point of style does not help locate v. 16 as traditional, because the other use of the verb with *meta* is also directly demanded by context. The previously isolated M sayings do not evidence this style.

In v. 17, the occurrence of *ho ethnikos kai ho telōnēs* 'Gentile and tax collector' as a precise designation of sinner (*hamartōlos*) is found here and in Matt 5.46-47 (par Luke 6.32-33). The use in Matt 5.46-47 probably comes from the redactor. Matt 6.7 (M saying no. 7) contains the single word *ethnikos*. Matthew's interest in the pairing of *ethnikos* and *telōnēs* is evident in a similar Q context in 5.46-47 and raises the suspicion that he is also responsible for this element in v. 17.[30] An apparent redactional pairing of *telōnai* and *pornai* in 21.31, 32 increases this suspicion. Matthew appears to favor pairs when designating those who are considered sinners. The use of *parakouō* 'to listen to' occurs only in this passage and in Mark 5.36 in the NT.

The content in vv. 15-17 cannot be established as disjunctive from Matthew's redactional interest in this immediate context. In ch. 18, Matthew weaves together two themes. The first, on seeking and forgiving the brother, is developed in 18.10-14 (par Luke 15.3-7) and 18.21-22 (par Luke 17.4) by the arrangement of Q traditions into Matthew's editorial pattern. The theme is concluded in 18.23-35 by the use of an unparalleled parable. A second theme, a warning against causing the little ones to stumble, comes at 18.6-9, which uses underlying Markan tradition (Mark 9.42-52). Verses 15-17 address the practical problem within the community of separating out in some way those who bring about stumbling, while at the same time providing for an honest attempt at seeking the brother. A solution is noted in v. 17, which does not call for complete separation of the offending brother from the community, but rather for a barrier of separation between the offended and the offender.[31] The singular *soi* can only refer to the original brother described in v. 15. The composition of vv. 15-17 in their present form is based upon a single Q logion (v. 15) and fits clearly the redactional intent of the immediate context. In fact, the presence of vv. 15-17 in this context limits the otherwise general and absolute authority granted in v. 18. Matthew agrees in other passages with this limit. He grants that the church is a *corpus mixtum* prior to the eschaton, and he does not provide for the exclusion of offenders from the Kingdom of Heaven prior to the return of the Son of Man (see Matt 13.24-30, 36-43; 25.31-46).

If vv. 15-17 cannot be assigned to pre-Matthean tradition on the basis of disjunction from Matthew's redactional intent expressed in the composition of ch. 18, neither is a similar process of community correction evident in the previously isolated M sayings. Matt 5.22 (saying no. 2) assigns a brother who offends by word (*raka, mōre*) to the eschatological court. There is no evidence of a local internal discipline in M like that described in vv. 15-17.

In conclusion, Matt 18.15-17 contains no clear evidence of M sayings. The unit is an expansion of a Q saying (v. 15), coming from the redactor or from a pre-Matthean tradent. The latter option would account for the non-Matthean vocabulary in the saying. Nevertheless, it is more probable that the unit is Matthew's own development of Q, since it fits clearly his own redactional intent. It may represent the current discipline practiced in Matthew's own time.

Verse 18

Verse 18 has a parallel in Matt 16.19 (C. 32; see John 20.23; in the case of John 20.23, no direct literary relationship with the passages in Matthew is evident). The parallel in Matt 16.19 differs from 18.18 in several ways. First, 18.18 uses the neuter form *hosa ean*, rather than the masculine singular form used in 16.19 (*ho ean*). The style of 16.19 is more usual in Matthew (33 times), and that of 18.18 is more unusual (3 times: Matt 7.12; 18.18; 22.9). Second, 18.18 is in the second person plural, while 16.19 is in the second person singular, as required by the narrative context, for 16.19 refers to Peter as the keeper of the keys to the Kingdom of Heaven (16.17-18). The narrative context of 18.18 is unclear. The subject of the preceding saying has been singular throughout (vv. 15-17). The subject is changed by the use of the formula *amēn legō hymin*. At the level of redaction, v. 18 is clearly meant to refer to a group, which in the narrative context would be the disciples. Third, the use of *en ouranō* (18.18) as compared with *en tois ouranois* (16.19) demonstrates no stylistic departure from Matthew 's usual use.

These comparisons lend support to the following conclusions: (1) both Matt 18.18 and 16.19 depend on earlier tradition that occurred without a narrative context. John 20.23 helps establish this conclusion, along with the evidence of adaptation (particularly in Matt 16.19) to the narrative context in Matthew. (2) Matt 16.19 shows a more thorough assimilation to Matthew's style in the use of *hos ean* than does 18.18. (3) The introductory formula *amēn legō hymin* is probably from Matthew; the disjunction of the second person plural from its preceding context may indicate that the logion underlying both 16.19 and 18.18 was available to Matthew in a plural form as a general legal rule that applied to the congregation. Matt 18.18 shows fewer signs of editorial adaptation to narrative context than does 16.19.[32]

The evidence from important vocabulary in 18.18 and 16.19 strengthens the probability that an M saying is present here. Only in these two verses and in 5.19 (M saying no. 1) does *lyō* occur in the sense of 'to allow, to release', with a quasi-legal or scribal connotation. Similarly, *didōmi* occurs only in 18.18 and 16.19 with the sense of 'to bind, or prohibit'.

Both 18.18 and 16.19 have the form of a community rule. Other than the introductory formula, which modifies the form into an amen-word/I saying, the verses lack any significant editorial modification of the form. On the basis of accumulated evidence, v. 18 may be designated as M saying no. 17.

Verses 19-20

The style of vv. 19-20 contains no peculiar elements that definitively distinguish these verses from Matthew's usual use. On the other hand, the use of the introductory formula (*amēn legō hymin*) appears to be a redactional attempt to associate vv. 19-20 with the style of the preceding statement. *Palin* 'again' seems to serve a similar function. In v. 20, the connecting particle *gar* may also be use by Matthew to associate two different pieces of tradition.

The vocabulary in v. 19 is not characteristic of Matthew. *Symphōneō* 'to agree' occurs only here and in an unparalleled parable in 20.2, 13 in Matthew. *Pragmatos* 'matter' is a *hapax legomenon* in Matthew. The use of *patēr ho en ouranois* 'father the one who is in the heavens' occurs both in M sayings and in other material throughout the Gospel. The use of *synagō* 'gather together' for Jesus' disciples is distinctive to v. 20. The verb is used in no other instance for Jesus' disciples. Elsewhere, it is used in reference to the enemies of Jesus (22.34, 41; 26.3, 57; 27.17, 62; 28.12). The use *eis to emon onoma* 'in my name' is found only here in Matthew.

In their content, vv. 19-20 are at least unusual among, if not disjunctive from, Matthew's usual concerns. The idea that what the disciples do on earth is mirrored or affirmed in heaven best approximates the conceptual perspective of the M saying contained in Matt 18.18 (16.19). The reference to two or three establishes some unity in content with the redactional verses in 18.15-17, but the gathering of the two or three in vv. 19-20 conveys no legal or quasi-legal indicators as in vv. 15-17. Verse 20 is coextensive with Matthew's own interests as expressed in 1.23 and 28.19. These two verses (the first a citation from Isa 7.14, which Matthew follows by explicitly translating Emmanuel as 'God with us'; and the second, an affirmation by the resurrected Christ of his continuing presence with his community to the end of the age) give the framework for one aspect of Matthew's Christology. Verse 20 fits within this conceptual framework. Verse 20, however, also fits with Matt 11.25-27 (par Luke 10.21-22), a Q passage. The identity between the father and the son implied by v. 20 in conjunction with v. 19 both fits Matthew's interests and has a conceptual parallel in traditional sayings.

This dual affinity opens the unity of vv. 19-20 to question. Above, *gar* was identified as a frequently used device for editorially linking two disparate pieces of tradition. Contrary to this conclusion, the close association in content between vv. 19 and 20 argues against their independence at the level of the tradition available to Matthew. The thought of v. 20 is associated logically and syntactically with v. 19 by the phrase 'two or three'. Conceptually, the identity of the father and the son implied by the two verses together could have come from either Matthew or the tradition available to him. The evidence of unusual vocabulary, coupled with the unity of style, syntax and content in vv. 19-20 appears strong enough to overrule the counter-evidence of *gar* here. Thus, a single M saying which we shall designate as no. 18 probably underlies vv. 19-20.[33]

c. *Life Setting*

Verse 18 is M saying no. 17; vv. 19-20 constitute saying no. 18. Saying no. 17 is a community rule that grants to the community the scribal and judicial power reserved only to the congregation leaders in the rabbinic literature and fits best in vocabulary with saying no. 1 (Matt 5.19). Saying no. 17 may well be influenced by a Christian group organized in direct opposition to the leadership and authority of a synagogue, and thus saying no. 17 conforms to the life setting of saying no. 12. Taken alone, the eschatological reference in saying no. 17 is ambiguous: it may mean that the decision of the community is sanctioned by the authority of heaven for the present time; or it may mean that the decision of the community is sanctioned by heaven for the final time. Without a context, the saying remains ambiguous; thus Matthew could easily adapt it to a non-eschatological context here in the composition of ch. 18. If (as its association in vocabulary with saying no. 1 indicates) the verse is located in the Christian group who adhere to sayings nos. 1, 2, 4, 5, 12, and 16, then the absolute reference to the eschatological time becomes clear. The association of v. 18 with this M tradition indicates a Christian group who took upon themselves both the interpretative and juridical functions with binding eschatological power. The granting of this power to the entire group accords well with saying no. 12 (Matt 23.10-12), which argues for no leadership hierarchy except the absolute authority of God and Jesus within the community.

The life setting of saying no. 18 (vv. 19-20) is difficult to determine in the absence of clear social indicators. In form, the saying is a community rule, although it does not clearly indicate the giving of a legal function to the community. In content, saying no. 18 fits well with saying no. 17. The immediate access to the Father through the Son also best fits conceptually with saying no. 12, as does the clear Christological claim of close identification of the Son with the Father. The difficulty in separating this saying from Matthew's own interest may be due simply to the close proximity between Matthew's ideology and life setting and that of sayings nos. 12 and 18. Saying 18 may have been phrased in opposition to the Jewish view preserved in *m. 'Aboth* that regards the *Shekhinah* as dwelling with those who study Torah. This opposition accords well with what we noted in the tradition represented by sayings nos. 1, 2, 4, 5, 12, 16 and 17.[34]

8. *Matt 19.10-12*

a. *Translation*

> (10) [His] disciples said [to him], 'If it is thus the case of a man with the woman, it is an advantage not to marry'. (11) But he said to them, 'Not all are able to accept [this] statement but those to whom it has been given. (12) For there are eunuchs such as those who are so begotten from the mother's womb, and those who are made eunuchs by men, and those who make themselves eunuchs because of the Kingdom of the Heavens. The one who is able to accept this, let him accept it.'

b. *Analysis*

Verses 10-11 establish the narrative tie between Matt 19.3-9 and 19.12. Verse 10 can only refer back to the preceding section; v. 11 in context refers back to the preceding scene. Even if *touton* is original to the text, the easiest reading refers back to the saying in v. 9. Matt 19.3-9 is a controversy story derived from Mark 10.2-12. Verses 10-11 are best regarded as Matthew's work, which joins the controversy story to the saying contained in v. 12. There is no necessary connection in content or syntax between v. 12 and vv. 10-11.

There are no parallels to v. 12 in either the Synoptics or the rest of the NT. Matthew nowhere else shows any knowledge of, or concern with, the subject of eunuchs, or the possibility of celibacy as a means of expressing dedication to the Kingdom of Heaven. While the content is somewhat similar to Matt 10.34-39, which holds that normal family relationships will be broken by discipleship, Matthew in his compositional placement of Q tradition at 10.34-39[35] in no way hints that becoming a eunuch, or celibate, is indicated by the situation of persecution by one's own family. The content of v. 12 is unique within Matthew's text and may be assigned as M saying no. 19.

c. *Life Setting*

A precise social location for saying no. 19 referring exclusively to the issue of castrated males is extremely difficult. Within Jewish tradition the eunuch is denied entry into the congregation in Deut 23.2-9. On the other hand Isa 56.3-5 foresees the overturning of this prescription in the formation of the eschatological congregation. The rabbis universally oppose the practice of castration; but they do recognize a distinction between those born sterile or without normal genitals and those made eunuchs by human operation. There are no known parallels in the Jewish literature to the phrase 'make themselves eunuchs because of the Kingdom of the Heavens'.[36]

Within the Greco-Roman culture the practice of castrating males for court service is attested. Josephus (*J.W.* 1.488) reports that three of Herod's chamberlains were eunuchs, so the practice was followed in some circles in Palestine. The practice of castration for religious purposes occurs among the Cybelene priesthood during the NT period.[37]

Some evidence that early Christians confronted the issue of the reception of eunuchs into their communities may be recorded in Acts 8.26-40—the conversion of the Ethiopian eunuch by Philip—but Luke records no hesitation on the part of Philip in baptizing this high court official.[38]

The clause, 'those who make themselves eunuchs because of the Kingdom of the Heavens', has traditionally been interpreted to refer to voluntary celibacy,[39] similar to that advocated by Paul (1 Cor 7.7). It may also have been practiced by segments of the Dead Sea Community. *Sifre Num* 99; 103 refers to the continence of Moses in relationship to Zipporah as justified by God in view of Moses' vocation, therefore the concept is not totally alien to rabbinic thought (cf. Jer 16.1). It is certainly probable that the redacted form of v. 12 in its Matthean context refers to such a practice. The unusually vivid language of the saying in the context of what is known of early Christian and Jewish traditions most probably is to be taken metaphorically and as indicative of the radical religious significance of celibacy for the Kingdom of Heaven. It *may* be a case of adopting language to describe celibacy that is calculated to be an affront to Jewish sensibilities, thereby setting the Christian adherent apart from Jewish views.[40]

Saying no. 19 may be associated with saying nos. 1, 2, 4, 5, 12, 16, 17, 18 on the suggestive evidence that the vocabulary of the saying is chosen in affront to Jewish sensibilities. It is further suggestive that the term 'Kingdom of Heaven' occurs only in sayings nos. 1 and 19 in the M sayings. Although saying no. 19 may represent an independent tradition, we suggest tentatively that it represents the same tradition as sayings nos. 1, 2, 4, 5, 12, 16, 17, 18. Since the vocabulary of castration (rather than celibacy) sets saying 19 apart from the views that appear to have characterized Judaism in the period, it probably comes from a Christian group some of whose members adopt a celibate life based upon a saying attributed to Jesus. These Christians understand their non-married status as a gift from God for the purposes of God's kingdom.

Conclusions

An investigation of eight unparalleled sayings in Matthew shows that five probably contain an M saying: Matt 7.6 (saying no. 15); Matt 12.36-37 (saying no. 16); Matt 18.18 (saying no. 17); Matt 18.19-20 (saying no. 18); Matt 19.12 (saying no. 19). An investigation of the content and life settings of each of these five M sayings suggests that saying no. 15 represents the same tradition as saying no. 8, and that sayings nos. 16-18 represent the same tradition as sayings nos. 1, 2, 4, 5, and 12. We find saying no. 19 more difficult to analyze but suggest the likelihood that it also should be aligned with the tradition represented by this last group of sayings.

If we tabulate the results of the investigation of ch. 6 with the results of ch. 5, the following picture results (sayings about which reservations have been expressed are followed by a '?').

Three distinct traditions are apparent in the M sayings.

Sayings nos. 1, 2, 4, 5, 12,[41] 16, 17, 18, 19(?)
Sayings nos. 7, 11
Sayings nos. 13, 14, 3(?)

Two other groups of sayings may be suggested that are representative of traditions exclusive of each other, but not apparently exclusive of one of the three traditions suggested above.

Sayings nos. 9, 10
Sayings nos. 8, 15

One saying remains. It is probably excluded from the same tradition as saying no. 5.

Saying no. 6.

As can be seen from the first tradition above (sayings nos. 1, 2, 4, 5, 12, 16, 17, 18, 19), the evidence of the M sayings points to an extensively represented tradition marked by significant christological claims and by legal sentences that appear to be formulated in antithesis to the viewpoints that might be expected from members of a Jewish synagogue in the first century, although here as elsewhere we must be cautious about conclusions drawn from evidence in texts compiled later than the first century, particularly rabbinic documents.

Chapter 7

THE HISTORY OF THE MATTHEAN COMMUNITY
AS REFLECTED IN THE M SAYINGS TRADITIONS

Introduction

The M sayings have been isolated and the traditions that they represent suggested. We are left with the question how and in what form these traditions were available to Matthew at the time of his writing of the First Gospel. Did Matthew receive these traditions in whole or in part in a written source or in an oral form? Further, is it possible to establish links between one tradition and another that allow us to suggest a history of the traditions that lies behind the M sayings? Does a history of the traditions imply or require a corresponding understanding of the history of the Matthean community?

We will answer these questions in five steps: (1) an examination of probable written sources in the M sayings traditions; (2) a hypothesis for oral and social continuity among the M sayings traditions; (3) an investigation of clues to Matthew's understanding of early Christian history to establish both a history of the traditions and the community or communities that preserved them; (4) relating these clues to the traditions represented in the M sayings; (5) a hypothesis about the history of the Matthean community reflected in the M sayings traditions based on the intersection of evidence in this chapter and that in Chapters 5 and 6.

1. The Evidence for Written Sources in the M Sayings Traditions

Critics encounter severe obstacles in discerning whether sayings in a Gospel come from an oral tradition or a written source. As regards Matthew, often they leave the nature of M unspecified. Bultmann maintains that in oral tradition there is a natural limit to cluster formations, which can only be superseded by written tradition.[1] This 'natural' limit, however, continues to elude precise definition.

Where parallels are lacking, a separation of written and oral traditions is rendered difficult by the way in which Gospel writers apparently viewed their material. Recently, W. Kelber has suggested that even texts,

> ... used for the composition of other texts were often assimilated through hearing and 'interim dictation', more than strict copying. Those textual aids could well be present to writers in an oral mode of apperception.[2]

Writers who stand on the border between an oral and written matrix might be expected to alternate between the two perspectives in their own compositions.

Kelber's observation appears to be accurate with regard to Matthew's use of Q. Clearly Matthew tends to rearrange and alter the Q sayings in a relatively more free way than Luke. Matthew also appears to write with a free attitude toward the use of Mark's Gospel.[3] For the M sayings, we may cautiously assume that, by analogy with what is known of Matthew's employment of Q and Mark, it is probable that Matthew freely adapted M traditions to his own purposes whether they were written or oral. That probability makes certitude on the question of written traditions in M extremely problematic.

The question is further complicated by form-critical studies that have found that the survival of sayings in an oral matrix depends to some extent upon orderliness and structure. Simple orderliness or careful parallel structures cannot be used as indicative of a written source. Accordingly we may propose criteria useful in discriminating oral from written tradition in the M sayings: (1) editorial connections between sayings would be expected in a written source; (2) a narrative structure and identifiable ideological consistency throughout the traditions might also indicate a written source; (3) style and vocabulary in a written source might be relatively consistent and distinguishable from the style and vocabulary of the final author.[4]

It is relatively clear from the analyses in chapters 5 and 6 that the hypothesis of a *single* written source to account for the M sayings traditions is untenable. (1) There are few indications of editorial connections between sayings that would lead to the postulate of a single written source. (2) Even the minor narrative touches in verses that set scenes or connect sayings into discourses reveal scant evidence of pre-Matthean tradition. Matthew appears to be responsible for the organization of various traditions into discourse settings. An understanding of the sayings never depends on a narrative context. Rather, the sayings survived and were incorporated into Matthew's text precisely because of their adaptability to multiple contexts. Ideological consistency, while discernable, is limited to single units or groups of sayings and depends more obviously on the life setting of the tradition rather than on its written nature. (3) While elements of style and vocabulary help to isolate specific sayings from Matthew's own work, these elements are neither consistent nor common within the traditional sayings in M, and so do not favor the postulate of a single written source in M.[5]

These considerations do not rule out the possibility that some of the traditions in M were written. Those sayings with extensive syntactical or structural integrity may have been available to Matthew in written form. Sayings nos. 1, 2, 4, 5 appear to represent a collection of the commandments of Jesus in antithetical form available to Matthew from a single tradition. The syntactical tie between saying no. 1 and nos. 2, 4, 5 established by the use of *toutōn* to refer forward may be a telltale sign of a written source. Unfortunately, within the other sayings assigned to the same tradition (nos. 12, 16, 17, 18, 19?) there are no observable editorial connections that might indicate a written source. Therefore, evidence is too scanty for the hypothesis of a written source underlying sayings nos. 1, 2, 4, 5, 12, 16, 17, 18, 19? in the M sayings.

Similarly the syntactical association that allows for the grouping of saying no. 9 with no. 10 is insufficient to suggest a probability of a written source. Nor is there compelling evidence in sayings nos. 7 and 11 to suggest that a written source underlies the M tradition represented there. The commonality of vocabulary between the two sayings (*pros to theathēnai*) is insufficient evidence to allow for the postulate of a written source.

While we cannot absolutely rule out the possibility that some or all the M sayings were taken by Matthew from written sources, there is no evidence that compels the postulate of written sources to account for the M sayings traditions.

2. *A Hypothesis for Oral and Social Continuity between the M Sayings Traditions*

In the face of the absence of positive evidence that written sources underlie the M sayings, we will proceed on the assumption that the M sayings available to Matthew immediately prior to his own editorial work were oral. Although Matthew uses several large units of M material that show signs of originating or being preserved in discrete social contexts, these M sayings lack an observable written matrix.

Where did these traditions come from? Kelber[6] postulates the law of 'social identification' as the means by which specific sayings are preserved and transmitted orally. According to this law, sayings that reflect similar social locators probably come from the same level of the history of tradition. The present study has adopted this approach in focusing on the immediately pre-Matthean level of the tradition. Kelber asserts that reconstruction of precise communal histories based on Gospel texts assumes 'an unbroken continuity in the function of contextuality from the oral to the written medium'.[7] In what follows, I hope to avoid the pitfall Kelber describes by not assuming unbroken continuity, but neither will I willingly fall into the pit of the absolute discontinuity he assumes.

The M sayings traditions indicate the existence of at least three social contexts in which sayings of Jesus were created or preserved to serve the interests of three discrete groups or communities at three distinct historical and social moments.[8] The survival of these sayings in the text of Matthew is probably due to their applicability to Matthew's own interests. It may be reasonably inferred that Matthew's community and its interests, exercised an influence on Matthew's use of tradition. Some sort of historical connection is probable between the Christian groups represented by the M traditions and Matthew's community in order for Matthew to know about and include representative sayings from these traditions. Hypothetically, these traditions that are unique to Matthew within the Gospels have a great probability of containing references to the history of a significant group of Christians within Matthew's community.[9] Matthew's own use of the M traditions shows an attitude that allows for a simultaneous preservation and reinterpretation of tradition. In this way, Matthew's handling of M sayings is continuous with the process of handing on tradition orally in his community, even though this continuity is to some extent interrupted by the fact of Matthew writing down his tradition. We can observe, for example, that Matthew clearly historicizes the sayings of Jesus into a pre-Easter framework.[10] While this historicizing phenomenon may already be at work in the pre-Synoptic stages of the oral transmission of traditions, the historicizing process first becomes evident to us in the Synoptic traditions with Mark's Gospel. It is not evident in Q. The Gospel form adopted by Matthew from Mark shows a closure of the generally more open communication of an oral culture. The absorption of the M sayings into the Gospel form allows for the relativizing of prescriptions attributed in an oral setting to Jesus (whether as earthly person or risen Lord) into a clearly historical 'once upon a time' setting of limited duration, namely, the active ministry of Jesus while present on earth prior to his resurrection and exaltation as the Son of God/Son of Man.[11] The form gives Matthew relative freedom in absorbing M sayings that might have been employed by others in contradiction to his own view.

3. *Matthew's Understanding of Early Christian History*

Taking as our starting point a general understanding of an oral continuity of traditions in the M sayings prior to and including the time of Matthew's writing, we may find that Matthew's composition implies assumptions about the history of early Christianity shared between Matthew and his readers. These assumptions have a strong probability of being informed by the experience of a significant group of Matthew's readers. They may further give us clues to a means of organizing the M traditions into a relative history. Such a tradition history then implies a history of the Christian groups who preserved or adhered to these traditions and whose descendants form a part of the audience of Matthew's Gospel.

It may be freely admitted that we cannot be sure that Matthew's knowledge of the history of early Christianity is accurate, or free from the prejudices of his own place and time of writing. Nevertheless, the most appropriate starting point in hypothesizing a history of the M traditions is the text of Matthew itself and not a set of presuppositions derived from the study of early Christianity outside of Matthew's text.[12]

Two contexts that include M traditions suggest Matthew's own understanding of early Christian history and may hold clues helpful

in the reconstruction of a history of the M traditions and the history
of the Matthean community that preserved them.

Matthew 23

The composition of Matthew 23 reveals shifts in the text of Matthew
that imply a readership familiar with a specific history of early
Christians. First, the narrative is clearly set in the ministry of Jesus
and addressed to both crowds and disciples (v. 1). In vv. 2-3a, the
authority of the interpretation of the leaders of the synagogue,
scribes and Pharisees, is recognized as binding. In the ensuing
discourse, however, this authority is progressively taken away. By
the end of the discourse, the authority of the Jewish leaders is no
longer upheld for those who organize themselves under the leadership
of Jesus as Christ, and God as Father.

The first shift in the process comes in vv. 3-7, where the actions of
the Jewish leadership are castigated. This castigation is followed in
vv. 8-12 by the explicit denial of all synagogue titles of respect to
those who consider themselves part of the community of God as
Father, and Jesus as teacher and Christ. The woes in vv. 13-28 then
give reasons for the unseating of the scribes and Pharisees from their
positions of authority over the community.

Verse 29 introduces a new theme that goes beyond the previous
woes in the indictment of the synagogue rulers. Here, the leaders are
judged neither for their interpretations nor for their behavior based
on those interpretations. Rather, the woe in vv. 29-33 serves as a
bridge to the saying in vv. 34-36, which holds the Jewish leadership
directly responsible for the persecution of Christian prophets, wise
men, and scribes.

At vv. 34-36, the discourse refers implicitly to a time not covered
in the historical ministry of Jesus with his disciples, for at no prior
point has Matthew narrated the persecution of any of Jesus'
followers. He assumes repeatedly, however, that his readers know of
such persecution (5.10; 10.17-20). In 23.34-36, the reference to the
sending of prophets, wise men, and scribes is dated explicitly at some
time after the life and ministry of Jesus and his disciples. Evidence
for this observation may be found in that Matthew is more specific
than the parallel in Luke 11.49 in stating that three groups are sent to
Jerusalem. The 'you' of v. 34 in context can only refer to the scribes
and Pharisees who have been the opponents named since v. 13.
Matthew knows, and assumes without further explanation that his

reader knows, about a mission from the community to the synagogue and its rulers that results in the persecution of the messengers. Matt 13.52 indicates that at least the scribes were still represented in Matthew's own community.[13]

Finally, in vv. 37-39, Matthew moves from indicting the synagogue authorities to claiming specifically that the entire nation is responsible for rejecting the mission of Jesus' followers. Once again, the context shifts forward, showing that after Jesus' crucifixion, his followers undertake their mission and as a group are also rejected by Israel.

The composition implies four distinct historical stages in the relationship between the contemporary readers of specific sayings and the Jewish authorities: (1) the reader's religious life is circumscribed by the authority of the Jewish synagogue leaders; (2) in antithesis to this circumscribed position, the reader is subject only to the authority of Jesus as teacher and Christ, and God as Father; (3) the reader is given an explanation of the new position, with reference first to the invalid interpretation and religious behavior of the synagogue rulers, and second to their overt persecution of members of the community of Jesus; (4) finally, the reader's ties with Judaism/ Israel are severed. Matthew depicts the final cause of the break with the synagogue and with Israel as the rejection by the synagogue authorities, and finally by all of Israel, of the messengers of Jesus. This rejection includes persecution to death, synagogue discipline, and some sort of pursuit from town to town, perhaps by official ban.[14]

Matthew 10

The composition of Matthew 10 supports this interpretation of Matthew 23. Matt 10.6 limits the mission of the disciples, who are the exclusive addressees of the discourse, to Israel. Matt 10.17-25 chronicles the move of the mission from Israel to the Gentiles (v. 18). According to vv. 21-22, this history of mission will coincide with the break-up of households. In this section, Matthew has taken material from Mark's apocalyptic discourse (specifically 13.9-13) and placed it within the ministry of Jesus and his disciples. As in Matthew 23, the reader implicitly recognizes that the persecution and mission described lie outside the historical ministry of Jesus and his disciples. Nowhere in the First Gospel are these events fulfilled or narrated. Instead, the reader must provide by his/her own knowledge the data that allow for the fulfillment of Jesus' prediction. Matthew apparently knows a time when his community was engaged exclusively in a mission to Israel.[15] For him, this mission is limited to the life and ministry of Jesus and his disciples. The discourse of Matthew 10 also points beyond the time of the life and ministry of Jesus to the time of a mission to the Gentiles. The mission, in Matthew's composition, occurs after persecution and witnessing before governmental authorities. The mission also results in the breaking up of households, as vv. 21-22, 34-38 make clear. This understanding is underscored by vv. 40-42, which in their present form come directly from Matthew. Verse 41 names prophets and righteous persons as specific groups who are sent and received. The content accords well with the viewpoint of Matt 23.34-36. While the use of 'the least' in 10.42 is clearly in reference to members of Matthew's own community and generation, the use of these two groups in 10.41 may refer to groups Matthew identifies with earlier stages of the community's history.

The composition in Matthew 10 yields an understanding of the history of early Christianity similar to that in Matthew 23: (1) the reader understands that mission activities are restricted to Israel by command of Jesus; (2) in antithesis to this command, the reader comes to know that mission activities will eventually be taken to the Gentiles; (3) the reader is given an explanation of this new position. The Gentile mission comes after the rejection by Israel of Christian missionaries (Jesus' messengers) evidenced by persecution on the part of Jewish authorities associated with the synagogues.

The construction of similar viewpoints on the history of early Christianity in both Matthew 23 and 10 suggests that the author and his readers share common assumptions about that history, otherwise the narrative becomes incomprehensible to the reader. In the narrative of Matthew 23 and 10, the disciples progress through two types of relationships to Jewish authorities based in the synagogue. (1) They positively relate to the leaders of a synagogue and accept their teaching authority, while they engage in a mission oriented exclusively to other Jews. (2) They later are forced to organize themselves in direct opposition to Jewish synagogue leaders and synagogue discipline and form their own community apart from non-Christian Jews, which engages in a mission to Gentiles.

Between these two relationships several things happen, according to Matthew. First, the interpretation of the synagogue leaders comes into conflict with specific teachings of Jesus. Second, the mission to Israel fails, resulting in persecution and death for the messengers of

Jesus. At the break with Israel family units are broken. Matthew's composition also hints that these occurrences are not limited to the history of the earthly Jesus and his disciples but are also characteristic of later Christian relationships with Judaism (see also Matt 21.42-46; 27.24-26).[16]

4. *Matthew's Understanding of Early Christian History May Reflect a History of the M Traditions* (C. 33)

I. In an earlier analysis, it was found that sayings nos. 7, 11 represent a tradition that comes from a Christian group that probably attends synagogue at a synagogue led by non-Christian Jews. We also suggested that sayings nos. 9-10 represent a tradition that comes from a Christian group who carried on a mission to Jews within Palestine in the first Christian generation. On the basis of the clues deduced from Matthew's own composition and employment of these sayings in Matthew 23 and 10, we may hypothesize that they represent the same tradition and are the earliest of the M sayings traditions.

II. The most extensively represented tradition in the M sayings is that of sayings nos. 1, 2, 4, 5, 12, 16, 17, 18, 19(?). These sayings apparently come from a tradition adhered to and preserved by a Christian group organized apart from and in antithesis to conceptions about Torah and community organization that characterized significant portions of Judaism in the first century. These sayings probably represent the latest of the M traditions.

There remain other M sayings that we have heretofore been unable to suggest as connected with these two traditions. Sayings nos. 13, 14 are used by Matthew in Matt 23.15-16 to explain, in part, the causes of separation between early Christians and Israel. We may suggest that sayings nos. 13, 14, 3(?) represent a period of conflict that occurs between the traditions grouped under I and II.

Sayings nos. 8, 15 are very difficult to align in this tradition history. Matthew believes that the genesis of the Gentile mission has its basis in the positive command of the risen Lord in Matt 28.16-20. It is probable that at least some significant part of Matthew's community was engaged in such a mission prior to the writing of the Gospel. We noted with regard to saying no. 13 that those who adhere to this saying may know of (engage in?) a proper Gentile mission on terms different from those employed by the blind guides, who according to our reconstruction are probably to be understood as Jewish leaders of a synagogue. Sayings nos. 8, 15 could represent this stage of the tradition history and belong to roughly the same period as sayings nos. 13, 14, 3(?). They probably do not belong to the period described under I. They possibly could come from period II of the history of the tradition, although none of the other sayings during this period discusses a Gentile mission.

5. *The History of the Matthean Community as Reflected in the M Sayings Traditions*

Two historical and social relationships to Jewish authorities represented primarily in a synagogue are evident for at least certain groups of the Matthean community prior to the composition of the Gospel.

I. A Christian Jewish group relatively at peace within the synagogue is constituted prior to 70 CE. The group affirms the teaching authority of its synagogue leadership, while being critical of the pious behavior of both the leadership and other synagogue members; this criticism is based on sayings attributed to Jesus. The group emphasizes religious practice for the exclusive reward that comes from God, whom it characterizes as the one who sees in secret. Its weekly observances of almsgiving, prayer, and fasting were probably similar to those of other synagogue members, except that they were conducted in careful concealment. The group also sends missionaries to other Jews, Israel. The precise nature of their preaching is not evident from the recovered tradition.[17] The group anticipates the imminent coming of the Son of Man, prior to the completion of its mission, which is geographically limited to Palestine.

II. The Christian Jewish group becomes a Jewish Christian community constituted apart from, and in ideological opposition to, the Jewish synagogue. It appears to have undergone persecution at the hands of the synagogue at the juncture of its break. It organizes itself exclusively under the authority of Jesus as the Christ, who is the eschatological promulgator of rules for the community. In this regard, it no longer has a positive relationship to the Jewish institutions of synagogue and Law. Some of the members of this community may also practice vocational celibacy as a means of service to the Kingdom of Heaven. A well developed Christology and theology based upon Jesus as the eschatological spokesperson for

God, with whom he is closely identified, is evident. Further, the presence of Jesus, the resurrected one, is assured to the community.

The history that occurs between these two clear configurations may be indicated by sayings nos. 13, 14, 3(?) and sayings nos. 8, 15. These sayings represent traditions that can be clearly distinguished from those of relationship I and also II. We cannot determine whether they represent the ancestors to Matthew's community while they are still a group within the synagogue (Christian Jews) or whether they are constituted apart from the synagogue (Jewish Christians). At some point, the Christian Jewish Group of I begins to experience tension with the synagogue authorities. Two factors in its open debate with the synagogue rulers are: (1) the belief in certain sayings of Jesus, whom it regards as the ultimate interpreter of Torah in competition with the *halakhic* role of the synagogue authorities; (2) the development of a mission to Gentiles in competition with that of the synagogue authorities. The shift in mission at this stage in the group's development is validated by reference to a saying of Jesus (no. 13). Awareness of this saying may have come from contact with other early Christian missionaries engaged in a mission to Gentiles, or the saying may have originated in the group in response to the reception of Gentiles into the synagogue community on the part of Jewish missionaries; or both factors may have played a role in the saying's emergence. Another factor in the shift in mission may have been increasing failure of a mission to Jews in Palestine and the delay in the return of the Son of Man hoped for in the first stage of the group's history. These sayings may have developed prior to the actual break with the parent synagogue or they may have been used polemically after the fact to justify the break. They must have been promulgated or adhered to at some point in the community's history earlier than the use of saying no. 5, however, since the respective contents of sayings nos. 5 and 14 are mutually exclusive. We cannot with certainty designate the Christian group represented by sayings nos. 13, 14, 3(?) as Christian Jewish or Jewish Christian; therefore this segment of the history is best referred to as an interim period.

Sayings nos. 3 and 14 indicate further that this group has a positive regard for the Jewish temple. Such a viewpoint might have been current in the group as early as I and have continued into II. The traditions survive because they represent the viewpoint of the group that adheres to them. Matthew's own text contains no noticeable departure from this positive regard for the temple and

Jerusalem. The viewpoint may go back to the earliest stages of his community's history.

Sayings nos. 8, 15 belong at some point after the development of a Gentile mission in the community. They may have arisen as early as the intermediate period of the community's history reflected in sayings nos. 13, 14, 3(?). Or they may belong to the Jewish Christian community of II.[18]

III. A third relationship may be added to this reconstruction: the time of the evangelist Matthew himself. Heir to the continuous community history outlined above, Matthew composes a Gospel. The Gospel reflects an angle of vision on the life and ministry of Jesus and the formulation of his church, an angle influenced by the shared history of the community. The use of Mark's Gospel and Q in Matthew may be partially understood as an assimilation of traditional material into the Matthean community's history. Thus, Matthew attempts to make sense of the community's history in terms of the traditions about Jesus. Two major themes throughout Matthew's Gospel are the Kingdom of Heaven and the development of the concept 'God the Father'. Both have profound theological importance for Matthew, at least in part because of the history of his community and its traditions. Further, the organization of the community under the exclusive authority of Jesus as Son of Man/Son of God owes a significant debt to the history of the M sayings traditions and the community that developed and preserved them.[19]

Conclusions

The hypothesis developed in ch. 7 is precisely that: a hypothesis. The hypothesis accounts only for the inclusion of the M traditions in Matthew's Gospel; it does not purport to represent a complete history of the Matthean community. The hypothesis argues from clues in Matthew's text that there is a probable historical and social continuity between a significant group in Matthew's own community and stages of that group's earlier history represented in the tradition which it preserved and which then was used as part of the traditions included in Matthew's Gospel. Matthew seems to have used blocks of sayings from his oral tradition that originated in the form of extended complexes of sayings. He also may have been quite selective about which of the M traditions he used. Therefore, our historical reconstruction can only give partial and probable conclusions based upon the evidence. In the formulation of the hypothesis we have sought to depend primarily on hints within Matthew's text. We hope that this hypothesis contributes to a fuller understanding of the message of the First Gospel.

NOTES

Notes to Chapter 1

1. B.H. Streeter, *The Four Gospels. A Study of Origins* (London: Macmillan, 1927) 223-70; T.W. Manson, *The Teachings of Jesus* (2nd edn; Cambridge: Cambridge University Press, 1935) 21-44; and *The Sayings of Jesus* (London: SCM, 1949) 21-26; G.D. Kilpatrick *The Origins of the Gospel According to St. Matthew* (Oxford: Oxford University Press, 1946) 8-36.

2. All charts are numbered consecutively (C. 1, C. 2, etc.) and provided in the Appendix. In the cases of Streeter and Manson, the chart is a deduction from their discussions, since neither gives in summary the exact contents of M. Manson's results are particularly difficult to discern since he does not always distinguish clearly between tradition and redaction in his commentary (*Sayings*, 149-240). Kilpatrick (*Origins*, 35) states his results explicitly.

3. Streeter (*Gospels*, 150) provides a chart of his hypothesis that is helpful here:

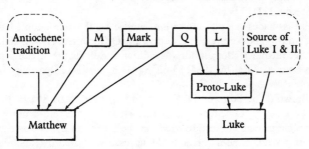

The elements enclosed in solid lines are documents, those in broken lines are oral traditions. The emphasis in Streeter's discussion is given to Q, L, and Proto-Luke (see his pp. 150-292).

4. Qmt is the designation used by some critics for a special recension of Q available to Matthew from his own tradition. See below for a fuller discussion of this option for accounting for the M material.

5. *Gospels*, 512. In this observation, Streeter introduces a hypothesis of the development of early Christianity to explain the text. The evidence derived from a study of the special Matthean sayings in and of themselves does not necessitate such a hypothesis of 'Judaistic reaction'. From Matthew's text, it is difficult to find a direct confrontation between the James and Paul groups in the early community.

6. *Teachings*, 36.

7. *Sayings*, 26.

8. *Origins*, 26.

9. Form-critical and redaction-critical studies frequently use the word 'redaction' in another sense to refer to the shaping of tradition at each point in its transmission, whether by oral rehearsal within a community, or by written editing. Redaction in this sense is present throughout the history of a tradition. Since the present study is interested in the discernment of material available to Matthew prior to his own writing, the use of the term 'redactional' is restricted to its primary sense, *edited*, i.e. material that Matthew himself first writes.

On the issue of 'redaction' at every stage of the development of tradition see R. Bultmann (*Die Geschichte der synoptischen Tradition* [3rd edn; Göttingen: Vandenhoeck & Ruprecht, 1957] 347-48); P. Hoffmann (*Studien zur Theologie der Logienquelle* [NtAbh, 8; Münster: Aschendorf, 1972] 3); D. Lührmann (*Die Redaktion der Logienquelle* (WMANT, 33; Neukirchen-Vluyn: Neukirchener Verlag, 1969] 15); and R.D. Worden ('Redaction Criticism of Q', *JBL* 94 [1975] 538). In different terms W. Kelber refers to 'social identification' and 'preventative censorship' to account for a similar process that he discerns in the shaping of oral tradition (*The Oral and the Written Gospel* [Philadelphia: Fortress, 1983] 14-34).

10. See pp. 111-13 below.

11. P. Vassiliades adopts a position similar to the one adopted in the present study ('The Nature and Extent of the Q Document', *NovT* 20 [1978] 49-73). See further J. Kloppenburg, 'Tradition and Redaction in the Synoptic Sayings Source', *CBQ* 46 (1984) 34-62, esp. n. 3. See also Kilpatrick, *Origins*, 11.

J.P. Brown ('The Form of 'Q' Known to Matthew', *NTS* 8 [1961] 27-42) argues for a source Qmt that was Q plus M, M being a commentary on Q with an ecclesiastical interest. In what may be seen as a variation on the Qmt hypothesis, W.D. Davies refers to M as casuistic *gemara* (rabbinic-type commentary) on Q (*The Setting of the Sermon on the Mount* [Cambridge: Cambridge University Press, 1964] 387-401). Davies does not specify whether this commentary was already in the form of written additions to Q at the time of the composition of the Gospel.

B.W. Bacon (*Studies in Matthew* [New York: Henry Holt, 1930] 120-30) proposes a similar theory, which accounts for virtually all of Matthew's special material by assigning it to S (a source larger than, but including, Q), oral tradition, and Matthew, the redactor. Similarly, F.P. Jones ('The Sources of the Material Peculiar to Matthew' [Th.D. dissertation, Union Theological Seminary, 1938]) assigns the unparalleled material to two different recensions of Q, both available to Matthew.

12. This method has affinities with the work of R.T. Fortna (*The Gospel of Signs. A Reconstruction of the Narrative Source Underlying the Fourth Gospel* [SNTSMS, 11; New York and Cambridge; Cambridge University Press, 1970]),

although the present study does not involve the reconstruction of a coherent source. See also R.E. Brown, *The Birth of the Messiah. A Commentary on the Infancy Narratives in Matthew and Luke* (Garden City: Doubleday, 1977) 105-108.

13. Streeter (*Gospels*) develops the classic case for the 'two document hypothesis', that Matthew and Luke drew on Mark and Q (defined in the next paragraph above). See W.G. Kümmel (*Introduction to the New Testament* [17th edn; Nashville: Abingdon, 1973] 38-80) for a recent statement of the two document hypothesis. Streeter's four source proposal (see n. 3) has not met with the same acceptance.

A significant minority of scholars has recently challenged the two document hypothesis. See W.R. Farmer, *The Synoptic Problem. A Critical Analysis* (New York: Macmillan, 1964); B. Orchard, *Matthew, Luke and Mark. The Griesbach Solution to the Synoptic Question* (Manchester: Koinonia Press, 1976); T.R.W. Longstaff, *Evidence of Conflation in Mark? A Study in the Synoptic Problem* (SBLDS, 28; Missoula: Scholars Press, 1977); H.-H. Stoldt, *History and Criticism of the Markan Hypothesis* (Macon, G.A.: Mercer University, 1980); see also reviews by W. Kelber, *CBQ* 41 (1979) 499-501 and H.C. Kee, *JBL* 98 (1979) 140-43. While some of the evidence, particularly the observations by Longstaff of alternating agreement of Matthew and Luke with Mark within pericopes, is significant, three objections remain unsatisfactorily resolved in these studies. First, those who adopt the Griesbach hypothesis that Matthew is the earliest Gospel used by Luke and that Mark is a conflation of Matthew and Luke (all except Stoldt, who advances no new hypothesis) have yet to make a satisfactory case to demonstrate reasons for Luke's redaction of Matthew. Second, a convincing life setting for the conflation of Matthew and Luke by Mark has yet to appear, although Farmer argues for a liturgical setting in Rome. Third, the exclusive appeal to literary sources fails to take account of the continuing influence of oral tradition. (See H. Koester, *Synoptische Überlieferung bei den Apostolischen Vätern* [TU, 65; Berlin: Akademie, 1957].) See W. Thompson (*Matthew's Advice to a Divided Community. Mt. 17,22–18,35* [AnBib, 44; Rome: Biblical Institute, 1970]), who begins his work with no theory of a solution to the Synoptic problem, but instead tests the various hypotheses pericope by pericope. His results tend to support the two *tradition* hypothesis adopted in the present study.

14. In addition to Streeter's work, cited above, see V. Taylor, 'The Order of Q', and 'The Original Order of Q', *New Testament Essays* (Grand Rapids: Eerdmans, 1968) 90-118. Worden ('Redaction', 532-46) provides a summary of scholarship on Q to 1975. In addition to Worden, see A. Polag, *Die Christologie der Logienquelle* (WMANT, 45; Neukirchen: Neukirchener Verlag, 1977); and *Fragmenta Q. Textheft zur Logienquelle* (Neukirchen: Neukirchener Verlag, 1979); S. Schulz, *Q die Spruchquelle der Evangelisten. Griechisch-deutsche Synopse der Q-Überlieferungen* (Zurich: Theologischer

Verlag, 1972); Vassiliades, 'Q Document'. Challenges to the Q hypothesis include W.R. Farmer, 'A Fresh Approach to Q', *SJLA* (1975) 39-50; L. Foster, 'The "Q" Myth in Synoptic Studies', *Bulletin of the Evangelical Theological Society* 7 (1964) 111-19.

15. For an example of one such complex source theory, see P. Benoit and M.-E. Boismard, *Synopse des quatre évangiles en français avec parallèles des apocryphes et des pères*, vol. II (Paris: Cerf, 1972).

16. See J.P. Meier (in R.E. Brown and J.P. Meier, *Antioch and Rome* [New York: Paulist, 1983] 51-57) for an outline of one hypothesis about the development of the Matthean tradition. His sketch suggests further research into the development of the Markan and Q traditions within Matthew's community prior to the composition of the First Gospel.

17. At a future date, I hope to be able to undertake such a study in the Matthean discourses.

18. Studies in the Fourth Gospel reveal the difficulties of the use of style as a means of recovering tradition in unparalleled material. For a summary and evaluation see R. Kysar (*The Fourth Evangelist and his Gospel. An Examination of Contemporary Scholarship* [Minneapolis: Augsburg, 1975] 13-29). In addition to the works cited there see also the remarks by J. Louis Martyn (*The Gospel of John in Christian History* [New York: Paulist, 1978] 91), who notes that the criterion of the aporia remains the starting point for the recovery of tradition in the Fourth Gospel.

Two recent studies in Matthew that use style as a criterion for the discussion of Matthean redaction (Thompson, *Advice*; and R.H. Gundry, *Matthew. A Commentary on his Literary and Theological Art* [Grand Rapids: Eerdmans, 1982] esp. p. 3) demonstrate the difficulties of the use of statistical observations in discussing Matthean redactional techniques.

19. F. Filson ('Broken Patterns in the Gospel of Matthew', *JBL* 75 [1 956] 227-31) suggests that the breaking of numerical patterns in Matthew shows an editorial tendency to sacrifice inherited patterns to an interest in the topical arrangement of material. Form-critical studies, such as that of H.D. Betz ('Eine judenchristliche Kult-Didache in Mt 6.1-18', in *Überlegungen und Fragen im Blick auf das Problem des historischen Jesus* [NT Festschrift for H. Conzelmann, ed. G. Strecker, Tübingen: Mohr, 1975] 445-47) use the detection of pre-Matthean patterns to separate tradition from redaction.

20. W. Bauer, *Orthodoxy and Heresy in Earliest Christianity*, ed. G. Strecker and R. Kraft (Philadelphia: Fortress, 1971). D. Harrington, 'The Reception of Walter Bauer's *Orthodoxy and Heresy in Earliest Christianity* During the Last Decade', *HTR* 73 (1980) 289-98; H.E.W. Turner, *The Pattern of Christian Truth. A Study in the Relations Between Orthodoxy and Heresy in the Early Church* (London: Mowbray, 1954). See the Appendix by Strecker and & Kraft (*Orthodoxy*, 286-316).

21. H. Koester, *Introduction to the New Testament*, vol. II (Philadelphia: Fortress, 1982); G. Strecker, *Das Judenchristentum in den Psuedoklementinen*

(2nd edn; TU, 70; Berlin: Akademie, 1981); and 'Appendix I. On the Problem of Jewish Christianity', *Orthodoxy*, 241-85; H.J. Schoeps, *Theologie und Geschichte des Judenchristentums* (Tübingen: Mohr, 1949).

22. R.E. Brown, 'Not Jewish Christianity and Gentile Christianity but Types of Jewish/Gentile Christianity', *CBQ* 45 (1983) 74-79; 'Introduction', *Antioch and Rome*, 1-9. J.P. Meier, in the latter volume, applies a similar classification system to groups he detects at Antioch.

23. 'Glimpses into the History of the Johannine Community', *L'Evangile de Jean, Sources, rédaction, théologie*, ed. M. de Jonge (BETL, 44; Leuven, 1977) 149-75; republished in Martyn, *Gospel* 90-121.

24. In addition to 'Glimpses', see Martyn, *History and Theology in the Fourth Gospel* (2nd edn; Nashville: Abingdon, 1979) esp. 64-81; R.E. Brown, *The Community of the Beloved Disciple* (New York: Paulist, 1979) also develops this theme into a detailed history of the Johannine community up to and past the period reflected in the Epistles of John.

25. In what follows, I am indebted to the summary by J.P. Meier (*Law and History in Matthew's Gospel. A Redactional Study of Mt. 5.17-48* [AnBib, 71; Rome: Biblical Institute, 1976] 9-13). Bornkamm's study, 'End-Expectation and Church in Matthew', occurs in G. Bornkamm, G. Barth and H.J. Held, *Tradition and Interpretation in Matthew* (Philadelphia: Westminster, 1963) 15-51. The programmatic form of Bornkamm's essay appeared as 'Matthäus als Interpret der Herrenworte', *TLZ* 79 (1954) 341-46. The essay in its conception and outworking may be seen as belonging to the early years of Bornkamm's redactional studies. The next essay to be considered, 'Der Auferstandene und Irdische', occurs in Bornkamm, Barth and Held, *Überlieferung und Auslegung im Matthäusevangelium* (5th edn; Neukirchen: Buchhandlung des Erziehungsvereins, 1968) 287-310; it is a decade later in its fundamental conceptuality. The final essay, 'Die Binde- und Lösegewalt in der Kirche des Matthäus', (*Geschichte und Glaube II* [Gesammelte Aufsätze, IV; München: Kaiser, 1971] 37-50) is nearly a decade later still. (See the English version, 'The Authority to "Bind" and "Loose" in the Church in Matthew's Gospel', in *Jesus and Man's Hope, I*, ed. D. Buttrick [Pittsburgh: Pittsburgh Theological Seminary, 1970] 37-50). The changes in Bornkamm's view are due in part to the refinements of redaction-critical research in Matthew over a quarter of a century.

26. Meier (*Law*, 11-13) outlines the various scholarly positions. The impasse of redaction criticism may be exemplified by a comparison of R. Hummel (*Die Auseinandersetzung zwischen Kirche und Judentum im Matthäusevangelium* [BEvT, 33; München: Kaiser, 1966]) and D. Hare (*The Theme of Jewish Persecution of Christians in the Gospel According to St. Matthew* [SNTSMS, 6; Cambridge: Cambridge University Press, 1967]). Hummel is closest to position 2 identified above, while Hare represents position 3.

27. As an aid to the reader, the results of this analysis are collected in C. 2,

in the Appendix.

28. 'The Original Order of Q', 118.

29. Bultmann divides the dominical sayings into four categories: logia, prophetic-apocalyptic sayings, legal and community rules, and similitudes (parables). The sayings involved in the present study fall into the first three categories (*The History of the Synoptic Tradition* [ET; rev. edn; New York: Harper & Row, 1963] 69-166).

30. To date a study of the entire body of Matthean parables has yet to appear. On the use of tradition in the Matthean parables, see E. Schweizer, 'Zur Sondertradition der Gleichnisse bei Matthäus', *Matthäus und seine Gemeinde* (Stuttgart: KBW, 1974) 98-105. On Matthew's use of parables see J. Kingsbury, *The Parables of Jesus in Matthew 13* (Richmond: John Knox, 1969).

Notes to Chapter 2

1. Redaction critics have discussed Matt 5.17-20 extensively. Frequently, en route to their exegeses, they have dealt with tradition history. The most important works for this analysis are G. Barth, 'Matthew's Understanding of the Law', in Bornkamm, Barth, and Held, *Tradition*, 58-164; W.D. Davies, 'Matthew 5.17-18', in *Mélanges bibliques redigés en l'honneur d'André Robert* (Travaux de l'Institute Catholique de Paris, 4; Paris: Bloud et Gay, 1957) 425-56; Hummel, *Auseinandersetzung*, 65-75; H. Ljungman, *Das Gesetz erfüllen: Matthäus 5, 17ff. und 3,15 untersucht* (Lund: Gleerup, 1954); U. Luz, 'Die Erfüllung des Gesetzes bei Matthäus', *ZTK* 75 (1978) 398-435; Meier, *Law*; E. Schweizer, 'Mt 5.17-20—Anmerkungen zum Gesetzverständnis des Matthäus', *TL* 77 (1952) 479-84; W. Trilling, *Das wahre Israel. Studien zur Theologie des Matthäusevangeliums* (Erfurter Theologische Studien, 7; Leipzig: St. Benno, 1959) 138-59. The work by I. Broer (*Freiheit vom Gesetz und Radikalisierung des Gesetzes* [SBS, 98; Stuttgart: KBW, 1980]) surveys the recent exegeses of the passage.

2. The majority of commentators assign v. 18 to Q. Bultmann, *History*, 138; G. Barth, 'Law', 65; Kilpatrick, *Origins*, 18; Meier, *Law*, 55; Trilling, *Israel*, 138. Recent reconstructions of the contents of Q have consistently included v. 18 (Schulz, *Synopse*, 14; Polag, *Fragmenta*, 74). H.-T. Wrege (*Die Überlieferungsgeschichte der Bergpredigt* [WUNT, 9; Tübingen: Mohr, 1968] 40) is among a minority of critics who do not hold the Q hypothesis. He regards v. 18 as traditional, nevertheless. E. Lohmeyer (*Das Evangelium des Matthäus*, ed. W. Schmauch [MeyerK Sonderband; Göttingen: Vandenhoeck & Ruprecht, 1967] 104-108) exemplifies those critics who do not explicitly assign v. 18 to Q, but use the parallel tradition in Luke 16.17 to recover Matthean redaction.

3. Barth, 'Law', 67-69; Lohmeyer, *Matthäus*, 107-108; Trilling, *Israel*, 143-45.

4. Barth, 'Law', 92-93; E. Klostermann, *Das Matthäusevangelium* (HNT, 4; Tübingen: Mohr, 1927) 41; Ljungman, *Gesetz*, 12-17; P. Bonnard, *L'Evangile selon St. Matthieu* (2nd edn; CNT, 1; Paris: Delachaux et Nestle, 1970) 61; J. Schmid, *Das Evangelium nach Matthäus* (5th edn; RNT, 1; Regensburg: Pustet, 1965) 86; Trilling, *Israel*, 145-47. For an opposing view, see W. Dumbrell, 'The Logic of the Role of the Law in Matthew V 1-20', *NovT* 23 (1981) 17.

5. On the citation formulas, see K. Stendahl, *The School of St. Matthew* (2nd edn; Philadelphia: Fortress, 1968); G. Strecker, *Der Weg der Gerechtigkeit. Untersuchung zur Theologie des Matthäus* (FRLANT, 82; Göttingen: Vandenhoeck & Ruprecht, 1962) 49-85; R.H. Gundry, *The Use of the Old Testament in St. Matthew's Gospel* (Leiden: Brill, 1967); W. Rothfuchs, *Die Erfüllungszitate des Matthäus-Evangeliums* (Stuttgart: Kohlhammer, 1969). R.E. Brown (*Birth*, 96-104) has a survey and evaluation of the history of scholarship on the formula citations.

6. Meier, *Law*, 82-89.

7. The infinitive *katalysai* may well have been suggested to Matthew by the use of *lyō* in Matt 5.19, which will be shown to be traditional. The interchangeability of *katalyō* with *lyō* in contexts with *nomos* is observed by A. Schlatter (*Der Evangelist Matthäus* [3rd edn; Stuttgart: Calwer, 1948] 157); see Josephus, *Ant.* 11.140.

8. Lohmeyer, *Matthäus*, 105.

9. In view of the discussion by Polag (*Christologie*, 79-84) and Lührmann (*Logienquelle*, 43-48), the foregoing statement needs some defense. The occurrences in Q of the term Pharisees are restricted to a single context of six verses (Matt 23.25, 23, 6-7a, 27, 4, 29-31 par Luke 11.39, 42-44, 46-48, 52, using Schulz's arrangement [*Synopse*, 10-14]). Within the context, Matthew and Luke agree in the use of the term only twice. While there appears to have been some anti-Pharisee polemic in Q, the data from Q do not account for the more widespread use of the term in Matthew and Luke.

10. Hummel, *Auseinandersetzung*, 13-25, 66.

11. Meier, *Law*, 116.

12. Barth, 'Law', 65; Trilling, *Israel*, 85; Lohmeyer, *Matthäus*, 113-14.

13. See H.W. Smyth (*Greek Grammar* [rev. edn; Cambridge, Mass.: Harvard, 1956] §1247) and BDF (§290) for examples in both Classical and Hellenistic texts. The LXX of Deut 1.1 uses *houtos* in referring forward to the *logoi* of Moses. Meier (*Law*, 102), Barth ('Law', 65), and Lohmeyer (*Matthäus*, 110) represent the variety of scholarly opinions. Meier thinks that *toutōn* refers to the iota and hook of v. 18. Barth suggests that the problem may be accounted for by the presence of an underlying Semitism. Lohmeyer thinks that the *toutōn* can only refer forward to 5.21-48. 1 Cor 7.29; 15.50; John 8.45 establish the syntactical possibility that *houtos* may refer forward in New Testament Greek. Coupled with the use in Deut 1.1 these texts give greater weight to Lohmeyer's case than he himself

developed. I am indebted to my colleague J. Marcus for pointing out the LXX use to me.

14. Meier (*Law*, 91) says, 'The synoptic tradition does not employ the noun *entolē* in the Johannine manner for the commandments of Jesus. *Entelomai*, the corresponding verb, is used of Jesus in Mt. 28.20, but it is also used in Mt. of God and Moses'. We must keep in mind, however, that Meier's discussion refers to the tradition as edited by Matthew. Are the uses of *entelomai* (28.20) and *entolai* (5.19) a remnant of a tradition that refers to Jesus' commandments in much the same way as parts of the Johannine tradition? See also Dumbrell, 'Logic', 20 n. 59.

15. In ch. 6, we will demonstrate on additional grounds of style, vocabulary, and content that Matt 16.19b and 18.18 contain an M saying that includes this peculiar use of *lyō*.

16. See Meier (*Law*, 98), who notes that '"Kingdom of Heaven" is a sign of Matthean redaction, *or at least of M*' (emphasis mine). It would be difficult to argue that in every case Matthew has employed an entirely new term of such theological importance in the composition of a Gospel intended for the use of a community.

17. See ch. 1, p. 16. Barth ('Law', 66), although he does not assign vv. 18 and 19 to Q, argues for their pre-Matthean unity, as does Trilling (*Israel*, 182-83), who further suggests that they were together in Q. Meier (*Law*, 102-104) works out this latter position in detail. P. Hoffmann (*Studien*, 4-5) and Schulz (*Synopse*) do not include Matt 5.19 in Q. Polag (*Christologie*) places 5.19 in his 'least likely' category. Lührmann (*Logienquelle*, 119) on the one hand assigns 5.17-19 to the larger tradition of pre-Matthean *logia*, but on the other cannot assign the verses to Q, because the Matthean developments in the tradition cannot be explained on the basis of a Q original reconstructed from a comparison of Matthew's text with the Lukan parallels.

18. Meier, *Law*, 120.

19. Subsequently, I intend to make such a suggestion, specifically, that v. 19 originally introduced a collection of commandments of Jesus preserved at least partially in Matt 5.21-48. See ch. 5, pp. 74-77.

20. Verse 18b,c is similar to Jewish tradition of the period. The phrase 'until heaven and earth pass away' in Jewish tradition could indicate two things. First, the phrase means 'forever' as midrashim on Deut 32.1 indicate (*Tg. Ps.-J.* on Deut 32.1; *Lev. Rab.* 29 [127c]; see H. Traub, 'οὐρανός', *TDNT*, V, 509-12). Second, the phrase, when it occurs in an apocalyptic context, indicates the end of the heaven and the earth (Isa 65.17; *1 Enoch* 91.16; 72.1). The two lines of interpretation occur together in *Sifre* on Deut 32.1. In either case, rabbinic exegeses argue for the eternal validity of the Torah (for a collection of texts, see Strack–Billerbeck, I, 244-47 and the analysis by W.D. Davies, *Torah in the Messianic Age and/or the Age to Come* [SBLMS, 7; Philadelphia: SBL, 1952].

21. This tension has led commentators to construct a life setting for the joining of the two verses in a community that included representatives of both a stricter 'Palestinian' and a more lenient 'Hellenistic' view of the Law. Bonnard (*Matthieu*, 62) is one of the few critics who do not recognize this tension.

22. Bultmann (*History*, 132) holds the Matthean version to be the more original based on its setting within the temple cult. A.H. McNeile regards Matthew's dependence on Mark as improbable (*The Gospel According to St. Matthew. The Greek Text with Introduction, Notes, and Indices* [New York: Macmillan, 1915; reprint edn; Grand Rapids: Baker, 1980] 63).

23. See Matt 21.41-46; 22.7; 23.38. E. Schweizer (*The Good News According to Matthew* [Atlanta: John Knox, 1975] 15) and Strecker (*Weg*, 36) articulate the case advanced by most critics.

24. The dominant view in the history of scholarship has regarded vv. 21-22d as an original unity, even though other antitheses have not been so regarded. (See Bultmann, *History*, 135; Klostermann, *Matthäusevangelium*, 42; Schweizer, *Good News*, 110-11; and the especially trenchant article by G. Strecker, 'Die Antithesen der Bergpredigt (Mt 5.21-48 par)', *ZNW* 69 [1978] 36-72). In opposition, M.J. Suggs argues that all of the antitheses are from the editor ('The Antitheses as Redactional Products', in *Überlegungen und Fragen im Blick auf das Problem des historischen Jesus*, 433-44). Thus, the antithetical formula originated with Matthew. Suggs correctly observes that 'Dissimilarity—the identification of elements distinctively characteristic of a speaker or author—is as valid for determining genuine Matthean material as it is for determining authentic Jesus tradition' (443). A unique *stylistic* device is a two-edged sword. The present study, however, attempts to determine whether each antithesis is editorial or existed before the Gospel. Bultmann's criterion that certain of the sentences that follow the formula 'But I say to you', could not have circulated independently of the previous antithesis has been shown to be inadequate (see the remarks by Strecker in 'Antithesen'). The present study shows (1) the style is consistent throughout vv. 21-22, and (2) the content is distinct in vocabulary from usual Matthean redaction.

25. Stendahl, *School*, 137.

26. K. Berger ('Zu den sogenannten Sätzen heiligen Rechts', *NTS* 17 [1970-71] 16-19) discusses such legal rules in relationship to the LXX. See particularly p. 18 n. 1.

27. Bultmann, *History*, 134.

28. With the genitive, *enochos* refers to punishment. See Matt 26.66. BAGD, 267-68.

29. A.T. Robertson, *A Grammar of the Greek New Testament in Light of Historical Research* (Nashville: Broadman, 1934) 535.

30. See ch. 4, p. 70. While 23.33 is assigned in whole to Matthew, the phrase is probably traditional.

31. Josephus uses the term especially in reference to the high council in

Jerusalem that appears to have had a civil administrative function prior to
the fall of Jerusalem in 70 CE. See H. Mantel, *Studies in the History of the
Sanhedrin* (HSM, 17; Cambridge: Harvard University, 1961) 54-101.

32. *Leg. Gaj.* 213; *Conf. Ling.* 86; *Vit. Ant.* 27; *Omn. Prob. Lib.* 11; *Ebr.*
165.

33. The possibility of a heavenly Sanhedrin is suggested by L. Ginsberg
(*The Legends of the Jews* [6 vols.; Philadelphia: The Jewish Publication
Society, 1909] I, 78; IV, 287; VI, 344). The earliest *aggadah* that seems to
refer to a heavenly Sanhedrin is *Gen. R.* 20.4. The term *sanhedrin* does not
occur here or in the parallel in *'Abot R. Nat.* 1.5. The concept of a properly
constituted court in heaven is well established in the Talmud, where the term
is either *bet din* or *dine šamayin* (*b. Mak.* 13b; *b. Yoma* 35b; *b. Git.* 53a; *b. B.
Qam.* 56a).

34. Reading with Papyrus 67 and Sinaiticus (original scribe), where the
pronoun is omitted. Nestle's 25th edition places the *autēn* in parentheses,
while the 26th edition makes it part of the text. The majority of witnesses
read *autēn*, but the first corrector of Sinaiticus and Family One manuscripts
read *autēs*. The genitive is preferred with verbs of desire in classical use
(Smyth, *Grammar*, §1349). The LXX use of the accusative in Ex 20.17
probably influenced the majority of manuscripts here. Philo uses the genitive
with *epithymeō* in *Leg. All.* 3.66. Luke also uses the genitive in Acts 2.33. The
omission of the pronoun should be the preferred reading because: (1) the
oldest witness does not have the pronoun; (2) the divergence in the later
manuscripts between *autēn* and *autēs* is best accounted for by the lack of any
pronoun in the original. For further use of the *pros to* construction with an
infinitive of purpose in the M material see Matt 6.1; 13.30; 23.5.

35. See Meier (*Law*, 140-50), who follows H. Baltensweiler ('Die
Ehebruchsklausen bei Matthäus. Zu Matth. 5,32; 19,9', *TZ* [1959] 340-56;
and *Die Ehe im Neuen Testament* [Zürich: Zwingli, 1967] 88-100) in
proposing that the exceptive clause refers to Gentiles who are entering the
Matthean community with spouses considered incestuous.

36. Reading with the majority of witnesses *kai hos ean apolelymenēn
gamēsȩ̄*. See B.M. Metzger, *A Textual Commentary on the Greek New
Testament* (London: United Bible Societies, 1971) 13-14.

37. Schweizer, *Good News*, 364-365. On the other hand, Lohmeyer
(*Matthäus*, 126) thinks that Matt 5.28-29 comes from tradition independent
of Matt 18.8-9.

38. Wrege, *Überlieferungsgeschichte*, 65-66. Josephus (*J.W.* 1.79) uses
kalon and the dative as in Matt 18.8-9. I have been unable to find other
attestations for the use of *kalon* and the accusative as in Mark 9.43-48. See
Strack-Billerbeck, I, 303; Schlatter, *Matthäus*, 178, 550. *Sympherō* is found
among the Synoptics only in Matthew, although the term occurs in Acts
(19.19; 20.20) so one would assume that Luke knew the term. Paul uses the
term (exclusively in 1 and 2 Corinthians) five times. John has the term three
times.

39. For the history of scholarship on the exceptive clause as well as an evaluation of the possible options for interpretation, see Meier, *Law*, 140-50. Meier holds that 5.32 draws on both Mark and Q.

40. See Meier, *Law*, 129-31. Meier may be correct that no great theological significance is to be understood by the abbreviated form in v. 31, but the variation is designed to communicate something to the Greek reader.

41. Smyth, *Grammar*, §§2834, 2836; BDF, §447.

42. Matthew uses *palin* 15 times outside of v. 33. See especially 22.1 and 27.50 where *palin* resumes the narrative after an interruption. Strecker ('Antithesen', 39) suggests that *palin* is used by Matthew to divide the antitheses into two groups. There appears to be no other use of this nature either in Matthew or the NT generally. Neither Smyth nor BDF mentions this use as a common editorial practice in Classical or Hellenistic Greek (see relevant sections noted above).

43. Stendahl, *School*, 137.

44. Most commentators do not directly comment on the number of paragraphs in 5.21-48, but discuss six antitheses as if there are six paragraphs in the unit. See D. Senior, *Invitation to Matthew* (Garden City, N.Y.: Doubleday, 1977) 66-72; D. Hill, *The Gospel of Matthew* (London: Oliphants, 1972) 124; Schweizer, *Good News*, 122-23.

D.H. Müller, (*Die Bergpredigt im Licht der Strophentheorie* [Vienna: Holder, 1908] 10) places vv. 31-32 together with vv. 27-30 and counts five antitheses. W.C. Allen (*A Critical and Exegetical Commentary on the Gospel According to S. Matthew* [3rd edn; Edinburgh: T. & T. Clark, 1912] 47-52) lists vv. 31-32 as a 'special application' subsumed under the second of five 'illustrations' (i.e. antitheses). J.C. Fenton (*Saint Matthew* [The Pelican Gospel Commentary; Baltimore: Penguin Books, 1963] 86) sees vv. 31-32 as an appendix to vv. 27-30. He proposes five antitheses. H.B. Green (*The Gospel According to Matthew* [Oxford: Oxford University Press, 1975] 81-82) includes vv. 31-32 as part of the second antithesis (vv. 27-30).

Filson ('Patterns', 227-31) suggests that vv. 31-32 are a subpoint, which Matthew added to a preexistent pattern of five antitheses. I am not prepared to suggest at this point that there were five antitheses before Matthew when he composed vv. 31-32, but it is probable that some collection of antitheses existed prior to Matthew in view of the discussion of vv. 21-22 above and the subsequent discussions of vv. 27-28, 33-37. See ch. 5, pp. 74-77.

45. Such an omission may be more apparent to the interpreter than it was to the ancient reader. The same Jesus who spoke vv. 21-22 speaks to the reader in vv. 27-28, and his power to legislate would carry with it an implicit threat. This understanding would hold especially if and when vv. 21-22 preceded 27-28.

46. M. Dibelius (*James, A Commentary on the Epistle of James*, rev. by H. Greeven [Hermeneia; Philadelphia: Fortress, 1976] 251) and Strecker ('Antithesen', 55-58) have nuanced discussions that find certain elements in James to be the more primitive form. The following discussion relies on the

main outlines of their inquiries.

P. Minear ('Yes or No: The Demand for Honesty in the Early Church', *NovT* 13 [1971] 1-13) locates Jas 5.12 near the earliest stage of the tradition.

47. Lohmeyer, *Matthäus*, 133.

48. Both Dibelius (*James*) and Strecker ('Antithesen') take this position. For the opposing view, albeit with different argumentation, see Schweizer (*Good News*, 111) and Suggs ('Antitheses', 436).

49. See L.L. Kline (*The Sayings of Jesus in the Pseudo-Clementine Homilies* [SBLDS, 14; Missoula: Scholars, 1975] 86-87), who contends that *Ps-Cl. Hom.* 3.55.1; 19.2.4 may rely on a harmony. On Justin, *Apol.* 16.5 see A.J. Bellinzoni, *The Sayings of Jesus in the Writings of Justin Martyr* (Leiden: Brill, 1967) 67. Strecker (*Judenchristentum*, 134) contends that *Ps-Cl. Hom.* 3.55.1; 19.2.4 reflect a modification of the more original Matthean form of 37a. The tendency is also found in Jas 5.12.

The formula in Matt 5.37 is frequently established as a form of swearing by reference to *2 Enoch* 49. 1. The passage is in the longer recension (designated A by Charles in *APOT*) and reads.

> I swear to you, my children, but I swear not by an oath, neither by heaven nor by earth, nor by any other creature which God created.
> The Lord said: 'There is no oath in me, nor injustice, but truth'. If there is no truth in men, let them swear by the words 'yea, yea', or else 'nay, nay' (*APOT* 2).

The passage is weak evidence for determining the background or meaning of Matt 5.37a. The A recension is usually regarded as the more corrupt. *2 Enoch* 49.1 is not found in the B recension nor in the critical edition by A. Vaillant (*Le Livre des Secrets d'Hénoch*, Paris: Institut d'Etudes Slaves, 1952). Both the date and venue of *2 Enoch* are unsure (G.W.E. Nickelsburg, *Jewish Literature Between the Bible and the Mishnah. A Historical and Literary Introduction* [Philadelphia: Fortress, 1981] 188). Therefore, *2 Enoch* 49.1 offers unreliable support for the argument that Matt 5.37a is a moralizing development on the original logion, perhaps better preserved in Jas 5.12. *2 Enoch* 49.1, however, might indicate that such a formula could be understood as an oath by late first-, second-, and third-century writers. The lines that appear to rely on Jas 5.12 in Justin and the *Pseudo-Clementines* may simply be a clarification of Matthew's text from this perspective and not directly dependent on James.

50. Strecker, 'Antithesen', 57 n. 54.

51. See below, where the redactional nature of 5.37b is established. The presence of editorial elements from Matthew in each of the parallels argues against the need to introduce a hypothesis of oral tradition to explain the later texts. On the Justin passage see the opposing views by Minear ('Yes or No', 1), who argues that Justin relies on oral tradition, and Sanders (*The*

Tendencies of the Synoptic Tradition [Cambridge: Cambridge University Press, 1969] 57, 67), who argues that Justin depends on Matthew.

52. See n. 46.

53. Matt 5.47 may be compared to Luke 6.34. The relevant phrases are: *ti perisson poieite* (Matt 5.47) and *poia hymin charis estin* (Luke 6.34).

54. The uses from Q are: 5.11 par Luke 6.22; 6.23 par Luke 11.34; 7.11 par Luke 11.13; 12.35 par Luke 6.45; 12.39 par Luke 11.29; 12.45 par Luke 11.24-26; 16.4 par Luke 11.29; 25.26 par Luke 19.22. The one use from Mark 7.21 is in Matt 15.19. All of the uses from Q are adjectival.

55. LSJ, 649. BAGD, 296. *Epiorkeō* occurs only in 1 Esdr 1.48 and Wis 14.28, which have no Hebrew parallels with which to compare its use.

56. Stendahl (*School*, 137) proposes that the scriptural allusions in v. 33 are based on catechetical material known to Matthew. See, however, his remarks in the 'Preface to the Second Edition' (1968, iv). In referring to the developments in OT textual criticism since his original work, Stendahl points out, 'It makes it more probable that readings found in Matthew could witness to text forms actually available in Greek, prior to Matthew. It makes recourse to testimonies less compelling as an explanation of textual peculiarities. It strengthens the suggestion that Hebrew texts continued to cause revision of Greek texts.' In the case of 5.33, the present study proposes that it is unnecessary to refer to 'catechesis', or midrash, in order to account for the scriptural reference.

57. J. Jeremias (*The Parables of Jesus* [2nd edn; New York: Scribners, 1972] 83-85) concludes that Matthew is responsible for the interpretation of the Parable of the Tares in 13.36-43 as well as the shortened and parallel interpretation of the Seine Net parable in 13.49-50. His study of style and vocabulary is convincing. See above p. 38 on the other uses of *ponēros* in Matthew with the article. All of these uses have now been attributed to the redactor.

58. Since this analysis is concerned only with M sayings, the lack of a complete logion satisfies its interest in v. 43. The scriptural quotation (Lev 19.18) in v. 43 is followed by the phrase *kai . . . sou*, which is not found in any known text. The scriptural use here is close to that of v. 38 (see the discussion above). This use may well be indicative of Matthew's editing. It is disjunctive from the use of the Decalogue in Antitheses 1, 2, 3, which are M sayings. Matthew's use of Lev 19.2 in the construction of 5.48 is noteworthy in this regard (Stendahl, *School*, 137).

The introductory formula *alla hymin legō* in Luke 6.27 has led some commentators to suggest that perhaps an antithesis existed in Q (Meier, *Law*, 127). Such a hypothesis is intriguing and would suggest that the antithetical formula was preserved in both Q and M traditions. Some further explanation, however, as to the lack of other evidence in Luke of his knowledge of the formula would help to make the hypothesis more probable.

It is clear, however, that the disjunctions noted throughout the foregoing pages between Antitheses 1, 2, 3, which are M sayings, and Antitheses 4, 5 along with v. 31, may be accounted for by postulating two levels of transmission: the M sayings and Matthew. The influence of Q on the M traditons that lie behind Matt 5.21-48 is an additional study suggested by the results of the present analysis and the hypothesis of these commentators.

59. Bultmann, *History*, 148.

60. This conclusion suggests only that vv. 9-13 come from a tradition common to Matthew and Luke. See p. 17 for the definition of Q used in this study, where we expressed some doubt as to whether the entirety of the tradition common to Matthew and Luke (Q) was written.

61. Betz ('Kult-Didache', 445-57) provides a different division, which depends on a topical pattern. The analysis offered here attempts to demonstrate the parallelism inherent in the organization of the Greek syntax.

62. Schweizer (*Good News*, 139) suggests that vv. 7-8 were originally in the singular and have been assimilated to the plurals of vv. 9-15 . Verses 16-17 would continue the assimilation. The disruption of pattern by vv. 7-8 seems to point rather in the direction that vv. 7-8 stood before Matthew in the plural. Schweizer is correct, however, that vv. 16-18 have probably been changed to the plural under the influence of the tradition in vv. 9-15.

63. Betz ('Kult-Didache', 453) assigns vv. 1-6, 16-18 to a thoroughly Jewish context with no trace of a Christian community life setting and assigns vv. 7-8 to a diaspora Jewish community. Both of these life settings are open to challenge. Verses 7-8 could certainly be located anywhere in the ancient world where Greco-Roman religions were practiced, including Palestine.

64. Among those who assign v. 1 to Matthew are Strecker (*Weg*, 152), Schweizer (*Good News*, 140), and J. Dupont (*Les Béatitudes* [3 vols.; 2nd edn; Paris: Gabalda, 1958, 1969, 1973] III, 260-72 especially p. 262 n. 8). Dupont reversed his position on the verse between his first and third volumes (cf. I, 159-63). Most recently, B. Przybylski (*Righteousness in Matthew and his World of Thought* [SNTSMS, 41; Cambridge: Cambridge University Press, 1980] 87-89) has assumed that 5.20 and 6.1 are free creations by the redactor and thus indicative of Matthew's understanding of *dikaiosynē* in 3.15; 5.6; 5.10; 6.33; 21.32. While the present study has already found that 5.20 is most likely redactional, it is not at all a certainty that 6.1 is also. Further, it appears that Przybylski has perhaps pressed all of the uses of *diakaiosynē* into too narrow a field of meaning. Certainly, a comparison of 5.20 and 6.1 to 6.33 would make the reader aware that *dikaiosynē* may mean both God's saving activity (6.33) and the norm of man's behavior (the interpretation Przybylski derives from 5.20 and 6.1). Focus on the full concept, *poiein dikaiosynēn*, may highlight the distinctiveness of the concept

within Matthew and the continuity of 6.1 with what is known of Jewish tradition before and after the NT period.

In opposition to Przybylski, Bultmann (*History*, 133) and Wrege (*Überlieferungsgeschichte*, 96-97) both assign 6.1 to pre-Matthean tradition. The following line of research is indebted to Wrege's drawing attention to the use of *poiein dikaiosynēn* in the LXX.

65. The passages with MT equivalents are: Gen 18.19; 20.5; 21.23; 2 Kgdms 8.15; 3 Kgdms 10.9; 1 Chron 18.14; 2 Chron 9.8; Ps 118.121; Isa 56.1; 58.2; Jer 9.23; 22.3; 22.15; 23.5; Ezek 18.5, 17, 19, 27; 33.14, 16, 19. 1 Kgdms 2.10. Tob 4.5; 12.9; Ezek 33.13 have no parallel in the MT. All the uses except Jer 9.23 have a human as the subject of *poiein dikaiosynēn*: thus, general use in the LXX refers to human acts towards God. In Jer 9.23 the subject is God.

66. Przybylski, *Righteousness*, 66-74.

Notes to Chapter 3

1. The agreement of Sinaiticus (first scribe) with witnesses from a variety of text types establishes good external evidence for deleting the *kai* before *Iakōbus*. Elsewhere in the paragraph, the disciples are grouped in twos by the use of *kai*. The inclusion of the *kai* at this juncture would break the internal pattern.

2. The development of the Markan and Q traditions within the Matthean community is the subject for another study. The assumption of such a development remains part of the working hypotheses of many commentators on Matthew. The critical leverage for analyzing the stages in such a development has yet to be firmly established. The present study attempts to test methods that could assist such an analysis. See the remarks on M in Meier (*Law*, 3-6), who articulates the present state of source and tradition history in Matthew.

On the intent of Matthew's editing of these verses in the broader context of the Gospel, see H.J. Held, 'Matthew as Interpreter of the Miracle Stories', in Bornkamm, Barth, and Held, *Tradition*, 250-51. Hare (*Persecution*, 96-97) has a succinct description of the use of Mark and Q in ch. 10, including his own historical reconstruction of the conditions that contributed to Matthew's editorial activity. Polag (*Fragmenta*, 44-46) presents a suggestion of the Q elements in this passage. Both he and Schulz (*Synopse*, 76-79) rely on the Lukan order to reconstruct the order of Q. In this particular passage, the application of the presupposition, current in studies on Q, that Luke has preserved the original order of Q, seems strained.

3. The asyndeton between v. 8a and v. 8b is not a sufficient disjunction to posit the use of tradition. Asyndeta characterize the styles of both Mark and

Matthew, particularly in passages of vivid description. Verse 8b is an example of the use of rhetorical asyndeton, where the following sentence advances the thought of the previous sentence (Smyth, *Grammar*, §2165). N. Turner (J.H. Moulton, *A Grammar of the Greek New Testament*, 4 vols. [Edinburgh: T. & T. Clark, 1908, 1929, 1963, 1976], vol. IV: *Style* by N. Turner, 31-32) attributes the asyndetic style in Mark and Matthew to Aramaic influence. The attestation of the style in Classical Greek (see Smyth) as well as in first-century Greek papyri and in Epictetus makes this attribution unnecessary and probably erroneous (R. Soulen, *Handbook of Biblical Criticism* [Atlanta: John Knox, 1976] 24; also E. Colwell, *The Greek of the Fourth Gospel* [Chicago: University of Chicago, 1931]).

Bultmann (*History*, 145) is unable to determine whether the saying is a Matthean or pre-Matthean expansion of Q.

4. *History*, 77.

5. Scholarly positions on Matt 10.5-6 may be conveniently divided into three categories: (1) the verses are redactional, i.e. a literary device designed to show that the ministry of Jesus was first connected to Israel exclusively; (2) the verses are from Q, even though they are only attested in Matthew; (3) the verses are traditional and from Matthew's special material.

(1) Barth, 'Law', 100 n. 4; H. Frankemölle, *Jahwebund und Kirche Christi: Studien zur Form- und Traditionsgeschichte des Evangelium nach Matthäus* (Münster: Aschendorff, 1974) 123-37; F. Beare, 'The Mission of the Disciples and the Mission Charge: Matthew 10 and Parallels', *JBL* 89 (1970) 1-13.

(2) G. Müller, *Zur Synopse. Untersuchungen über die Arbeitsweise des Lukas und Matthäus und ihrer Quellen* (FRLANT, 11; Göttingen: Vandenhoeck & Ruprecht, 1908) 10; B. Weiss, *Die Quellen des Lukasevangelium* (Stuttgart: Cotta, 1907) 130; J. Hawkins, 'Probabilities as to the So-Called Double Tradition of St. Matthew and St. Luke', in *Studies in the Synoptic Problem by Members of the University of Oxford*, William Sanday, ed. (Oxford: Clarendon, 1911) 134, with reservations; Strecker, *Weg*, 194, with reservations; H. Schürmann, 'Mt 10,5b-6 und die Vorgeschichte des synoptischen Aussendungsberichtes', *Traditionsgeschichtliche Untersuchungen zu den synoptischen Evangelien* (Düsseldorf: Patmos, 1968) I, 137-49, who places 10.5-6 after Luke 10.7 in Q; Polag, *Fragmenta*, 44, who places the saying after Luke 12.12 and rates it as 'probable'. J. Lange, *Das Erscheinen des Auferstandenen im Evangelium nach Matthäus* (Würzburg: Echter, 1973) 251-52.

(3) Kilpatrick, *Origins*, 26-27; Trilling, *Israel*, 82; Meier, *Law*, 27; Hummel, *Auseinandersetzung*, 138; S. Brown, 'The Two-Fold Representation of the Mission in Matthew's Gospel', *ST* 31 (1977) 21-32.

6. Bultmann (*History*, 145) designates vv. 5b-6 as a legal-church rule. The introductory phrase, on the principles of form criticism, may well be a secondary expansion of the original logion. Sanders (*Tendencies*, 275) regards

direct discourse and first-person address as very strong indicators of development in a tradition.

7. Samaritans or Samaria occurs as follows: Mark, never; Luke, three times; John, four times.

8. *Probaton* occurs at 7.15; 9.36; 10.16; 12.11, 12; 15.24; 18.12; 25.32, 33; 26.31 outside of this passage. Only in 15.24 is it in context with *oikou Israēl*. Attention to the entire phrase is important here.

9. Luke in Acts uses the concept twice: once in Acts 2.36, and once in a quotation from Amos 5.25 at Acts 7.42. Hebrews uses *oikou Israēl* at 8.8 in reliance on Jer 31.31 and at 8.10, which repeats the use from the quotation.

On the LXX background to the formulation in vv. 5b-6 see also Isa 53.6; Ps 118.176; Isa 11.12; 1 Kgdms 22.17.

10. Strecker (*Weg*, 194-95), for example, holds that Matt 15.24 better preserves the original tradition. Although 15.24 is a shorter saying, 10.5b-6 is not cast in the form of an 'I' saying, which form criticism usually considers an indication of development in the tradition. Given Matthew's redaction of the Markan pericope in 15.21-28 (par Mark 7.24-30), the simpler explanation would be that Matthew constructed 15.24 on the model of 10.5b-6. I am in agreement, therefore, with Frankemölle's argument that 15.24 is a Matthean redactional product, although I do not agree that 10.5b-6 is redactional as well (see *Jahwebund*, 123-37). Frankemölle has taken insufficient account of both the problem that the tradition contained in 10.5b-6 caused the editor, and the finesse with which the editor circumvented its implications. For an analysis similar to Frankemölle's see the article by Beare cited above. In response to Frankemölle, see Strecker, *Weg*, 107-109; Meier, *Law*, 23 n. 118; S. Brown, 'Two-Fold', 25 n. 16.

11. O. Michel, 'Der Abschluss des Matthäus-Evangeliums', *EvT* 10 (1950) 16-26, seems to have been the first to observe that 28.16-20 was the key to understanding the Gospel. See the below cited studies of salvation-history in Matthew, which treat 28.16-20 as a key text.

12. The analysis could, of course, be expanded to other passages within the Gospel, in which Matthew's view of the Gentiles is apparent. I have chosen three passages which seem to relate to one another conceptually. See also the citations in Matt 4.15, 12.18-21 and the interpretation of the Parable of the Wicked Tenants in Matt 21.42-43. Brown (*Birth*, 178-88) demonstrates Matthew's interest in the extension of the Gospel to the Gentiles from a consideration of Matt 2.1-12.

In their very different attempts to read Matt 10 in reference to the practice of Matthew's community at the time the Gospel was written, Hare and S. Brown take insufficient account of the composition and placement of the three sections analyzed above. The underlined phrases in the analysis above highlight the difference between the mission before and after the resurrection. The clear differences resist the attempt to read ch. 10 as a reflection of the mission practice of Matthew's community. In describing a community-building commission, which from its context and content applies to the reader, 28.18-20 probably reveal the mission practice of Matthew's church. Chapter 10, however, gives no indication that the command in 5b-6 extends beyond the mission of the disciples while Jesus is present with them in the flesh.

Analyses usually relate Matthew's understanding of the mission to the Gentiles to his understanding of (what is often called) salvation-history. On this, see Strecker, *Weg*, 86-123; and 'Das Geschichtsverständnis des Matthäus', *EvT* 26 (1966) 57-74 (available in English, though abbreviated, as 'The Concept of Salvation-History in Matthew', *JAAR* 35 [1967] 219-30); J. Kingsbury, 'The Structure of Matthew's Gospel and his Concept of Salvation History', *CBQ* 35 (1973) 451-74; Meier, *Law*, 25-40 (reproduced in 'Salvation-History in Matthew: In Search of a Starting Point', *CBQ* 37 [1975] 203-15).

13. There is a possibility of an overlap of Q with Mark at Matt 10.19. The elements *hotan de* and *merimnēsēte pōs* may come from Q (see Luke 12.11-12). The overlap appears in this case insufficient to posit an underlying Q saying. See below on Schürmann's view.

14. Compare the findings of J. McDermott with those of the present investigation. He argues that 23a is traditional, while 23b is Matthew's own construction ('Mt 10.23 in Context', *BZ* 28 [1984] 230-40). See M. Kunzi for the history of interpretation and a thorough bibliography (*Das Naherwartungslogion Matthäus 10,23. Geschichte seiner Auslegung* [Tübingen: Mohr, 1970]).

15. K. Berger, *Die Amen-Worte Jesu. Eine Untersuchung zum Problem der Legitimation in apokalyptischer Rede* (Berlin: Walter de Gruyter, 1970) 71-86, especially p. 72; H. Tödt, *The Son of Man in the Synoptic Tradition* (Philadelphia: Westminster, 1965) 67-94, especially p. 90.

16. *Hotan* (Matthew 19 times, Mark 1 time, Luke 29 times, John 17 times) begins a sentence in Matthew on eight occasions. Three are redactional (10.19[?]; 21.40; 25.31), one is from Q (Matt 12.43 par Luke 11.24) four are M (6.2, 5, 6, 16). The distribution allows no firm conclusions.

Heteros, the form less common than *allos* in NT Greek (BDF, §306), occurs nine times in Matthew at 6.24; 8.21; 10.23; 11.3, 16; 12.45; 15.30; 16.14; 21.30 (Mark 1 time, Luke 33 times, John 1 time). No significant pattern is observable here. *Allos* is used 29 times by Matthew (Mark 22 times, Luke 11 times, John 36 times).

17. Contra McDermott ('Mt. 10.23', 237), there is no reason to posit an underlying Aramaism in order to account for the use of *tautē*. See Schürmann ('Zur Traditions- und Redaktionsgeschichte von Mt 10.23', *Untersuchungen*, I, 150 n. 2).

18. At 16.28, Matthew apparently changes the Markan saying about the Kingdom of God to a Son-of-Man saying. Son-of-Man sayings, like Amen-

Words, occur at all levels of the Synoptic tradition (see Tödt, *Son of Man*).

19. A similar form occurs in Matt 23.39 without the *amēn*. Matt 23.39 comes from Q (Luke 13.35).

20. Berger (*Amen-Worte*, 71-86) gives a thorough consideration to Matthew's use of the form. His study indicates that the use of Amen-Words is present at every level of tradition. The use of an amen formula to introduce the Son-of-Man sayings where he acts as world judge is prevalent in Matthew. The simple occurrence of the amen formula does not indicate the use of tradition in v. 23b. Berger believes, however, that Matthew 10.23b is a traditional saying, '... der Auftrag an Israel kann in der gegenwärtigen Generation schon nicht mehr ganz erfüllt werden' (p. 72). Furthermore, Berger regards the concrete expectation of the end ('betonte Naherwartung') as characteristic of the older tradition of Amen-Words. He assigns 10.23b to Matthew's 'Sondergut'.

21. LSJ, 1772. BAGD, 810.

22. Smyth, *Grammar*, §2098; BDF, §414.2; Robertson, *Grammar*, 1120-21.

23. As will be noted below, vv. 5b-6, which have been shown to be a M saying, are continuous in content with v. 23b. If we conjecture that within the M material v. 23b followed vv. 5b-6, then the reader would understand, 'Do not go in the way of the Gentiles and do not enter the city of the Samaritans; but rather go out to the lost sheep of the nation of Israel. For, amen, I say to you, you will not finish (going [*poreumenoi*] to [*pros*] the cities of Israel...'. The advantage to this third solution grammatically and conceptually is that the reader can easily supply both the participle and preposition from the immediately preceding context. See below p. 80.

24. The limitation of mission to Israel in vv. 5b-6 fits with the eschatological promise in v. 23b. The conceptual continuity, as well as the possibility of a syntactical continuity (see note above), are good indications that both sayings come from the same tradition.

25. Schürmann ('Mt 10.23') includes v. 23a-b in the Q tradition. In addition to the argument already given in the present work, a further response to Schürmann's position is that no doubly attested saying between Matthew and Luke (= Q) provides evidence for the limitation of the mission to Israel or limitation of the activities of the disciples to the cities of Israel. Indeed, the story of the Centurion's Servant (Matt 8.5-13; Luke 7.1-10) would argue against such a motif in Q. The idea of the limitation of the mission (vv. 5b-6), as well as the limitation of the disciple's activity to the cities of Israel, is unique to Matthew's special material and may not be assigned with confidence to Q.

26. On *eis/en*, see BDF, §206.

27. Matthew uses *dechomai* 10 times; *lambanō* 53 times. By comparison: Mark uses *dechomai* 6 times, *lambanō* 20 times; Luke *dechomai* 16 times,

lambanō 22 times; John *dechomai* 1 time, *lambanō* 46 times.

28. Kilpatrick (*Origins*, 26-27) assigns vv. 5-6, 8b, 16b, 23, 24-25a, and 'in part' 25b and 41 to M (see C. 1). The difference between his results and the results here primarily comes from a difference in method. Kilpatrick employs only source criticism in Matt 10 and did not explore either redaction or form criticism as a means of separating tradition from the work of the editor.

Notes to Chapter 4

1. The omission of *kai dysbastakta* in Regius (L) and Family One manuscripts is probably due to stylistic refinement or to accidental oversight, i.e. the eye of the scribe jumping over one *kai* (Metzger [*Commentary*, 59] reports that the majority of the committee at work on the United Bible Society's third edition supports this opinion). The extent and variety of witnesses that attest the inclusion of the term is strong evidence against the term being an interpolation from Luke 11.46 (but see Metzger [*Commentary*, 60] for the argument for interpolation).

2. The grammar of the sentence requires that a *tis* be supplied after *kalesēte*. The genitive *hymōn* may then be understood in the partitive sense. This appears to be A. Robertson's understanding (*Word Pictures in the New Testament*, 6 vols. [Nashville: Broadman, 1930] I, 179). Schweizer (*Good News*, 431-32) denies, without explanation, that the text can mean, 'You must not call anyone among you "father"'. His suggestion that the grammatical confusion in the text is a result of the presence of independent tradition about Abraham related to Matt 3.19 will be taken up below.

3. Scholars have assigned different verses in Matt 23.1-12 to M. Bultmann (*History*, 113) includes vv. 2-3, 5, 11, 12 in Matthew's special source. He remains undecided whether vv. 8-10 are from the special source or the redactor. Manson (*Sayings*, 95) provisionally assigns vv. 2-3, 5, 7b-12 to M, since they are without parallel in Mark or Luke, but goes on to suggest that M, rather that Q, underlies the entirety of ch. 23. It will be apparent in the following analysis that Manson's view of Q has been judged too wooden. He appears to rely on a source-critical principle of a written Q and does not allow for the oral development of Q within the communities of Matthew and/or Luke. Kilpatrick (*Origins*, 30) assigns vv. 2-3, 5, 7b-10 to M. E. Haenchen ('Matthäus 23', *ZTK* 48 [1951] 38-63) assigns vv. 2-3, 5b, 8-10 to Matthew's *Sondergut*. D. Garland (*The Intention of Matthew 23* [NovTSupp 52; Leiden: Brill, 1979] 8-20) does not explicitly define the M material as opposed to the redactional material in the passage, but does maintain that vv. 2-3, 5b-7a, 8-10 comprise pre-Matthean Jewish Christian material (p. 19 n. 29). He assigns vv. 4, 6, 7a, 12 to Q (with Markan overlap at 7a). The lack of consensus about vv. 5, (7b)8-10, 11-12 indicates the

tradition-historical complexity of the passage.

4. Schweizer, *Good News*, 431.

5. Haenchen, 'Matthäus 23', 39-40; Garland, *Matthew 23*, 19 n. 29; Polag, *Fragmenta*, 56; Schulz, *Synopse*, 12.

6. Bultmann, Haenchen, and Garland, along with most commentators, regard v. 1 as redactional. Neither Polag nor Schulz assigns the verse to Q. (See above n. 3.)

7. The uses of Moses in Matt 8.4; 17.3, 4; 19.7, 8; 22.24 depend on Mark 1.4; 9.4,5; 10.3,5; 12.19, respectively. 'Seat of Moses' is unattested until the fourth century outside of the NT (*Pesiq. R.* 7a; McNeile, *Matthew*, 329).

8. Garland, *Matthew 23*, 41-46. Q may have suggested 'scribes' to Matthew. Luke 11.52 names the 'lawyers' as Jesus' opponents.

9. Matt 12.50 par Mark 3.34; Matt 7.3, 4, 5 par Luke 6.41, 42; Matt 18.15, 21 par Luke 17.3, 4. Matthew is probably responsible for the term at 5.47; 18.15 (one use), 35; 25.40; 28.10. The uses in 5.22 (twice), 23, 24 are likely from M material.

10. The conclusion applies to the entire phrase, 'heavenly father'. On the basis of further considerations, particularly with regard to the parallel structure of the passage, I will suggest below that 'father' is part of the M material.

11. Matt 22.42 par Mark 12.35; Matt 24.23, 24 par Mark 13.21, 22; Matt 26.63 par Mark 14.61. Matthew adds the term at Matt 11.22 see Luke 7.18-19; Matt 16.20 see Mark 8.30 and Luke 9.21; Matt 24.5 see Mark 13.6; Matt 26.68 see Mark 14.65. The unparalleled, but likely redactional, use is at Matt 2.4. See J.D. Kingsbury, *Matthew: Structure, Christology, Kingdom* (Philadelphia: Fortress, 1975) 96-99.

12. Kingsbury, *Structure*, 92-93.

13. The uses from Mark are: Matt 19.16 par Mark 10.20; Matt 22.16 par Mark 12.14; Matt 22.24 par Mark 12.19. Matthew is responsible for the term at Matt 8.19 (see Luke 9.57-62); Matt 9.11 (see Mark 2.13-17); Matt 12.38 (see Mark 8.11-12); Matt 22.36 (see Mark 12.28); Matt 17.24. See Kingsbury, *Matthew* (Philadelphia: Fortress, 1977) 43-44; J.P. Meier, *The Vision of Matthew. Christ, Church and Morality in the First Gospel* (New York: Paulist, 1978) 48-49.

14. Meier (*Vision*, 48-49; also Kingsbury, *Structure*, 92-93) points out that Jesus is the one teacher, despite Matthew's refusal of the title *didaskalos* except in the mouths of unbelievers. It is precisely this tension that is one indication of the presence of M material here. The tradition behind v. 8 may be the conceptual source for Matthew's opposition to the use of the title *didaskalos* during Jesus' ministry. The redactional addition of *ho Christos* in v. 10 may indicate that Jesus becomes designated the one teacher only after the resurrection, when he is manifested as Son of Man and Son of God (Matt 28.16-20).

15. LSJ, 852; Lohmeyer, *Matthäus*, 339-41. Meier (*Vision*, 48) renders

kathēgētēs as 'instructor', as does the translation given above.

16. The results may be compared with Schweizer's conclusion (*Good News*, 431-32). Schweizer separates vv. 8-10 into three non-homogeneous sayings. He regards v. 9 as originally independent and possibly from Jesus himself. He thinks that v. 9 originally might have read, 'You must not call Abraham your father' (see Matt 3.19). The verse could not have meant, according to Schweizer, 'You must not call anyone among you "father"'. It appears, contrary to Schweizer, that the parallelism between the three verses argues for an original unity. The simpler and more probable option is to supply a *tina* before the *hymon* and read, 'And do not call someone among you "Father. . ."'. Although an intriguing guess, supposition of a reference to Abraham lacks evidence from the text itself.

17. Verse 14 is not present in the strongest manuscript tradition (Sinaiticus, Vaticanus, Family One, etc.). Some manuscripts have the verse after v. 12, others include it after v. 13. The weakness of the reading, as well as the confusion among those manuscripts that do contain v. 14, leads most commentators to omit the verse as an interpolation from Mark 12.40 (Manson, *Sayings*, 233; Schweizer, *Good News*, 433).

18. For the reconstructions of Streeter, Manson, and Kilpatrick, see C.I. Bultmann (*History*, 113) regards vv. 15, 16-22, 24 as from Matthew's special source, and vv. 28, 33 as from Matthew. Haenchen ('Matthäus 23') argues that vv. 13, 23, 25-26, 27, 29-31 are from Q; that the redactor is responsible for vv. 28, 32-33[34?]; and that Matthew's *Sondergut* includes vv. 15-22, 24. Garland (*Matthew 23*, 29 n. 19) argues that vv. 13, 23, 25, 26, 27, 29-31 are from Q. He does not explicitly define M. Polag (*Fragmenta*) places vv. 25, 26, 23, 27, 28, 29-31, 13 in Q. Schulz (*Synopse*) places vv. 25, 23, 27, 29-31, 13 in Q. Apparently, there is a consensus that at least vv. 15, 16-22 are unparalleled and from pre-Matthean material.

19. Haenchen, 'Matthäus 23', 50. Garland (*Matthew 23*, 150-62) has a thorough discussion of the possibilities for interpretation of the verse. He argues convincingly that Matt 23.27 depends on Q, but with extensive reformulation by Matthew. He further concludes that v. 28 is redactional.

20. Garland (*Matthew 23*, 9-18) theorizes that Q contains seven woes in the order: (1) you tithe; (2) you cleanse; (3) you love chief seats; (4) you are like graves; (5) you bind heavy burdens; (6) you build tombs; (7) you take the key. The first four were directed against the Pharisees, the last three against the scribes (= lawyers). Luke preserved Q, except in adapting number one to his setting (Luke 11.39). Matthew deconstructed numbers five and three (Matt 23.4, 6). He then added two more woes to the remaining five from Q (vv. 15, 16-22), thereby filling out a sevenfold woe pattern. Garland suggests that v. 15 might have been created by Matthew, and that the woe formula in vv. 16-22 was not included in the M material. Thus, he concludes that the woe formulas in vv. 15, 16 are the work of Matthew.

The analysis given here and developed below regarding vv. 15 and 16 agrees with Garland that the woes in Matt 23.13, 23, 25, 27, 29 are from Q. Further, Garland has demonstrated that the full woe formula, which combines scribes with Pharisees, comes from Matthew. Despite this finding, Q probably exercises an influence on Matthew's formulation. Luke 11.52 names the *nomikoi* (= *grammateis*) as the opponents, and Luke 11.44, 47 name the *Pharisaioi*. *Pace* Garland, it seems to me probable that vv. 15 and 16 were already woes prior to Matthew's composition (see below). Critical probability for the form of Q that underlies Matt 23.4, 6 is difficult to establish. Here again, the question of the development of Q within the Matthean community arises. Perhaps it is best to observe, as has Bonnard (*Matthieu*, 337), that the complexity of the tradition history in Matt 23.13-31 cannot be explained simply by recourse to the hypothesis of two written sources. Some account must be taken of the respective milieux of Matthew and Luke.

21. Haenchen, 'Matthäus 23', 50. Garland, *Matthew 23*, 150-62.

22. The proselyte was a full convert to Judaism (*b. Yebam.* 46b, 47b; *b. Qidd.* 62a,b; for Greco-Roman texts see: Juvenal, *Sat.* 14.96-106; Horace, *Sat.* 1.4.133-143; 1.9.60-61; Tacitus, *History*, 5.5; B. Bamberger, *Proselytism in the Talmudic Period* (New York: KTAV, 1968 [1939]) 31-97; G. Moore, *Judaism in the First Centuries of the Christian Era*, 2 vols. (New York: Schocken, 1971 [1927, 1930]) I, 323-53. See also T. Finn, 'The God-fearers Reconsidered', *CBQ* 47 (1985) 75-84.

23. Compare Haenchen's division of the pericope ('Matthäus 23', 47).

1. Verse 16—Rabbinic opinion number 1.
2. Verse 17—Refutation in the form of a question.
3. Verse 18—Rabbinic opinion number 2.
4. Verse 19—Refutation in the form of a question.
5. Verse 20—Proposed opinion based on case 2.
6. Verse 21—Proposed opinion based on case 1.
7. Verse 22—An opinion concerning a case not mentioned previously that has been added in order to round out a count of seven.

He draws attention to the possibility of growth within this M saying prior to Matthew. It is improbable that Matthew is responsible for v. 22 (see the evidence on vocabulary and content given below).

24. On Matthew's redaction in 15.1-20, see Barth, 'Law', 86-89. He regards vv. 13-14 as Matthew's insertions, although he leaves unclear whether the two sayings are Matthew's or depend on traditional material. Given Matthew's editorial activity in this pericope, it appears likely that v. 13 is from Matthew, and that the phrase 'Let them alone, they are blind guides' is Matthew's adaptation of the following Q saying to his context. The use of 'blind guides' as a designation for the opponent leaders may well have come to Matthew from M through the saying that underlies v. 16.

25. The hypothesis that 5.33-37 and 23.16-22 come from two different

traditions within M seems preferable to a hypothesis that one or the other represents a free creation from the redactor. An editor would be less likely to create a contradiction than to use two variant traditions within his composition for his own purposes.

26. Klostermann, *Matthäusevangelium*, 187. Haenchen ('Matthäus 23', 49) sees this verse as a polemic against the cultic practices of purity and assigns the verse to Matthew's *Sondergut*.

27. The evidence concerning v. 33 is further complicated by its similarity to Matt 3.7, a Q statement (Luke 3.7). It is possible that Matthew formulated v. 33 in imitation of this Q statement.

Notes to Chapter 5

1. See pp. 15-17 for a discussion of the view of traditions that informs our work here.

2. See p. 22. Chapter 7 will propose a hypothesis about the history of the traditions represented by the M sayings.

3. See p. 28.

4. The debate appears to have been initiated by Bultmann (*History*, 135-36). See Meier, *Law*, 135, nn. 24, 25 for the positions taken by various scholars. The tendency to regard Jesus as 'New Moses' is best illustrated by Davies ('Matthew 5.17-18'; *Setting*, 25-108). Barth ('Law') and Hummel (*Auseinandersetzung*) regard Jesus as 'Supreme Rabbi'.

5. Much of the following analysis is indebted to Meier's insights into the importance of the antithetical formulation for interpreting the antitheses (*Law*, 131-35). The structure of the antithetical formulas in the sayings discussed implies an extraordinary christological claim. In the antitheses, Jesus is neither New Moses nor Supreme Rabbi. He is quintessentially God's spokesperson in the eschatological age.

6. Here, as throughout this chapter, we will presuppose the arguments already given in previous chapters where these sayings were isolated. See p. 31, on the antithetical formula.

7. The rabbis maintained that the *oral* Law was also given on Sinai (*m. 'Abot* 1.1). The date of this tradition is difficult to determine, since it occurs in documents written no earlier than 200 CE. The antithetical formula is constructed with the written Mosaic Torah in view and betrays no reference to rabbinic-type views with regard to the oral Law. I have referred to the oral tradition of the rabbis as *halakhah*.

8. M. Smith's examples of rabbinic parallels to the antithetical formula involve the citation of rabbinic opinion, not written Torah (*Tannaitic Parallels to the Gospels* [Philadelphia: SBL, 1951] esp. 27-29). The difference is decisive for the interpretation of the antithetical formula. As will be seen below, the use of the formula makes a claim for Jesus that is not made by

rabbis for themselves when developing interpretation (*halakhah*) (Meier, *Law*, 133-34, n. 21).

9. Here and throughout the analyses of the chapter, the assumption is that the group who originated or preserved these traditions understood the sayings. The sayings themselves imply certain shared assumptions between speaker (or writer) and audience in order for communication to take place. These implications may give us clues to the social and historical situation of the communication.

10. Following here the LXX text. The MT has no variants significant for our analysis.

11. *Houtos* refers forward as in Deut 1.1. The use is similar to that of saying no. 1.

12. These two options apply at the pre-Matthean level of the tradition. Within Matthew's text, *errethē* is probably to be read as a divine passive. As Meier shows, the full force of the antithetical formula for Matthew is, 'God said to the ancients at Sinai . . . but I say to you' (*Law*, 131-35). At the pre-Matthean level, I suspect that *errethē* also should be read as a divine passive, but the evidence suggested by the saying itself does not allow a secure conclusion.

13. I prefer to leave the designation 'hearers or readers' ambiguous. The formula may have been spoken by Jesus during his lifetime to an audience not unlike that depicted by Matthew's narrative. The formula may have arisen within a Christian group after Easter and only later have been attributed to the ministry of Jesus. The origin of the formula is not our concern here, but the probable meaning that it had at the level of tradition prior to the work of Matthew. I would maintain that either at the level of the historical Jesus, or at any other level of the tradition up to and including Matthew's own work, the content of the antitheses and the meaning of the antithetical formula implies a hearer or reader who would understand the formula in a way consistent with the reconstruction that I have offered. On the possibility that the antithetical sayings (nos. 2, 4, 5) were in written form prior to Matthew's editing see Chapter 7, §1 below.

14. See Meier, *Law*, 135-61.

15. E. Käsemann ('Sentences of Holy Law in the New Testament', *New Testament Studies of Today* [Philadelphia: Fortress, 1969] 66-81) seeks to distinguish the form 'sentence of holy law' from other legal sayings. The pure form of these sentences consists of a chiastic correspondence between the protasis and apodosis of a conditional sentence. The same verb is used to denote both transgression and punishment. The punishment is designated to be future. In this last point, Käsemann argues for a distinction between gnomic and eschatological future. The assignment of punishment exclusively to the eschatological court arises, according to Käsemann, only in contexts where early Christian prophets are present. Käsemann's view has been attacked by K. Berger in two articles ('Zu den sogenannten Sätzen heiligen

Rechts', *NTS* 17 [1970-71] 10-40; and 'Die sogenannten Sätze heiligen Rechts im Neuen Testament. Ihre Funktion und ihr Sitz im Leben', *ThZ* 28 [1972] 305-30). Berger tries to show a pre-Christian trajectory of the development of the form from wisdom sayings, concerned with reward in this world (Prov 13.13, 20; 22.8; Sir 4.10; 7.1) toward apocalyptic passages that propose reward and judgment in the end time (2 *Enoch* 2.2; 59.1-60.2; 60.3f.; *T. Rub.* 4.11; *T. Levi* 13.5-6; 6.6; *T. Zeb.* 7.1; 8.3). Within these examples, however, only *T. Levi* 13.5 refers to eschatological reward and even it does not fit the form proposed by Käsemann. See the criticisms of Berger's method by J. Baumgarten (*Paulus und die Apokalyptik. Die Auslegung apokalyptischer Überlieferungen in den echten Paulusbriefen* [Neukirchen-Vluyn: Neukirchener Verlag, 1975] 31 n. 87).

Even if Berger's critique misses the mark, Käsemann's proposal founders on two points. First, he finds the pure form only in 1 Cor 3.17; 14.38a; Mark 8.38 (par Matt 10.32); Luke 9.26; Matt 6.14. Second, a distinction between gnomic and eschatological future cannot be made purely on the evidence of the saying itself. In every case adduced by Käsemann, the literary context provides the key to interpretation. In the case of Matt 6.14, the saying is so similar to Sir 4.10 and *T. Levi* 13.5, 6 that it is difficult to see the peculiarly Christian emphasis of eschatological judgment and reward hypothesized by Käsemann.

The failure of Berger to show a clear pre-Christian example of legal sayings that assign only eschatological punishment or reward for breaking a community rule demonstrates negatively that early Christian legal sayings that do assign such punishment are, seen from a history of religions standpoint, unique. The paucity of evidence for the particular form 'sentence of holy law' as defined by Käsemann leads to doubt about both his formal analysis and his reconstruction of the life setting in which these sentences arose. The occurrences of such legal sentences cannot be assigned exclusively to early Christian prophets. I would suggest, however, that sentences with a clear reference to the eschatological court might best be described as 'sentences of holy law' in order to differentiate them from wisdom sayings, or legal sentences that refer the offender to a human court. The idea that certain sins are punishable only at the final judgment, and not by a human court, certainly seems to characterize M sayings (sayings nos. 1, 2, and 16).

See also the discussion by M.E. Boring (*Sayings of the Risen Jesus. Christian Prophecy in the Synoptic Tradition* [SNTSMS, 46; Cambridge: Cambridge University Press, 1982] 130-32). He cautiously concludes that the form is somewhat characteristic of prophetic speech, but not unique to Christian prophets. Thus, the life setting cannot be specified as prophetic on the basis of form alone. By the designation 'sentence of holy law', then, the present study indicates a particular ideology expressed in some legal sentences in early Christian tradition without specifying the life setting as Käsemann does.

16. See above pp. 31-33.

17. On the rabbinic evidence, see Davies, *Torah*. While the Teacher at Qumran apparently was regarded as the quintessential interpreter of Torah, he does not appear to be considered the giver of Torah in a manner that transcends the place of Moses in the Exodus traditions. The highest affirmation of the Teacher in relationship to the Law appears in CD 6.1-11 where he is referred to as the 'rod of the Law'.

18. See n. 20 below. CD 9.8-12; 15.1-16.19. W.S. LaSor, *The Dead Sea Scrolls and the New Testament* (Grand Rapids: Eerdmans, 1972) 243.

19. Contra Bultmann, who asserts that this saying comes from early Palestinian Christianity prior to 70 (*History*, 132). Brown points out that Josephus (*Against Apion* 2.77) and *1 Clement* 40.4-5 as well as Mishnaic tractates speak of the temple in the present tense although the temple has been destroyed (*Antioch and Rome*, 150). See for example the fifth division of the Mishnah, 'Kodashim'.

20. *M. Sanh.* 3.2 contains the only rabbinic parallel that even approximates saying no. 6. Saying no. 6 is certainly an injunction against frivolous oath taking, and such a view is consistent with rabbinic argument (Strack–Billerbeck, I, 328-32; Meier, *Law*, 155-56; Schneider, 'ὀμνύω', *TDNT*, V, 176-85 on oaths in the Jewish and Greco-Roman sources generally). Schneider and Meier both recognize that Matt 5.34-37 places the Christian community outside Judaism by prohibiting oaths entirely. Verse 36 (saying no. 6), however, in its content does not necessitate such an assumption and may belong to a group that practices some form of oath taking for religious purposes.

21. Betz, 'Kult-Didache'. In designating these sayings as 'teaching about cult' (*Kult-Didache*) Betz misses the point of the sayings. The sayings are more accurately described as rules for secret piety because they deny by their very content the practice of these particular acts of piety in a public fashion. Hence no 'cult' is involved as cult is commonly understood in the study of religions.

22. Bultmann, *History*, 145-46.

23. Przybylski, *Righteousness*; Moore, *Judaism*, II, 166-73; 212-36; 291-96; 55-69; 257-66. Strack–Billerbeck (I, 396-406; 426-29) collect a considerable number of rabbinic texts concerned with these issues of synagogue piety. The rabbis are in favor of circumspection with regard to public displays of piety. Considerable debate appears after the fall of the temple over whether or not prayer was allowed outside of Jerusalem and/or outside of synagogue (*m. Berakh.* 4.8b, 31; *Midr. Ps.* 4.9 [23b]). Proper posture in prayer is also discussed (*m. Berakh.* 1, 3; Strack–Billerbeck I, 403-404). Apparently after the fall of the temple the acts of piety associated with the temple service are becoming absorbed into the synagogue life. The intensity of the arguments indicates that the rabbis frequently deal with the regulation of synagogue members who are overly public or hypocritical in their piety, a situation also

reflected by M saying no. 7. The problem may well have existed within Judaism and Christianity prior to the date of the documents in which these traditions are embedded.

24. Moore (*Judaism*, II, 55-69, 257-66) reconstructs the practice during public fasts. Such fasts included a refusal to bathe or to anoint the head (*m. Yoma* 8, 1). Whether such rules also applied to weekly voluntary fasts, which were becoming part of the synagogue piety during the NT period, remains unclear. The earliest indication of the Jewish practice of weekly voluntary fasts comes from *Did.* 8. 1. Voluntary fasts may have been much less circumscribed by official synagogue regulation than the older and more established practice of public fast days. A Christian Jew's practice of private fasting most likely would not have conflicted—either openly or specifically—with other synagogue members' practice. See also Strack–Billerbeck I, 426-29; IV, 77; J. Behm, 'νῆστις', *TDNT*, IV, 931.

In the reconstruction of this type of religious practice for first- century Judaism, we are hampered as always by the problem of dating specific practices to specific eras on the basis of documents collected and edited much later than the first century. The reconstruction hypothesized here seems to be indicated by a critical reading of the later Jewish sources.

25. Compare Betz, 'Kult-Didache', 453.

26. See above p. 44.

27. *M. Ed.* 1.4 refers to Shammai and Hillel as 'the fathers of the world'. It may be upon this basis that *m. 'Aboth* receives its title. Those tradents in the Jewish tradition up to Shammai and Hillel may be referred to as *Abba*. The prevalence of this title at the time of Matthew's composition remains uncertain. See Strack Billerbeck I, 918-19.

28. See the conclusions in Chapter 6.

29. See above pp. 66-69.

30. Both Acts and Galatians offer evidence of arguments within early Christianity over the proper terms of the incorporation of Gentiles into early Christian communities (see Brown, 'Not Jewish Christianity');

On Jewish proselytizing activities see Bamberger, *Proselytism*; W. Braude , *Jewish Proselytizing in the First Five Centuries of the Common Era: The Age of the Tannaim and Ammoraim* (Providence: Brown University, 1940); Moore, *Judaism*, I, 323-53; F. Derwacter, *Preparing the Way for Paul. The Proselyte Movement in Later Judaism* (New York: Macmillan, 1930). These four works cover the Jewish and Greco-Roman literature on the subject. Only Derwacter argues that there is some mission literature and organized mission activities. He bases his views on Philo, *Address to Gaius.* 31; *De. Man.* 2.3 ; Josephus *Ant.* 18. 9.1; Epiphanius, *Adv. Haer.* 30.4.11; *b. Meg.* 18b; *b. Sanh.* 26a. The other authors find no organized dispatching of missionaries, but do find proselytizing activities extending from the base provided by synagogues. Derwacter's evidence may be strengthened if the polemic in Matt 23.15 refers at the pre-Matthean level to the activities of certain synagogue leaders. See also E. Lerle, *Proselytenwerbung und Urchristentum* (Berlin: Evangelische Verlagsanstalt, 1960); Garland, *Matthew 23*, 129-31, esp. n. 23, for further discussion and bibliography.

31. See above pp. 67-68. This saying shows a clear unity and parallelism and probably was conceived of and transmitted in its entirety at the level of tradition immediately preceding Matthew's writing.

32. Matthew by his composition of ch. 23 obviously believes the argument to be between Jesus and the Jewish leadership of a synagogue (Matt 23.1-2). We cannot, however, at this level of analysis utilize Matthew's redaction as a means for determining whether sayings 13 and 14 come from a conflict between Christian Jews and non-Christian Jews or between two different groups of Christian Jews. We will in Chapter 7 critically use Matthew's viewpoint as a means of helping to resolve the problems presented by the evidence of all the M sayings and the traditions that they represent.

33. Contra Bultmann who sees no substantive difference between the antithetical formula and this legal debate form (*History*, 145-50).

Notes to Chapter 6

1. Matt 6.34, while not paralleled in Luke (see Luke 12.22-32), will not be treated. First, the saying shows no disjunction in context with the preceding verses (Matt 6.25-33). Second, it forms an inclusion as to content with v. 25. These observations lead to three possible explanations: the verse may be Q, which Matthew has preserved better than Luke (see Luke 12.32); the verse may have been added to Q in Matthew's community prior to Matthew's editing; or the verse may be Matthew's own creation. (The passage raises again the question of the development of the Q tradition within Matthew's community prior to Matthew's editing. That question is outside the scope of this study.) Redaction may account best for v. 34, which lacks any evidence suggesting M sayings. Wrege (*Überlieferungsgeschichte*, 123-24) contends that the entirety of Matt 6.25-34 comes from tradition independent of the parallel in Luke 12.22-32. Kilpatrick (*Origins*, 22, 35) lists Matt 6.34 as an M fragment, although he does not critically demonstrate the isolation. Dupont (*Béatitudes*, I, 171 n. 3) finds that the verse is redactional. Neither Polag nor Schulz lists Matt 6.34 in his reconstruction of Q.

2. Kilpatrick (*Origins*, 15-17) shows v. 5 to be original to Matthew's text. See Dupont, *Béatitudes*, I, 255-63; 223-27 on these verses; Wrege, *Überlieferungsgeschichte*, 19-24.

3. 9.27 par Mark 10.47; 20.30-31 par Mark 10.47 depend on Mark. 15.22 par Mark 7.25; 17.15 par Mark 9.17 are added by Matthew.

4. See above pp. 27-28, 45-46 on 5.20; 6.1. Also see 3.15; 5.6; 21.32.

5. Dupont (*Béatitudes*, I, 223-27) sees v. 10 as a transition from vv. 7-9 to vv. 11-12, the latter being Q tradition. He holds that vv. 5-9 are best

attributed to the redactor.

6. In this Chapter, the translation of *Gospel of Thomas* is from H. Koester and T. Lambdin in *The Nag Hammadi Library in English*, ed. J. Robinson (New York: Harper & Row, 1977).

7. Sanders, *Tendencies*, 275.

8. Bornkamm assigns the verse to Matthew's *Sondergut* primarily on this basis ('Der Aufbau der Bergpredigt', *NTS* 24 [1978] 419-32).

9. Jeremias, *Parables*, 199-200.

10. Bultmann, *History*, 77.

11. *Lev. R.* 13(114c); *Gen. R.* 65 (40d); *Midr. Ps.* 80 §6 (182a); *Midr. Qoh.* 1.9(9b); *Mid. Esth.* 1.15 (90 b); *'Abot R. Nat.* 34; *b. Hag.* 13a; Schweizer, *Good News*, 169-170; Klostermann, *Matthäusevangelium*, 66.

12. Bornkamm, 'Aufbau', 429.

13. Kilpatrick (*Origins*, 22, 24, 35) asserts, though never demonstrates, that v. 15 is M. Schweizer (*Good News*, 177), Bonnard (*Matthieu*, 103-104), Dupont (*Béatitudes*, I, 171), and Barth ('Law', 162-63) all see v. 15 as redactional.

14. Verses 2-6 par Luke 7.18-23; vv. 7-11 par Luke 7.24-28; vv. 12-15 par Luke 16.16; vv. 16-19 par Luke 7.31-35; vv. 20-24 par Luke 10.12-15; vv. 25-27 par Luke 10.21-22.

15. See above p. 19, on the use of vocabulary as a criterion for distinguishing redactional from traditional material. The analysis of uncharacteristic vocabulary in 11.28-30 is different from Gundry's (*Matthew*, 218-20). A critical methodological difference accounts for most of the disagreements: unlike Gundry's, this study does not assume all unparalleled uses of words come from Matthew.

16. For example, Strecker, *Weg*, 172; Stendahl, *School*, 141-42; Meier, *Vision*, 80 n. 60.

17. Stendahl, *School*, 141-42.

18. Schweizer, 'Christus und Gemeinde im Matthäusevangelium', in *Matthäus*, 9-69, esp. 42-57; M. Suggs, *Wisdom Christology and Law in Matthew's Gospel* (Cambridge, MA: Harvard University, 1970) 31-97; Koester, 'The Structure of Early Christian Beliefs', in J.M. Robinson and H. Koester, *Trajectories through Early Christianity* (Philadelphia: Fortress, 1971) 221; Meier, *Vision*, 76-83; F. Christ, *Jesus Sophia* (Zürich: Zwingli, 1970).

19. Bultmann, *History*, 159-60; Barth, 'Law', 103-31.

20. Considerable scholarly argument has occurred over the extent to which Matthew's Christology can be viewed as a Wisdom Christology. As indicated above, Matthew never refers to Jesus as the Wisdom of God, nor does he use motifs that would imply his knowledge or acceptance of a Wisdom myth that included the descent and incarnation of Wisdom. Meier's argument that Matthew masterfully combines wisdom and apocalyptic elements in ch. 11 is the most persuasive. Suggs insists that a Wisdom

Christology solves the problem of the relationship between Jesus and the Law in Matthew, but his position ultimately exceeds the evidence of the text. While Matthew knows about, and draws on, wisdom motifs for his own purposes, he uses them selectively and subsumes them to both a Son of God and Son of Man Christology: they do not dominate his conceptualization of Jesus. Only a sophisticated acquaintance with a broad spectrum of wisdom literature would have prepared Matthew's contemporary readers for interpreting his Jesus as Wisdom incarnate. Stendahl's findings, cited above, militate against assuming such an acquaintance.

21. See above p. 149n. 15 on sentences of holy law.

22. *CD* 10.22; *m. 'Aboth* 1.17; 3.14. Davies, *Setting*, 238-39. Strack–Billerbeck I, 639-40.

23. Both its affinity with Jewish types of reasoning and its affiliation with saying no. 2 suggest that saying no. 16 comes from the same tradition.

24. Bornkamm, 'Bind and Loose', 38. Strecker, *Weg*, 223. Trilling, *Israel*, 92-95.

25. Stendahl, *School*, 138-39.

26. Strack–Billerbeck, I, 791-92. The closest parallels are found at Qumran (1QS 5.25–6.1; CD 9.2-4), although even these are more juridical in their content and do not appear to depend directly on Deut 19.15. See Thompson, *Advice*, 183 n. 29; J. Schmitt, 'Contribution à l'étude de la discipline penitentielle dans l'église primitive à la lumière des textes de Qumran', *Les Manuscrits de la Mer Morte* (Colloque de Strasbourg, 25-27 Mai 1955; Paris, 1957) 96-100 .

27. Barth, 'Law', 84.

28. Thompson, *Advice*, 182.

29. Strecker maintains that the citation formulas are from a pre-Matthean level of the tradition (*Weg*, 49-85). His evaluation has not persuaded all critics (Gundry, *Use*; Rothfuchs, *Erfüllungszitate*). Brown concludes, after a survey of scholarship and an evaluation of the evidence in Matthew, that some of the citations may have come from tradition and some probably come from Matthew himself (*Birth*, 96-104).

30. Hummel, *Auseinandersetzung*, 25-26.

31. Thompson, *Advice*, 200-202; Bonnard, *Matthieu*, 275.

32. Brown *et al.* eds. (*Peter in the New Testament* [Minneapolis: Augsburg, 1973] 75-107) do not decide which verse represents the older form; however, they regard 16.19 as dependent on pre-Matthean tradition. See also O. Cullmann, *Peter, Disciple, Apostle, Martyr. A Historical and Theological Study* (2nd edn; Philadelphia: Westminster, 1962) 210; Thompson, *Advice*, 193.

33. Bornkamm, 'Bind and Loose', 38.

34. While at the end of Chapter 5 we left undecided the clear association of saying no. 12 with the tradition of sayings nos. 1, 2, 4, 5, the evidence that is emerging in this chapter with regard to sayings nos. 16, 17, 18 makes the

connection between all of these sayings at the pre-Matthean level progressively more probable.

35. See Luke 12.51-52; 14.25-27; 17.33.

36. Schneider, 'εὐνοῦχος', *TDNT*, II, 763-68; Strack–Billerbeck I, 807; *Sifre Lev.* on 22.24; *m. Yebam.* 8.4-6; *m. Nid.* 5. 9. The prohibition for the entry of the physically debilitated into the congregation at Qumran may also have applied to eunuchs, although they are not specifically named (1QSa 2.3-10).

37. Schneider, 'εὐνοῦχος'.

38. The reference in Acts 8.27 may mean nothing more than a high court official, *eunouchos* not being meant literally (A. Sand, *Reich Gottes und Eheverzicht im Evangelium nach Matthäus* [SBS, 109; Stuttgart: Katholisches Bibelwerk, 1983] 61).

39. McNeile, *Matthew*, 276; Manson, *Sayings*, 215; Hill, *Matthew*, 281-83; Schweizer, *Good News*, 382-84; Davies, *Setting*, 393-95; Q. Quesnell, '"Made themselves Eunuchs for the Kingdom of Heaven" (Mt 19,12)', *CBQ* 30 (1968) 335-58. On the whole issue in Matthew see Sand, *Reich Gottes*.

40. Bonnard (*Matthieu*, 284) appears to be alone in suggesting that the last phrase may refer to those who emasculate themselves, an allusion to contemporary ascetic practices among oriental cults, as well as referring figuratively to the renunciation of sexual life. The lack of other references to such a practice within early Christian documents allows for little critical probability to this view. Boring (*Sayings*, 93-94) sees the verse as referring to the ascetic practices of early Christian prophets primarily with reference to the renunciation of marriage.

41. The analysis of the M sayings isolated in Chapter 6 makes it possible to suggest the inclusion of saying no. 12 with sayings nos. 1, 2, 4, 5 as representative of the same tradition on a more critically secure basis than in the analysis of Chapter 5.

Notes to Chapter 7

1. *History*, 322. Bultmann's evolutionary model, which is followed by Robinson and Koester, has been carefully criticized by Kelber (*Oral*, 2-8). The present study does not assume an evolutionary model for the development of oral and written tradition. It does, however, investigate linguistic and historical/social ties between isolated traditions. By such investigations, the hypotheses of Bultmann and Kelber can be tested with regard to specific studies in Matthew. The difficulty with both Kelber and Bultmann is that they compose general theories based on a philosophical/ linguistic presupposition, not on a survey of the evidence. This is placing the cart before the horse.

2. Kelber, *Oral*, 23.

3. See Kelber's remarks on the orality of Mark's text in *Oral*, 44-80.

4. Compare the methods used by Streeter, Manson, Kilpatrick cited on pp. 12-15 above.

5. These findings directly contradict the hypotheses of Streeter and Kilpatrick with regard to M. See pp. 12-15, above.

6. *Oral*, 24.

7. *Ibid.*, 115.

8. See the conclusions in Chapter 6.

9. We cannot rule out the possibility that Matthew's community is composed of more than one early Christian group. Meier has proposed such a hypothesis for the community of Matthew at Antioch (*Antioch and Rome*). The results of the analysis of the M sayings and the hypothesis proposed below are not wholly incompatible with his hypothesis, if the location of Matthew's community at Antioch is accepted.

10. Strecker, *Weg*, 86-122; 'Geschichtsverständnis', 57-74; 'Concept', 219-30; Meier, *Law*, 25-40.

11. In distinction to Kelber, I would argue that Matthew shows signs of anticipating from his readers perceptions of the traditions about Jesus that are determined both by an open form of oral communication as well as by the more closed form of written communication. Kelber has, it seems to me, drawn too clear a ceasura between oral and written hermeneutics in describing Mark's Gospel, and has thereby set up a relationship of antipathy between Mark and his traditions. Whether Kelber is correct or not with regard to Mark's Gospel, Matthew shows little antipathy for oral traditions; indeed his Gospel may well be an outgrowth of a congenial collegiality between both oral and written processes of handing on the traditions about Jesus.

12. In Chapter 1, we found that earlier approaches to the M material developed hypotheses about the material that were informed by certain presuppositions about the history of early Christianity. Later studies in other NT literature have shown the productivity of a method that investigates early Christian history based in the first instance on a critical reading of the texts available to us. It has become apparent in recent critical study that early Christianity contained a wide variety of groups each with its own peculiar history. The hypothesis developed here is not exhaustive of all the *possibilities*; it develops a probable case. It is hoped that this hypothesis will stimulate modifications or competing hypotheses that more adequately account for the M traditions.

13. On the importance of this text for the interpretation and life setting of Matthew see O. Lamar Cope, *Matthew: A Scribe Trained for the Kingdom of Heaven* (CBQMS, 5; Washington: CBA, 1976).

14. I suggest this as a possibility. See Hare, *Persecution*; and Hummel, *Auseinandersetzung*. Hare argues for a restricted persecution of Christian missionaries. When Matthew's composition is analyzed, however, in view of

the tradition history outlined so far, grounds emerge for a more general community experience of persecution by Matthew's forebears. Martyn (*Gospel*, 119; and *History*, 32-41) has established the broadness of the persecution against the Johannine community. The experience of the Matthean community may reflect a similarly general form of persecution.

15. The coming of the Son of Man referred to in v. 23 may in Matthew's view, be accomplished in the crucifixion and resurrection. On this view, see Meier, *Law*, 25-35.

16. See Hare, *Persecution*, 129.

17. Brown (*Birth*, 109) isolates an underlying tradition within the Birth narrative that, by relating Jesus to the figure of Moses, would have well suited the mission of this group. Matthew's use of the citation formulas may relate in some way to the preaching of this group.

18. Saying no. 6 cannot be critically aligned with the tradition history proposed here. It may belong to this interim period, but may just as well represent another tradition otherwise unrepresented in the M sayings.

19. This configuration accords with those suggested by Bornkamm ('Bind and Loose'), Strecker (*Weg*, 15-48), and Meier (*Law*, 7-24; *Vision*, 12-25).

APPENDIX

Charts 1-33

C. 1

Streeter	*Manson*	*Kilpatrick*
Discourse: 5.1–6.21; 6.34–7.6; 7.12-29. 10.5-8, 23, 24-25, 41. 18.12-14, 15, 17, 21-22. 23.1-36.	(3.14-15)	I. 5.21-24, 27-28, 33-37, 38-41, 19-20; 6.1-8, 16-18. 5.23-24, 36; 6.7-8 from other contexts.
Parables: 13.24-30, 44-50 (M or some other source).	SM:* 5.7-10, 13-24, 27-48; 6.1-21, 34; 7.1, 13-14, 21-23.	II. 10.5-6, 8b, 16b, 23, 24-25a, 25b, 41(?).
Other: 12.9-13; 15:22b-24; 16.18-19; 19.3-12.	Mission: 10.5-16, 23-25, 10.40-11.1.	III. Parables: (a) Kingdom Parables: 13.24-30, 36-52; 18.23-34; 20.1-15; 22.2, 11-14; 25.1-10. (b) Others: 21.28-32; 25.31-45.
	Various: 11.14-15, 28-30, 12.5-7, 11-12, 34a, 36-37.	
	Parables: 13:24-30, 36-43, 44-46, 47-50, 51-53.	IV. Against Religious Leaders: 23.2-3, 5, 7b-10, 15-22, 24, 26(?), 27.
	Various: 15.12-13, 22-25: 16.2-3, 17-19, 20.	V. Fragments: 5.7-9 with possibly 4 and 10, 14, 16-17; 6.34; 7.6, 13, 14, 15; 11.28-30; 12.5-6, 7, 36-37; 15.12-13; 18.10, 18-20; 19.10-12.
	Christian Fellowship: 18.10, 12-14, 15-22, 23-35.	
	Service and Reward: 19.10-12, 28; 20.1-16.	
	Refusers: 21.14-16, 28-32, 43, (44); 22.1-14.	
	Pharisees: 23.1-36.	
	Eschatological: 24.10-12, 30a; 25.1-46.	

*Sermon on the Mount

C. 2

The M Sayings

Translation

1.   (Matt 5.19) Therefore, if anyone abolishes a single one of the least of these commandments and teaches others likewise then he will be called least in the Kingdom of Heaven. But if anyone should do one of the least of these commandments and teach others likewise he will be called great in the Kingdom of Heaven.

2.   (Matt 5.21-22) You have heard that it was said to the ancients, 'Do not kill, whoever kills is liable to the judgment'. But I say to you that everyone who is angry with his brother is liable to the judgment; whoever says to his brother *'raka'*, is liable to the court; whoever says *'fool'*, is liable to the Gehenna of fire.

3.   (Matt 5.23-24) If, therefore, you are taking your gift up to the altar and if you remember that your brother has something against you leave your gift there before the altar and go, first be reconciled to your brother, and then when you have come offer your gift.

4.   (Matt 5.27-28) You have heard that it was said, 'Do not commit adultery'. But, I say to you that anyone who looks at a woman for the purpose of desire already commits adultery with her in his heart.

5.   (Matt 5.33-35, 37) You have heard that it was said to the ancients, 'You shall not break your oath, but offer your oath to the Lord'. But, I say to you that you are not to swear at all; neither by the heaven, because it is the throne of God; nor by the earth, because it is a footstool for his feet; nor by Jerusalem, because it is the city of the great king. But let your word be yes, yes, no, no. (Beyond this is from the evil one.)

6.   (Matt 5.36) Nor may you swear by your head, because you are unable to make a single hair white or black.

7.   (Matt 6.1-6, 16-18) Beware that you do not perform your righteousness in front of people in order to be seen by them. But if you do not heed this, you do not have a reward from your father, the one who sees in secret. Therefore, when you give alms, do not sound a trumpet before you like the hypocrites do in the synagogues and roadways in order that they might receive glory from people. Amen, I say to you, they have their reward. But when you give alms do not let your left (hand) know what your right (hand)

does, thus your alms may be in secret and your father who sees in secret will reward you.

And when you pray, do not be like the hypocrites who love to pray while standing in the synagogues and on the street corners that they may be seen be people. Amen, I say to you, they have their reward. But when you pray, go into your inner room and when you have closed your door, pray to your father, the one who is in secret, and your father who sees in secret will reward you.

And when you fast, do not be downcast like the hypocrites, for they disfigure their faces so that they might be seen by people when they fast. Amen, I say to you, they have their reward. But when you fast, anoint your head and wash your face, so that you might not be seen by people while you are fasting, but rather that you might be seen by your father who is in secret and your father who sees in secret will reward you.

8.   (Matt 6.7-8) But when you pray do not babble like the Gentiles, for they suppose that by their running off at the mouth that they will be listened to. Therefore, do not be like them, for your father knows the things of which you have need before you ask him.

9.   (Matt 10.5b-6) Do not go in the way of the Gentiles and do not enter the city of the Samaritans; but rather go out to the lost sheep of the nation of Israel.

10.   (Matt 10.23b) For amen, I say to you, you will not finish the cities of Israel before the Son of Man comes.

11.   (Matt 23.2-3, 5) (The scribes and the Pharisees) sit upon the chair of Moses. Therefore, do and keep whatever they say to you, but do not do according to their works; for they speak, yet they do not act. And they do all of their works in order to be seen by people; for they make their phylacteries broad and they lengthen their tassels.

12.   (Matt 23.8-10) But you, do not be called 'Rabbi'; for your teacher is one. And do not call someone among you 'Father'; for your father is one. Nor be called 'Instructors'; for your instructor is one.

13.   (Matt 23.15) Woe to you, blind guides, because you travel around the sea and the land in order to make one proselyte, and when he becomes one you make him twice as much a child of Gehenna as yourselves.

14.   (Matt 23.26-22, 24, 33) Woe to you, blind guides, the ones saying, 'Whoever swears by the temple, it is nothing; but whoever swears by the gold of the temple is obligated'. Fools and blind ones, because what is greater, the

gold or the temple that makes the gold holy? And, 'whoever swears by the altar, it is nothing; but whoever swears by the gift on it, is obligated'. Blind ones, for what is greater, the gift or the altar that makes the gift holy? Therefore, the one who swears by the altar swears by it and by everything on it; and the one who swears by the temple swears by it and by the one who inhabits it; and the one who swears by heaven swears by the throne of God and the one who sits upon it. Blind guides, those who strain out the gnat and gulp down a camel.

15.   (Matt 7.6) Do not give what is holy to dogs, neither cast your pearls before swine, lest they trample them with their feet and afterwards turn to attack you.

16.   (Matt 12.36-37) And I say to you, in the day of judgment people will render account for every careless word which they have spoken. For out of your words, you will be judged, and out of your words, you will be condemned.

17.   (Matt 18.18) Whatever you bind upon the earth will be bound in heaven, and whatever you loose upon the earth, will be loosed in heaven.

18.   (Matt 18.19-20) I say to you that if two of you should agree about any matter upon the earth, which they should ask, it will be done for them by my father the one who is in the heavens. (20) For where two or three are gathered in my name, there I am in their midst.

19.   (Matt 19.12) For there are eunuchs such as those who are so begotten from the mother's womb, and those who are made eunuchs by men, and those who make themselves eunuchs because of the Kingdom of the Heavens.

The Greek Text

1.   (Matt 5.19) ὃς ἐὰν οὖν λύσῃ μίαν τῶν ἐντολῶν τούτων τῶν ἐλαχίστων καὶ διδάξῃ οὕτως τοὺς ἀνθρώπους, ἐλάχιστος κληθήσεται ἐν τῇ βασιλείᾳ τῶν οὐρανῶν· ὃς δ᾽ ἂν ποιήσῃ καὶ διδάξῃ, οὗτος μέγας κληθήσεται ἐν τῇ βασιλείᾳ τῶν οὐρανῶν.

2.   (Matt 5.21-22) ἠκούσατε ὅτι ἐρρέθη τοῖς ἀρχαίοις· οὐ φονεύσεις· ὃς δ᾽ ἂν φονεύσῃ, ἔνοχος ἔσται τῇ κρίσει. ἐγὼ δὲ λέγω ὑμῖν ὅτι πᾶς ὁ ὀργιζόμενος τῷ ἀδελφῷ αὐτοῦ ἔνοχος ἔσται τῇ κρίσει· ὃς δ᾽ ἂν εἴπῃ τῷ ἀδελφῷ· ρακα, ἔνοχος ἔσται τῷ συνεδρίῳ· ὃς δ᾽ ἂν εἴπῃ· μωρέ, ἔνοχος ἔσται εἰς τὴν γέενναν τοῦ πυρός.

3. (Matt 5.23-24) ἐὰν οὖν προσφέρῃς τὸ δῶρόν σου ἐπὶ τὸ θυσιαστήριον κἀκεῖ μνησθῇς ὅτι ὁ ἀδελφός σου ἔχει τι κατὰ σοῦ, ἄφες ἐκεῖ τὸ δῶρόν σου ἔμπροσθεν τοῦ θυσιαστηρίου καὶ ὕπαγε πρῶτον διαλλάγηθι τῷ ἀδελφῷ σου, καὶ τότε ἐλθὼν πρόσφερε τὸ δῶρόν σου.

4. (Matt 5.27-28) ἠκούσατε ὅτι ἐρρέθη· οὐ μοιχεύσεις. ἐγὼ δὲ λέγω ὑμῖν ὅτι πᾶς ὁ βλέπων γυναῖκα πρὸς τὸ ἐπιθυμῆσαι ἤδη ἐμοίχευσεν αὐτὴν ἐν τῇ καρδίᾳ αὐτοῦ.

5. (Matt 5.33-35, 37) ἠκούσατε ὅτι ἐρρέθη τοῖς ἀρχαίοις· οὐκ ἐπιορκήσεις, ἀποδώσεις δὲ τῷ κυρίῳ τοὺς ὅρκους σου. ἐγὼ δὲ λέγω ὑμῖν μὴ ὀμόσαι ὅλως· μήτε ἐν τῷ οὐρανῷ, ὅτι θρόνος ἐστὶν τοῦ θεοῦ, μήτε ἐν τῇ γῇ, ὅτι ὑποπόδιόν ἐστιν τῶν ποδῶν αὐτοῦ, μήτε εἰς Ἱεροσόλυμα, ὅτι πόλις ἐστὶν τοῦ μεγάλου βασιλέως. ἔστω δὲ ὁ λόγος ὑμῶν ναὶ ναί, οὒ οὔ· τὸ δὲ περισσὸν τούτων ἐκ τοῦ πονηροῦ ἐστιν.

6. (Matt 5.36) (μήτε) ἐν τῇ κεφαλῇ σου ὀμόσῃς, ὅτι οὐ δύνασαι μίαν τρίχα λευκὴν ποιῆσαι ἢ μέλαιναν.

7. (Matt 6.1-6, 16-18) προσέχεις τὴν δικαιοσύνην σου μὴ ποιεῖν ἔμπροσθεν τῶν ἀνθρώπων πρὸς τὸ θεαθῆναι αὐτοῖς· εἰ δὲ μή γε, μισθὸν οὐκ ἔχεις παρὰ τῷ πατρί σου τῷ βλέποντι ἐν τῷ κρυπτῷ. ὅταν οὖν ποιῇς ἐλεημοσύνην, μὴ σαλπίσῃς ἔμπροσθέν σου, ὥσπερ οἱ ὑποκριταὶ ποιοῦσιν ἐν ταῖς συναγωγαῖς καὶ ἐν ταῖς ῥύμαις, ὅπως δοξασθῶσιν ὑπὸ τῶν ἀνθρώπων· ἀμὴν λέγω ὑμῖν, ἀπέχουσιν τὸν μισθὸν αὐτῶν. σοῦ δὲ ποιοῦντος ἐλεημοσύνην μὴ γνώτω ἡ ἀριστερά σου τί ποιεῖ ἡ δεξιά σου, ὅπως ᾖ σου ἡ ἐλεημοσύνη ἐν τῷ κρυπτῷ· καὶ ὁ πατήρ σου βλέπων ἐν τῷ κρυπτῷ ἀποδώσει σοι.

καὶ ὅταν προσεύχησθε, οὐκ ἔσεσθε ὡς οἱ ὑποκριταί, ὅτι φιλοῦσιν ἐν ταῖς συναγωγαῖς καὶ ἐν ταῖς γωνίαις τῶν πλατειῶν ἑστῶτες προσεύχεσθαι, ὅπως φανῶσιν τοῖς ἀνθρώποις· ἀμὴν λέγω ὑμῖν, ἀπέχουσιν τὸν μισθὸν αὐτῶν. σὺ δὲ ὅταν προσεύχῃ, εἴσελθε εἰς τὸ ταμεῖόν σου καὶ κλείσας τὴν θύραν σου πρόσευξαι τῷ πατρί σου τῷ ἐν τῷ κρυπτῷ· καὶ ὁ πατήρ σου ὁ βλέπων ἐν τῷ κρυπτῷ ἀποδώσει σοι.

ὅταν δὲ νηστεύητε, μὴ γίνεσθε ὡς οἱ ὑποκριταὶ σκυθρωποί, ἀφανίζουσιν γὰρ τὰ πρόσωπα αὐτῶν ὅπως φανῶσιν τοῖς ἀνθρώποις νηστεύοντες· ἀμὴν λέγω ὑμῖν, ἀπέχουσιν τὸν μισθὸν αὐτῶν. σὺ δὲ νηστεύων ἄλειψαί σου τὴν κεφαλὴν καὶ τὸ πρόσωπόν σου νίψαι, ὅπως μὴ φανῇς τοῖς ἀνθρώποις νηστεύων ἀλλὰ τῷ πατρί σου τῷ ἐν τῷ κρυφαίῳ καὶ ὁ πατήρ σου ὁ βλέπων ἐν τῷ κρυφαίῳ ἀποδώσει σοι.

8. (Matt 6.7-8) προσευχόμενοι δὲ μὴ βατταλογήσητε ὥσπερ οἱ ἐθνικοί, δοκοῦσιν γὰρ ὅτι ἐν τῇ πολυλογίᾳ αὐτῶν εἰσακουσθήσονται. μὴ οὖν ὁμοιωθῆτε αὐτοῖς· οἶδεν γὰρ ὁ πατὴρ ὑμῶν ὧν χρείαν ἔχετε πρὸ τοῦ ὑμᾶς αἰτῆσαι αὐτόν.

9.   (Matt 10.5b-6) εἰς ὁδὸν ἐθνῶν μὴ ἀπέλθητε καὶ εἰς πόλιν Σαμαριτῶν μὴ εἰσέλθητε· πορεύεσθε δὲ μᾶλλον πρὸς τὰ πρόβατα τὰ ἀπολωλότα οἴκου Ἰσραήλ.

10.   (Matt 10.23b) ἀμὴν γὰρ λέγω ὑμῖν, οὐ μὴ τελέσητε τὰς πόλεις τοῦ Ἰσραὴλ ἕως ἂν ἔλθῃ ὁ υἱὸς τοῦ ἀνθρώπου.

11.   (Matt 23.2-3, 5) ἐπὶ τῆς Μωϋσέως καθέδρας ἐκάθισαν (οἱ γραμματεῖς καὶ οἱ Φαρισαῖοι). πάντα οὖν ὅσα ἐὰν εἴπωσιν ὑμῖν ποιήσατε καὶ τηρεῖτε, κατὰ δὲ τὰ ἔργα αὐτῶν μὴ ποιεῖτε· λέγουσιν γὰρ καὶ οὐ ποιοῦσιν. πάντα δὲ τὰ ἔργα αὐτῶν ποιοῦσιν πρὸς τὸ θεαθῆναι τοῖς ἀνθρώποις· πλατύνουσιν γὰρ τὰ φυλακτήρια αὐτῶν καὶ μεγαλύνουσιν τὰ κράσπεδα.

12.   (Matt 23.8-10) ὑμεῖς δὲ μὴ κληθῆτε ῥαββί· εἷς γάρ ἐστιν ὑμῶν ὁ διδάσκαλος. καὶ πατέρα μὴ καλέσητε ὑμῶν, εἷς γάρ ἐστιν ὑμῶν ὁ πατήρ. μηδὲ κληθῆτε καθηγηταί, εἷς γάρ ἐστιν ὑμῶν ὁ καθηγητής.

13.   (Matt 23.15) οὐαὶ ὑμῖν, ὁδηγοὶ τυφλοί, ὅτι περιάγετε τὴν θάλασσαν καὶ τὴν ξηρὰν ποιῆσαι ἕνα προσήλυτον, καὶ ὅταν γένηται ποιεῖτε αὐτὸν υἱὸν γεέννης διπλότερον ὑμῶν.

14.   (Matt 23.16-22, 24) οὐαὶ ὑμῖν, ὁδηγοὶ τυφλοὶ οἱ λέγοντες· ὃς ἂν ὀμόσῃ ἐν τῷ ναῷ, οὐδέν ἐστιν· ὃς δ᾽ ἂν ὀμόσῃ ἐν τῷ χρυσῷ τοῦ ναοῦ, ὀφείλει. μωροὶ καὶ τυφλοί, τίς γὰρ μείζων ἐστίν, ὁ χρυσὸς ἢ ὁ ναὸς ὁ ἁγιάσας τὸν χρυσόν; καὶ ὃς ἂν ὀμόσῃ ἐν τῷ θυσιαστηρίῳ, οὐδέν ἐστιν· ὃς δ᾽ ἂν ὀμόσῃ ἐν τῷ δώρῳ τῷ ἐπάνω αὐτοῦ, ὀφείλει. τυφλοί, τί γὰρ μεῖζον, τὸ δῶρον ἢ τὸ θυσιαστήριον τὸ ἁγιάζον τὸ δῶρον; ὁ οὖν ὀμόσας ἐν τῷ θυσιαστηρίῳ ὀμνύει ἐν αὐτῷ καὶ ἐν πᾶσι τοῖς ἐπάνω αὐτοῦ· καὶ ὁ ὀμόσας ἐν τῷ ναῷ ὀμνύει ἐν αὐτῷ καὶ ἐν τῷ κατοικοῦντι αὐτόν, καὶ ὁ ὀμόσας ἐν τῷ οὐρανῷ ὀμνύει ἐν τῷ θρόνῳ τοῦ θεοῦ καὶ ἐν τῷ καθημένῳ ἐπάνω αὐτοῦ. ὁδηγοὶ τυφλοί, οἱ διϋλίζοντες τὸν κώνωπα, τὴν δὲ κάμηλον καταπίνοντες.

15.   (Matt 7.6) μὴ δῶτε τὸ ἅγιον τοῖς κυσίν, μηδὲ βάλητε τοὺς μαργαρίτας ὑμῶν ἔμπροσθεν τῶν χοίρων, μήποτε καταπατήσουσιν αὐτοὺς ἐν τοῖς ποσὶν αὐτῶν καὶ στραφέντες ῥήξωσιν ὑμᾶς.

16.   (Matt 12.36-37) πᾶν ῥῆμα ἀργὸν ὃ λαλήσουσιν οἱ ἄνθρωποι ἀποδώσουσιν περὶ αὐτοῦ λόγον ἐν ἡμέρᾳ κρίσεως· ἐκ γὰρ τῶν λόγων σου δικαιωθήσῃ, καὶ ἐκ τῶν λόγων σου καταδικασθήσῃ.

17.   (Matt 18.18) ὅσα ἐὰν δήσητε ἐπὶ τῆς γῆς ἔσται δεδεμένα ἐν οὐρανῷ, καὶ ὅσα ἐὰν λύσητε ἐπὶ τῆς γῆς ἔσται λελυμένα ἐν οὐρανῷ.

18.   (Matt 18.19-20) λέγω ὑμῖν ὅτι ἐὰν δύο συμφωνήσωσιν ἐξ ὑμῶν ἐπὶ τῆς

γῆς περὶ παντὸς πράγματος οὗ ἐὰν αἰτήσωνται, γενήσεται αὐτοῖς παρὰ τοῦ πατρός μου τοῦ ἐν οὐρανοῖς. οὗ γάρ εἰσιν δύο ἢ τρεῖς συνηγμένοι εἰς τὸ ἐμὸν ὄνομα, ἐκεῖ εἰμι ἐν μέσῳ αὐτῶν.

19. (Matt 19.12) εἰσὶν γὰρ εὐνοῦχοι οἵτινες ἐκ κοιλίας μητρὸς ἐγεννήθησαν οὕτως, καὶ εἰσὶν εὐνοῦχοι οἵτινες εὐνουχίσθησαν ὑπὸ τῶν ἀνθρώπων, καὶ εἰσὶν εὐνοῦχοι οἵτινες εὐνούχισαν ἑαυτοὺς διὰ τὴν βασιλείαν τῶν οὐρανῶν.

C. 3

Matt 5.18   Luke 16.17

ἀμὴν γὰρ λέγω ὑμῖν
ἕως ἂν παρέλθῃ   εὐκοπώτερον δέ ἐστιν
ὁ οὐρανὸς καὶ ἡ γῆ,   τὸν οὐρανὸν καὶ τὴν γῆν
ἰῶτα ἓν ἢ μία κεραία   παρελθεῖν ἢ τοῦ νόμου
οὐ μὴ παρέλθῃ ἀπὸ τοῦ νόμου,   μίαν κεραίαν πεσεῖν.
ἕως ἂν πάντα γένηται.

Key:

Precise verbal agreement is indicated by _____
The same word in a different form   _ _ _ _ _ _ _ _ _
Different words but synonymous   . . . .

C. 4

οὐκ ἦλθον καταλῦσαι τὸν νόμον·
οὐκ ἦλθον καταλῦσαι ἀλλὰ ποιεῖν.

C. 5

Matt 11.13   Luke 16.16a

πάντες γὰρ οἱ προφῆται   ὁ νόμος καὶ οἱ προφῆται
καὶ ὁ νόμος ἕως Ἰωάννου   μέχρι Ἰωάννου
ἐπροφήτευσαν·

C. 6

Matt 5.19

19a   ὃς ἐὰν οὖν λύσῃ μίαν τῶν ἐντολῶν τούτων τῶν ἐλαχίστων καὶ
       διδάξῃ οὕτως τοὺς ἀνθρώπους,
19b   ἐλάχιστος κληθήσεται ἐν τῇ βασιλείᾳ τῶν οὐρανῶν·

Matt 16.19c

       καὶ ὃ ἐὰν λύσῃς ἐπὶ τῆς γῆς ἔσται λελυμένον ἐν τοῖς οὐρανοῖς.

Matt 18.18b

       καὶ ὅσα ἐὰν λύσητε ἐπὶ τῆς γῆς ἔσται λελυμένα ἐν οὐρανῷ.

C. 7

Matt 5.18b, c, 19a, b

ἕως ἂν παρέλθῃ ὁ οὐρανὸς καὶ ἡ γῆ, ἰῶτα ἓν ἢ μία κεραία οὐ μὴ παρέλθῃ
ἀπὸ τοῦ νόμου.
ὃς ἐὰν οὖν λύσῃ μίαν τῶν ἐντολῶν τούτων τῶν ἐλαχίστων καὶ διδάξῃ
οὕτως τοὺς ἀνθρώπους, ἐλάχιστος κληθήσεται ἐν τῇ βασιλείᾳ τῶν
οὐρανῶν·

C. 8

Matt 5.23-24

ἐὰν οὖν προσφέρῃς τὸ δῶρόν σου ἐπὶ τὸ θυσιαστήριον κἀκεῖ μνησθῇς ὅτι ὁ ἀδελφός σου ἔχει τι κατὰ σοῦ, <u>ἄφες</u> ἐκεῖ τὸ δῶρόν σου ἔμπροσθεν τοῦ θυσιαστηρίου καὶ ὕπαγε πρῶτον διαλλάγηθι τῷ ἀδελφῷ. καὶ τότε ἐλθὼν πρόσφερε τὸ δῶρόν σου.

Mark 11.25

καὶ ὅταν στήκετε προσευχόμενοι, ἀφίετε εἴ τι ἔχετε κατά τινος, ἵνα καὶ ὁ πατὴρ ὑμῶν ὁ ἐν τοῖς οὐρανοῖς ἀφῇ ὑμῖν τὰ παραπτώματα ὑμῶν.

Matt 5.25-26

ἴσθι εὐνοῶν <u>τῷ ἀντιδίκῳ σου</u> ταχύ, ἕως ὅτου εἶ μετ' αὐτοῦ ἐν τῇ <u>ὁδῷ</u>, μηποτέ σε παραδῷ ὁ ἀντίδικος <u>τῷ κριτῇ καὶ ὁ κριτὴς τῷ ὑπερέτῃ</u>, <u>καὶ εἰς φυλακὴν βληθήσῃ</u>· ἀμὴν <u>λέγω σοι, οὐ μὴ ἐξέλθῃς ἐκεῖθεν</u>, <u>ἕως ἂν ἀποδῷς τὸν ἔσχατον</u> κοδράντην.

Luke 12.58-59

ὡς γὰρ ὑπάγεις μετὰ τοῦ ἀντιδίκου σου ἐπ' ἄρχοντα, ἐν τῇ ὁδῷ δὸς ἐργασίαν ἀπηλλάχθαι ἀπ' αὐτοῦ, μήποτε κατασύρῃ σε πρὸς τὸν κριτήν, καὶ ὁ κριτής σε παραδώσει τῷ πράκτορι, καὶ ὁ πράκτωρ σε βαλεῖ εἰς φυλακήν. λέγω σοι, οὐ μὴ ἐξέλθῃς ἐκεῖθεν, ἕως καὶ τὸ ἔσχατον λεπτὸν ἀποδῷς.

C. 9

Matt 5.21-22

21a ἠκούσατε ὅτι ἐρρέθη τοῖς ἀρχαίοις·
  b   οὐ φονεύσεις·   οὐ φονεύσεις. (Exod 20.13)
  c   ὃς δ' ἂν φονεύσῃ,
  d   ἔνοχος ἔσται τῇ κρίσει.
22a ἐγὼ δὲ λέγω ὑμῖν ὅτι
  c   πᾶς ὁ ὀργιζόμενος τῷ ἀδελφῷ αὐτοῦ
  d   ἔνοχος ἔσται τῇ κρίσει·
  e   ὃς δ' ἂν εἴπῃ τῷ ἀδελφῷ αὐτοῦ· ῥακά,
  f   ἔνοχος ἔσται τῷ συνεδρίῳ·
  g   ὃς δ' ἂν εἴπῃ· μωρέ,
  h   ἔνοχος ἔσται εἰς τὴν γέενναν τοῦ πυρός.

C. 10

Matt 5.29-30	Matt 18.8-9	Mark 9.43, 45, 47

29 εἰ δὲ ὁ ὀφθαλμός σου ὁ δεξιὸς σκανδαλίζει σε, ἔξελε αὐτὸν καὶ βάλε ἀπὸ σοῦ· συμφέρει γάρ σοι ἵνα ἀπόληται ἓν τῶν μελῶν σου καὶ μὴ ὅλον τὸ σῶμά
30 σου βληθῇ εἰς γέενναν. καὶ εἰ ἡ δεξιά σου χεὶρ σκανδαλίζει σε, ἔκκοψον αὐτὴν καὶ βάλε ἀπὸ σοῦ· συμφέρει γάρ σοι ἵνα ἀπόληται ἓν τῶν μελῶν σου καὶ μὴ ὅλον τὸ σῶμά σου εἰς γέενναν ἀπέλθῃ.

8 εἰ δὲ ἡ χείρ ἢ ὁ πούς σου σκανδαλίζει σε, ἔκκοψον αὐτὸν καὶ βάλε ἀπὸ σοῦ· καλόν σοί ἐστιν εἰσελθεῖν εἰς τὴν ζωὴν κυλλὸν ἢ χωλὸν ἢ δύο χεῖρας ἢ δύο πόδας ἔχοντα βληθῆναι
9 εἰς τὸ πῦρ τὸ αἰώνιον. καὶ εἰ ὁ ὀφθαλμός σου σκανδαλίζει σε, ἔξελε αὐτὸν καὶ βάλε ἀπὸ σοῦ· καλόν σοί ἐστιν μονόφθαλμον εἰς τὴν ζωὴν εἰσελθεῖν ἢ δύο ὀφθαλμοὺς ἔχοντα βληθῆναι εἰς τὴν γέενναν τοῦ πυρός.

43 καὶ ἐὰν σκανδαλίζῃ σε ἡ χείρ σου, ἀπόκοψον αὐτήν· καλόν ἐστίν σε κυλλὸν εἰσελθεῖν εἰς τὴν ζωὴν ἢ τὰς δύο χεῖρας ἔχοντα ἀπελθεῖν εἰς τὴν γέενναν, εἰς τὸ πῦρ
45 τὸ ἄσβεστον. καὶ ἐὰν ὁ πούς σου σκανδαλίζῃ σε, ἀπόκοψον αὐτόν· καλόν ἐστίν σε εἰσελθεῖν εἰς τὴν ζωὴν χωλὸν ἢ τοὺς δύο πόδας ἔχοντα βληθῆναι εἰς τὴν γέενναν. καὶ ἐὰν ὁ ὀφθαλμός σου σκανδαλίζῃ σε, ἔκβαλε αὐτόν· καλόν σέ ἐστιν μονόφθαλμον εἰσελθεῖν
47 εἰς τὴν βασιλείαν τοῦ θεοῦ ἢ δύο ὀφθαλμοὺς ἔχοντα βληθῆναι εἰς τὴν γέενναν,

C. 11

Matt 5.32

ἐγὼ δὲ λέγω ὑμῖν ὅτι πᾶς ὁ
ἀπολύων τὴν γυναῖκα αὐτοῦ
παρεκτὸς λόγου πορνείας ποιεῖ
αὐτὴν μοιχευθῆναι, καὶ ὃς ἐὰν
ἀπολελυμένην γαμήσῃ, μοιχᾶται.

Mark 10.11-12

καὶ λέγει αὐτοῖς· ὃς ἂν ἀπολύσῃ
τὴν γυναῖκα αὐτοῦ καὶ γαμήσῃ
ἄλλην μοιχᾶται ἐπ᾽ αὐτήν· καὶ
ἐὰν αὐτὴ ἀπολύσασα τὸν ἄνδρα
αὐτῆς γαμήσῃ ἄλλον μοιχᾶται.

Matt 5.32

ἐγὼ δὲ λέγω ὑμῖν ὅτι πᾶς ὁ
ἀπολύων τὴν γυναῖκα αὐτοῦ
παρεκτὸς λόγου πορνείας ποιεῖ
αὐτὴν μοιχευθῆναι, καὶ ὃς ἐὰν
ἀπολελυμένην γαμήσῃ, μοιχᾶται.

Luke 16.18

πᾶς ὁ ἀπολύων τὴν γυναῖκα
αὐτοῦ καὶ γαμῶν ἑτέραν μοιχεύει,
καὶ ὁ ἀπολελυμένην ἀπὸ ἀνδρὸς
γαμῶν μοιχεύει.

C. 12

		Matt 5.33-37	James 5.12
33	A	Πάλιν ἠκούσατε ὅτι ἐρρέθη τοῖς ἀρχαίοις·	πρὸ πάντων δέ, ἀδελφοί μου,
	B	οὐκ ἐπιορκήσεις,	
	C	ἀποδώσεις δὲ τῷ κυρίῳ τοὺς ὅρκους σου.	
34	A'	ἐγὼ δὲ λέγω ὑμῖν	μὴ ὀμνύετε
	B'	μὴ ὀμόσαι ὅλως·	μήτε τὸν οὐρανὸν
	a	μήτε ἐν τῷ οὐρανῷ,	
	b	ὅτι θρόνος ἐστὶν τοῦ θεοῦ,	
35	a	μήτε ἐν τῇ γῇ,	μήτε τὴν γῆν
	b	ὅτι ὑποπόδιόν ἐστιν τῶν ποδῶν αὐτοῦ,	
	a	μήτε εἰς Ἱεροσόλυμα,	μήτε ἄλλον τινὰ ὅρκον·
	b	ὅτι πόλις ἐστὶν τοῦ μεγάλου βασιλέως,	
36	c	μήτε ἐν τῇ κεφαλῇ σου ὀμόσῃς,	
	d	ὅτι οὐ δύνασαι μίαν τρίχα λευκὴν ποιῆσαι ἢ μέλαιναν.	
37a	C'	ἔστω δὲ ὁ λόγος ὑμῶν ναί, ναί, οὔ, οὔ·	ἤτω δὲ ὑμῶν τὸ ναὶ ναί, καὶ τὸ οὒ οὔ,
37b	C	τὸ δὲ περισσὸν τούτων ἐκ τοῦ πονηροῦ ἐστιν.	ἵνα μὴ ὑπὸ κρίσιν πέσητε.

C. 13

Justin, *Apol.* 1.16.5

περὶ δὲ τοῦ μὴ ὀμνύναι ὅλως, τἀληθῆ δὲ λέγειν ἀεί, οὕτως παρεκελύσατο·
μὴ ὀμόσητε ὅλως
ἔστω δὲ ὑμῶν τὸ ναὶ ναί, καὶ τὸ οὒ οὔ.
τὸ δὲ περισσὸν τούτων ἐκ τοῦ πονηροῦ.

Ps. Cl. Hom. 3.56.3

τοῖς δὲ αὐτὸν διαβεβαιουμένοις ἐν ναῷ εἶναι ἔφη
μὴ ὀμόσητε τὸν οὐρανὸν ὅτι θρόνος θεοῦ ἐστιν
μήτε τὴν γῆν ὅτι ὑποπόδιον τῶν ποδῶν αὐτοῦ ἐστιν.

Ps. Cl. Hom. 3.55.1 (par 19.2.4)

τοῖς δὲ νομίζουσιν (ὡς αἱ γραφαὶ διδάσκουσιν) ὅτι ὁ θεὸς ὀμνύει ἔφη·
ἔστω ὑμῶν τὸ ναὶ ναί, τὸ οὒ οὔ
τὸ γὰρ περισσὸν τούτων ἐκ τοῦ πονηροῦ ἐστιν.

Epiphanius, *Pan. Haer.* 19.6.2

καὶ πάλιν ἐν τῷ εὐαγγελίῳ λέγοντος,
μὴ ὀμνύναι
μήτε τὸν οὐρανὸν
μήτε τὴν γῆν
μήτε ἕτερόν τινα ὅρκον
ἀλλ᾽ ἤτω ὑμῶν τὸ ναὶ ναί, καὶ τὸ οὒ οὔ,
τὸ περισσότερον γὰρ τούτων ἐκ τοῦ πονηροῦ ὑπάρχει.

C. 14

Exod 20.16	Matt 5.33
οὐ ψευδομαρτυρήσεις	οὐκ ἐπιορκήσεις

Ps 49.14

ἀπόδος τῷ ὑψίστῳ τὰς εὐχάς σου.	ἀποδώσεις δὲ τῷ κυρίῳ τοὺς ὅρκους σου.

C. 15

Matt 5.39b-42   Luke 6.29-30

ἀλλ᾽ ὅστις σε ῥαπίζει εἰς τὴν   τῷ τύπτοντί σε ἐπὶ τὴν σιαγόνα
δεξιὰν σιαγόνα, στρέψον αὐτῷ   πάρεχε καὶ τὴν ἄλλην, καὶ ἀπὸ
καὶ τὴν ἄλλην· καὶ τῷ θέλοντί   τοῦ αἴροντός σου τὸ ἱμάτιον καὶ
σοι κριθῆναι καὶ τὸν χιτῶνά σου   τὸν χιτῶνα μὴ κωλύσῃς.
λαβεῖν, ἄφες αὐτῷ καὶ τὸ ἱμάτιον·
καὶ ὅστις σε ἀγγαρεύσει μίλιον
ἕν, ὕπαγε μετ᾽ αὐτοῦ δύο.
τῷ αἰτοῦντί σε δός, καὶ τὸν   παντὶ αἰτοῦντι σε δίδου, καὶ ἀπὸ
θέλοντα ἀπὸ σοῦ δανείσασθαι   τοῦ αἴροντος τὰ σὰ μὴ ἀπαίτει.
μὴ ἀποστραφῇς.

C. 16

Matt 5.44-48   Luke 6.27-28, 35b, 32-33, 36

ἐγὼ δὲ λέγω ὑμῖν, ἀγαπᾶτε τοὺς   ἀλλὰ ὑμῖν λέγω τοῖς ἀκούουσιν·
ἐχθροὺς ὑμῶν καὶ προσεύχεσθε   ἀγαπᾶτε τοὺς ἐχθροὺς ὑμῶν,
ὑπὲρ τῶν διωκόντων ὑμᾶς· ὅπως   καλῶς ποιεῖτε τοῖς μισοῦσιν
γένησθε υἱοὶ τοῦ πατρὸς ὑμῶν   ὑμᾶς, προσεύχεσθε περὶ τῶν
τοῦ ἐν οὐρανοῖς, ὅτι τὸν ἥλιον   ἐπηρεαζόντων ὑμᾶς. καὶ ἔσεσθε
αὐτοῦ ἀνατέλλει ἐπὶ πονηροὺς   υἱοὶ ὑψίστου, ὅτι αὐτὸς χρηστός
καὶ ἀγαθοὺς καὶ βρέχει ἐπὶ   ἐστιν ἐπὶ τοὺς ἀχαρίστους καὶ
δικαίους καὶ ἀδίκους.   πονηρούς.
ἐὰν γὰρ ἀγαπήσητε τοὺς   καὶ εἰ ἀγαπᾶτε τοὺς ἀγαπῶντας
ἀγαπῶντας ὑμᾶς, τίνα μισθὸν   ὑμᾶς, ποία ὑμῖν χάρις ἐστίν; καὶ
ἔχετε; οὐχὶ καὶ οἱ τελῶναι τὸ   γὰρ οἱ ἁμαρτωλοὶ τοὺς
αὐτὸ ποιοῦσιν; καὶ ἐὰν   ἀγαπῶντας αὐτοὺς ἀγαπῶσιν.
ἀσπάσησθε τοὺς ἀδελφοὺς ὑμῶν   καὶ γὰρ ἐὰν ἀγαθοποιῆτε τοὺς
μόνον, τί περισσὸν ποιεῖτε; οὐχὶ   ἀγαθοποιοῦντας ὑμᾶς, ποία ὑμῖν
καὶ οἱ ἐθνικοὶ τὸ αὐτὸ ποιοῦσιν;   χάρις ἐστίν; καὶ οἱ ἁμαρτωλοὶ τὸ
                                       αὐτὸ ποιοῦσιν.
                                       (cf. 34-35a)
ἔσεσθε οὖν ὑμεῖς τέλειοι ὡς ὁ   γίνεσθε οἰκτίρμονες, καθὼς ὁ
πατὴρ ὑμῶν ὁ οὐράνιος τέλειός   πατὴρ ὑμῶν οἰκτίρμων ἐστίν.
ἐστιν.

C. 17

Matt 6.9-13

Luke 11.2-4

οὕτως οὖν προσεύχεσθε ὑμεῖς·
πάτερ ἡμῶν ὁ ἐν τοῖς οὐρανοῖς,
ἁγιασθήτω τὸ ὄνομά σου·
ἐλθάτω ἡ βασιλεία σου·
γενηθήτω τὸ θέλημά σου, ὡς ἐν
οὐρανῷ καὶ ἐπὶ γῆς·
τὸν ἄρτον ἡμῶν τὸν ἐπιούσιον
δὸς ἡμῖν σήμερον·
καὶ ἄφες ἡμῖν τὰ ὀφειλήματα
ἡμῶν,
ὡς καὶ ἡμεῖς ἀφήκαμεν τοῖς
ὀφειλέταις ἡμῶν· καὶ μὴ
εἰσενέγκῃς ἡμᾶς εἰς πειρασμόν,
ἀλλὰ ῥῦσαι ἡμᾶς ἀπὸ τοῦ
πονηροῦ.

εἶπεν δὲ αὐτοῖς· ὅταν προσεύχησθε,
λέγετε· πάτερ,
ἁγιασθήτω τὸ ὄνομά σου·
ἐλθάτω ἡ βασιλεία σου·

τὸν ἄρτον ἡμῶν τὸν ἐπιούσιον
δίδου ἡμῖν τὸ καθ᾽ ἡμέραν
καὶ ἄφες ἡμῖν τὰς ἁμαρτίας ἡμῶν,
καὶ γὰρ αὐτοὶ ἀφίομεν παντὶ
ὀφείλοντι ἡμῖν·
καὶ μὴ εἰσενέγκῃς ἡμᾶς εἰς
πειρασμόν.

Matt 6.14-15

Mark 11.25

ἐὰν γὰρ ἀφῆτε τοῖς ἀνθρώποις
τὰ παραπτώματα αὐτῶν, ἀφήσει
καὶ ὑμῖν ὁ πατὴρ ὑμῶν ὁ
οὐράνιος· ἐὰν δὲ μὴ ἀφῆτε τοῖς
ἀνθρώποις, οὐδὲ ὁ πατὴρ ὑμῶν
ἀφήσει τὰ παραπτώματα ὑμῶν.

καὶ ὅταν στήκετε προσευχόμενοι,
ἀφίετε εἴ τι ἔχετε κατά τινος, ἵνα
καὶ ὁ πατὴρ ὑμῶν ὁ ἐν τοῖς
οὐρανοῖς ἀφῇ ὑμῖν τὰ
παραπτώματα ὑμῶν.

C. 18

Matt 6.1-8, 16-18

1   προσέχετε δὲ τὴν δικαιοσύνην ὑμῶν ποιεῖν ἔμπροσθεν τῶν
          ἀνθρώπων πρὸς τὸ θεαθῆναι αὐτοῖς·
          εἰ δὲ μή γε, μισθὸν οὐκ ἔχετε παρὰ τῷ πατρὶ ὑμῶν τῷ ἐν τοῖς
          οὐρανοῖς.

2 A   ὅταν οὖν ποιῇς ἐλεημοσύνην,
    B   μὴ σαλπίσῃς ἔμπροσθεν σου,
    a   ὥσπερ οἱ ὑποκριταὶ ποιοῦσιν ἐν ταῖς συναγωγαῖς καὶ
             ἐν ταῖς ῥύμαις,
    b   ὅπως δοξασθῶσιν ὑπὸ τῶν ἀνθρώπων·
    c   ἀμὴν λέγω ὑμῖν, ἀπέχουσιν τὸν μισθὸν αὐτῶν.
3 A′   σοῦ δὲ ποιοῦντος ἐλεημοσύνην
    B′   μὴ γνώτω ἡ ἀριστερά σου τί ποιεῖ ἡ δεξιά σου,
4 b′   ὅπως ᾖ σου ἡ ἐλεημοσύνη ἐν τῷ κρυπτῷ·
    c′   καὶ ὁ πατήρ σου ὁ βλέπων ἐν τῷ κρυπτῷ ἀποδώσει
             σοι.
5 A   καὶ ὅταν προσεύχησθε,
    B   οὐκ ἔσεσθε
    a   ὡς οἱ ὑποκριταί, ὅτι φιλοῦσιν ἐν ταῖς συναγωγαῖς
             καὶ ἐν ταῖς γωνίαις τῶν πλατειῶν ἑστῶτες
             προσεύχεσθαι,
    b   ὅπως φανῶσιν τοῖς ἀνθρώποις·
    c   ἀμὴν λέγω ὑμῖν, ἀπέχουσιν τὸν μισθὸν αὐτῶν.
6 A′   σὺ δὲ ὅταν προσεύχῃ,
    B′   εἴσελθε εἰς τὸ ταμεῖόν σου καὶ κλείσας τὴν θύραν σου
    b′   πρόσεξαι τῷ πατρί σου τῷ ἐν τῷ κρυπτῷ
    c′   καὶ ὁ πατήρ σου ὁ βλέπων ἐν τῷ κρυπτῷ ἀποδώσει
             σοι.
7 A   προσευχόμενοι δὲ
    B   μὴ βατταλογήσητε
    a   ὥσπερ οἱ ἐθνικοί, δοκοῦσιν γὰρ ὅτι ἐν τῇ πολυλογίᾳ
             αὐτῶν εἰσακουσθήσονται.
8 B′   μὴ οὖν ὁμοιωθῆτε αὐτοῖς·
    c′   οἶδεν γὰρ ὁ πατὴρ ὑμῶν ὧν χρείαν ἔχετε πρὸ τοῦ
             ὑμᾶς αἰτῆσαι αὐτόν.
16 A   ὅταν δὲ νηστεύητε,
    B   μὴ γίνεσθε
    a   ὡς οἱ ὑποκριταὶ σκυθρωποί, ἀφανίζουσιν γὰρ τὰ
             πρόσωπα αὐτῶν
    b   ὅπως φανῶσιν τοῖς ἀνθρώποις νηστεύοντες·
    c   ἀμὴν λέγω ὑμῖν, ἀπέχουσιν τὸν μισθὸν αὐτῶν.

17 Α' σὺ δὲ νηστεύων
    Β' ἄλειψαί σου τὴν κεφαλὴν καὶ τὸ πρόσωπόν σου νίψαι,
18 b'   ὅπως μὴ φανῇς τοῖς ἀνθρώποις νηστεύων ἀλλὰ τῷ
          πατρί σου τῷ ἐν τῷ κρυφαίῳ
    c'   καὶ ὁ πατήρ σου ὁ βλέπων ἐν τῷ κρυφαίῳ
          ἀποδώσει σοι.

C. 19

Tobit 12.9

ἐλεημοσύνη γὰρ ἐκ θανάτου ῥύεται, καὶ αὐτὴ ἀποκαθαριεῖ
πᾶσαν ἁμαρτίαν· οἱ ποιοῦντες ἐλεημοσύνας καὶ δικαιοσύνας
πλήσθησονται ζωῆς·

C. 20

Hypothetical Reconstruction of an 'M' Saying in Matt 6.1

προσέχεις τὴν δικαιοσύνην σου μὴ ποιεῖν ἔμπροσθεν τῶν ἀνθρώπων πρὸς
τὸ θεαθῆναι αὐτοῖς· εἰ δὲ μή γε, μισθὸν οὐκ ἔχεις παρὰ τῷ πατρί σου τῷ
βλέποντι ἐν τῷ κρυπτῷ.

C. 21

Matt 10.1-16	Mark 6.7
καὶ <u>προσκαλεσάμενος τοὺς</u> <u>δώδεκα</u> μαθητὰς αὐτοῦ ἔδωκεν αὐτοῖς ἐξουσίαν πνευμάτων ἀκαθάρτων ὥστε ἐκβάλλειν αὐτὰ καὶ θεραπεύειν πᾶσαν νόσον καὶ πᾶσαν μαλακίαν. τῶν δὲ δώδεκα ἀποστόλων τὰ ὀνόματά ἐστιν ταῦτα· πρῶτος <u>Σίμων</u> ὁ λεγόμενος <u>Πέτρος</u> καὶ Ἀνδρέας ὁ ἀδελφὸς αὐτοῦ, <u>καὶ Ἰάκωβος ὁ τοῦ</u> <u>Σεβεδαίου καὶ Ἰωάννης ὁ</u> <u>ἀδελφὸς αὐτοῦ,</u> Φίλιππος καὶ <u>Βαρθολομαῖος, Θωμᾶς, καὶ Μαθ-</u>	καὶ προσκαλεῖται τοὺς δώδεκα καὶ ἤρξατο αὐτοὺς ἀποστέλλειν δύο δύο καὶ ἐδίδου αὐτοῖς ἐξουσίαν τῶν πνευμάτων τῶν ἀκαθάρτων, **Mark 3.13-19** καὶ ἀναβαίνει εἰς τὸ ὄρος καὶ προσκαλεῖται οὓς ἤθελεν αὐτός, καὶ ἀπῆλθον πρὸς αὐτόν. καὶ ἐποίησεν δώδεκα οὓς καὶ ἀποστόλους ὠνόμασεν ἵνα ὦσιν

θαῖος ὁ τελώνης, Ἰάκωβος ὁ τοῦ Ἀλφαίου καὶ Θαδδαῖος, Σίμων ὁ Καναναῖος καὶ Ἰούδας ὁ Ἰσκαριώτης ὁ καὶ παραδοὺς αὐτόν.

Τούτους τοὺς δώδεκα ἀπέστειλεν ὁ Ἰησοῦς παραγγείλας αὐτοῖς λέγων· εἰς ὁδὸν ἐθνῶν μὴ ἀπέλθητε καὶ εἰς πόλιν Σαμαριτῶν μὴ εἰσέλθητε· πορεύεσθε δὲ μᾶλλον πρὸς τὰ πρόβατα τὰ ἀπολωλότα οἴκου Ἰσραήλ. πορευόμενοι δὲ κηρύσσετε λέγοντες ὅτι ἤγγικεν ἡ βασιλεία τῶν οὐρανῶν. ἀσθενοῦντας θεραπεύετε, νεκροὺς ἐγείρετε, λεπροὺς καθαρίζετε, δαιμόνια ἐκβάλλετε· δωρεὰν ἐλάβετε, δωρεὰν δότε. Μὴ κτήσησθε χρυσὸν μηδὲ ἄργυρον μηδὲ χαλκὸν εἰς τὰς ζώνας ὑμῶν, μὴ πήραν εἰς ὁδὸν μηδὲ δύο χιτῶνας μηδὲ ὑποδήματα μηδὲ ῥάβδον· ἄξιος γὰρ ὁ ἐργάτης τῆς τροφῆς αὐτοῦ. εἰς ἣν δ᾽ ἂν πόλιν ἢ κώμην εἰσέλθητε, ἐξετάσατε τίς ἐν αὐτῇ ἄξιός ἐστιν· κἀκεῖ μείνατε ἕως ἂν ἐξέλθητε. εἰσερχόμενοι δὲ εἰς τὴν οἰκίαν ἀσπάσασθε αὐτήν· καὶ ἐὰν μὲν ᾖ

μετ᾽ αὐτοῦ καὶ ἵνα ἀποστέλλῃ αὐτοὺς κηρύσσειν καὶ ἔχειν ἐξουσίαν ἐκβάλλειν τὰ δαιμόνια· καὶ ἐποίησεν τοὺς δώδεκα, καὶ ἐπέθηκεν ὄνομα τῷ Σίμωνι Πέτρον, καὶ Ἰάκωβον τὸν τοῦ Ζεβεδαίου καὶ Ἰωάννην τὸν ἀδελφὸν τοῦ Ἰακώβου καὶ ἐπέθηκεν αὐτοῖς ὀνόματα Βοανηργές, ὅ ἐστιν υἱοὶ βροντῆς· καὶ Ἀνδρέαν καὶ Φίλιππον καὶ Βαρθολομαῖον καὶ Μαθθαῖον καὶ Θωμᾶν καὶ Ἰάκωβον τὸν τοῦ Ἀλφαίου καὶ Θαδδαῖον καὶ Σίμωνα τὸν Καναναῖον καὶ Ἰούδαν Ἰσκαριώθ, ὃς καὶ παρέδωκεν αὐτόν.

Mark 6.12-13

καὶ ἐξελθόντες ἐκήρυξαν ἵνα μετανοῶσιν, καὶ δαιμόνια πολλὰ ἐξέβαλλον, καὶ ἤλειφον ἐλαίῳ πολλοὺς ἀρρώστους καὶ ἐθεράπευον.

Mark 6.8-10

καὶ παρήγγειλεν αὐτοῖς ἵνα μηδὲν αἴρωσιν εἰς ὁδὸν εἰ μὴ ῥάβδον μόνον, μὴ εἰς τὴν ζώνην χαλκόν, ἀλλὰ ὑποδεδεμένους σανδάλια, καὶ μὴ ἐνδύσησθε δύο χιτῶνας. καὶ ἔλεγεν αὐτοῖς· ὅπου ἐὰν εἰσέλθητε εἰς οἰκίαν, ἐκεῖ μένετε ἕως ἂν ἐξέλθητε ἐκεῖθεν.

Mark 6.11

καὶ ὃς ἂν τόπος μὴ δέξηται ὑμᾶς

ἡ οἰκία ἀξία, ἐλθάτω ἡ εἰρήνη
ὑμῶν ἐπ᾿ αὐτήν, ἐὰν δὲ μὴ ᾖ
ἀξία, ἡ εἰρήνη ὑμῶν πρὸς ὑμᾶς
ἐπιστραφήτω. <u>καὶ ὃς ἂν μὴ</u>
<u>δέξηται ὑμᾶς μηδὲ ἀκούσῃ</u> τούς
λόγους <u>ὑμῶν, ἐξερχόμενοι ἔξω</u>
τῆς οἰκίας ἢ τῆς πόλεως ἐκείνης
<u>ἐκτινάξατε τὸν κονιορτὸν τῶν</u>
<u>ποδῶν ὑμῶν.</u> ἀμὴν λέγω
ὑμῖν, ἀνεκτότερον ἔσται γῇ
Σοδόμων καὶ Γομόρρων ἐν ἡμέρᾳ
κρίσεως ἢ τῇ πόλει ἐκείνῃ.
    Ἰδοὺ ἐγὼ ἀποστέλλω ὑμᾶς ὡς
πρόβατα ἐν μέσῳ λύκων· γίνεσθε
οὖν φρόνιμοι ὡς οἱ ὄφεις καὶ
ἀκέραιοι ὡς αἱ περιστεραί.

μηδὲ ἀκούσωσιν ὑμῶν,
ἐκπορευόμενοι ἐκεῖθεν ἐκτινάξατε
τὸν χοῦν τὸν ὑποκάτω τῶν
ποδῶν ὑμῶν εἰς μαρτύριον
αὐτοῖς.

Matt 10.1-16

    Τούτους τοὺς δώδεκα ἀπέστειλεν
ὁ Ἰησοῦς παραγγείλας αὐτοῖς
λέγων· εἰς ὁδὸν ἐθνῶν μὴ ἀπέλθητε
καὶ εἰς πόλιν Σαμαριτῶν μὴ
εἰσέλθητε· πορεύεσθε δὲ μᾶλλον
πρὸς τὰ πρόβατα τὰ ἀπολωλότα
οἴκου Ἰσραήλ. πορευόμενοι δὲ
κηρύσσετε <u>λέγοντες ὅτι ἤγγικεν</u>
<u>ἡ βασιλεία τῶν οὐρανῶν.</u>
<u>ἀσθενοῦντας</u> θεραπεύετε, νεκρούς
ἐγείρετε, λεπροὺς καθαρίζετε,
δαιμόνια ἐκβάλλετε· δωρεὰν
ἐλάβετε, δωρεὰν δότε. <u>Μὴ</u>
<u>κτήσησθε χρυσὸν μηδὲ ἄργυρον</u>
<u>μηδὲ χαλκὸν εἰς τὰς ζώνας ὑμῶν,</u>
<u>μὴ πήραν</u> εἰς ὁδὸν μηδὲ δύο
χιτῶνας μηδὲ ὑποδήματα μηδὲ
ῥάβδον· ἄξιος γὰρ ὁ ἐργάτης τῆς
<u>τροφῆς αὐτοῦ.</u> εἰς ἣν δ᾿ ἂν πόλιν
ἢ κώμην εἰσέλθητε,
ἐξετάσατε τίς ἐν αὐτῇ ἄξιός
ἐστιν· κἀκεῖ μείνατε ἕως ἂν

Luke 10.9

καὶ θεραπεύετε τοὺς ἐν αὐτῇ
ἀσθενεῖς καὶ λέγετε αὐτοῖς·
ἤγγικεν ἐφ᾿ ὑμᾶς ἡ βασιλεία τοῦ
θεοῦ.

Luke 10.4-8
μὴ βαστάζετε βαλλάντιον, μὴ
πήραν, μὴ ὑποδήματα, καὶ
μηδένα κατὰ τὴν ὁδὸν ἀσπάσησθε.
εἰς ἣν δ᾿ ἂν εἰσέλθητε οἰκίαν,
πρῶτον λέγετε· εἰρήνη τῷ οἴκῳ
τούτῳ. καὶ ἐὰν ἐκεῖ ᾖ υἱὸς
εἰρήνης, ἐπαναπαήσεται ἐπ᾿ αὐτὸν
ἡ εἰρήνη ὑμων· εἰ δὲ μή γε, ἐφ᾿
ὑμᾶς ἀνακάμψαι. ἐν αὐτῇ δὲ τῇ
οἰκίᾳ μένετε ἐσθίοντες καὶ
πίνοντες τὰ παρ᾿ αὐτῶν· ἄξιος

ἐξέλθητε. εἰσερχόμενοι δὲ εἰς τὴν
οἰκίαν ἀσπάσασθε αὐτήν· καὶ
ἐὰν μὲν ᾖ ἡ οἰκία ἀξία, ἐλθάτω ἡ
εἰρήνη ὑμῶν ἐπ᾽ αὐτην, ἐὰν δὲ
μὴ ᾖ ἀξία, ἡ εἰρήνη ὑμῶν πρὸς
ὑμᾶς ἐπιστραφήτω. καὶ ὃς ἂν μὴ
δέξηται ὑμᾶς μηδὲ ἀκούσῃ τοὺς
λόγους ὑμῶν, ἐξερχόμενοι ἔξω
τῆς οἰκίας ἢ τῆς πόλεως ἐκείνης
ἐκτινάξατε τὸν κονιορτὸν τῶν
ποδῶν ὑμῶν. ἀμὴν λέγω ὑμῖν,
ἀνεκτότερον ἔσται γῇ Σοδόμων
καὶ Γομόρρων ἐν ἡμέρᾳ κρίσεως
ἢ τῇ πόλει ἐκείνῃ.
    Ἰδοὺ ἐγὼ ἀποστέλλω ὑμᾶς ὡς
πρόβατα ἐν μέσῳ λύκων· γίνεσθε
οὖν φρόνιμοι ὡς οἱ ὄφεις καὶ
ἀκέραιοι ὡς αἱ περιστεραί.

γὰρ ὁ ἐργάτης τοῦ μισθοῦ αὐτοῦ.
μὴ μεταβαίνετε ἐξ οἰκίας εἰς
οἰκίαν. καὶ εἰς ἣν ἂν πόλιν
εἰσέρχησθε καὶ δέχωνται ὑμᾶς,
ἐσθίετε τὰ παρατιθέμενα ὑμῖν.

Luke 10.10-12

εἰς ἣν δ᾽ ἂν πόλιν εἰσέλθητε καὶ
μὴ δέχωνται ὑμᾶς, ἐξελθόντες εἰς
τὰς πλατείας αὐτῆς εἴπατε· καὶ
τὸν κονιορτὸν τὸν κολληθέντα
ἡμῖν ἐκ τῆς πόλεως ὑμῶν εἰς
τοὺς πόδας ἀπομασσόμεθα ὑμῖν·
πλὴν τοῦτο γινώσκετε ὅτι ἤγγικεν
ἡ βασιλεία τοῦ θεοῦ. λέγω ὑμῖν
ὅτι Σοδόμοις ἐν τῇ ἡμέρα ἐκείνῃ
ἀνεκτότερον ἔσται ἢ τῇ πόλει
ἐκείνῃ.

Luke 10.3

ὑπάγετε· ἰδοὺ ἀποστέλλω ὑμᾶς
ὡς ἄρνας ἐν μέσῳ λύκων.

C. 22

Matt 10.17-25	Mark 13.9-13

Προσέχετε δὲ ἀπὸ τῶν ἀνθρώπων·
παραδώσουσιν γὰρ ὑμᾶς εἰς
συνέδρια καὶ ἐν ταῖς συναγωγαῖς
αὐτῶν μαστιγώσουσιν ὑμᾶς· καὶ
ἐπὶ ἡγεμόνας δὲ καὶ βασιλεῖς
ἀχθήσεσθε ἕνεκεν ἐμοῦ εἰς
μαρτύριον αὐτοῖς καὶ τοῖς ἔθνεσιν.
ὅταν δὲ παραδῶσιν ὑμᾶς, μὴ
μεριμνήσητε πῶς ἢ τί λαλήσητε·
δοθήσεται γὰρ ὑμῖν ἐν ἐκείνῃ τῇ
ὥρᾳ τί λαλήσητε· οὐ γὰρ ὑμεῖς
ἐστε οἱ λαλοῦντες ἀλλὰ τὸ
πνεῦμα τοῦ πατρὸς ὑμῶν τὸ
λαλοῦν ἐν ὑμῖν.

Παραδώσει δὲ ἀδελφὸς ἀδελφὸν
εἰς θάνατον καὶ πατὴρ τέκνον,
καὶ ἐπαναστήσονται τέκνα ἐπὶ
γονεῖς καὶ θανατώσουσιν αὐτούς,
καὶ ἔσεσθε μισούμενοι ὑπὸ
πάντων διὰ τὸ ὄνομά μου· ὁ δὲ
ὑπομείνας εἰς τέλος οὗτος
σωθήσεται.

Ὅταν δὲ διώκωσιν ὑμᾶς ἐν τῇ
πόλει ταύτῃ, φεύγετε εἰς τὴν
ἑτέραν· ἀμὴν γὰρ λέγω ὑμῖν, οὐ
μὴ τελέσητε τὰς πόλεις τοῦ
Ἰσραὴλ ἕως ἂν ἔλθῃ ὁ υἱὸς τοῦ
ἀνθρώπου.

Οὐκ ἔστιν μαθητὴς ὑπὲρ τὸν
διδάσκαλον οὐδὲ δοῦλος ὑπὲρ
τὸν κύριον αὐτοῦ. ἀρκετὸν τῷ
μαθητῇ ἵνα γένηται ὡς ὁ
διδάσκαλος αὐτοῦ καὶ ὁ δοῦλος
ὡς ὁ κύριος αὐτοῦ. εἰ τὸν
οἰκοδεσπότην Βεελζεβοὺλ
ἐπεκάλεσαν, πόσῳ μᾶλλον τοὺς
οἰκιακοὺς αὐτοῦ.

Βλέπετε δὲ ὑμεῖς ἑαυτούς·
παραδώσουσιν ὑμᾶς εἰς συνέδρια
καὶ εἰς συναγωγὰς δαρήσεσθε
καὶ ἐπὶ ἡγεμόνων καὶ βασιλέων
σταθήσεσθε ἕνεκεν ἐμοῦ εἰς
μαρτύριον αὐτοῖς. καὶ εἰς πάντα
τὰ ἔθνη πρῶτον δεῖ κηρυχθῆναι
τὸ εὐαγγέλιον. καὶ ὅταν ἄγωσιν
ὑμᾶς παραδιδόντες, μὴ
προμεριμνᾶτε τί λαλήστε, ἀλλ᾽ ὃ
ἐὰν δοθῇ ὑμῖν ἐν ἐκείνῃ τῇ ὥρᾳ
τοῦτο λαλεῖτε· οὐ γάρ ἐστε ὑμεῖς
οἱ λαλοῦντες ἀλλὰ τὸ πνεῦμα τὸ
ἅγιον. καὶ παραδώσει ἀδελφὸς
ἀδελφὸν εἰς θάνατον καὶ πατὴρ
τέκνον, καὶ ἐπαναστήσονται
τέκνα ἐπὶ γονεῖς καὶ
θανατώσουσιν αὐτούς· καὶ ἔσεσθε
μισούμενοι ὑπὸ πάντων διὰ τὸ
ὄνομά μου. ὁ δὲ ὑπομείνας εἰς
τέλος οὗτος σωθήσεται.

Luke 6.40

οὐκ ἔστιν μαθητὴς ὑπὲρ τὸν
διδάσκαλον, κατηρτισμένος δὲ
πᾶς ἔσται ὡς ὁ διδάσκαλος
αὐτοῦ.

C. 23

Matt 10.26-39

Luke 12.2-9

Μὴ οὖν φοβηθῆτε αὐτούς·
οὐδὲν γάρ ἐστιν κεκαλυμμένον ὃ
οὐκ ἀποκαλυφθήσεται καὶ
κρυπτὸν ὃ οὐ γνωσθήσεται. ὃ
λέγω ὑμῖν ἐν τῇ σκοτίᾳ εἴπατε ἐν
τῷ φωτί, καὶ ὃ εἰς τὸ οὖς ἀκούετε
κηρύξατε ἐπὶ τῶν δωμάτων. καὶ
μὴ φοβεῖσθε ἀπὸ τῶν
ἀποκτεννόντων τὸ σῶμα, τὴν δὲ
ψυχὴν μὴ δυναμένων ἀποκτεῖναι·
φοβεῖσθε δὲ μᾶλλον τὸν
δυνάμενον καὶ ψυχὴν καὶ σῶμα
ἀπολέσαι ἐν γεέννῃ. οὐχὶ δύο
στρουθία ἀσσαρίου πωλεῖται;
καὶ ἓν ἐξ αὐτῶν οὐ πεσεῖται ἐπὶ
τὴν γῆν ἄνευ τοῦ πατρὸς ὑμῶν.
ὑμῶν δὲ καὶ αἱ τρίχες τῆς
κεφαλῆς πᾶσαι ἠριθμημέναι εἰσίν.
μὴ οὖν φοβεῖσθε πολλῶν
στρουθίων διαφέρετε ὑμεῖς.

Πᾶς οὖν ὅστις ὁμολογήσει ἐν
ἐμοὶ ἔμπροσθεν τῶν ἀνθρώπων,
ὁμολογήσω κἀγὼ ἐν αὐτῷ
ἔμπροσθεν τοῦ πατρός μου τοῦ
ἐν τοῖς οὐρανοῖς· ὅστις δ᾿ ἂν
ἀρνήσηταί με ἔμπροσθεν τῶν
ἀνθρώπων, ἀρνήσομαι κἀγὼ
αὐτὸν ἔμπροσθεν τοῦ πατρός μου
τοῦ ἐν τοῖς οὐρανοῖς.

Οὐδὲν δὲ συγκεκαλυμμένον
ἐστὶν ὃ οὐκ ἀποκαλυφθήσεται
καὶ κρυπτὸν ὃ οὐ γνωσθήσεται.
ἀνθ᾿ ὧν ὅσα ἐν τῇ σκοτίᾳ εἴπατε
ἐν τῷ φωτὶ ἀκουσθήσεται καὶ ὃ
πρὸς τὸ οὖς ἐλαλήσατε ἐν τοῖς
ταμείοις κηρυχθήσεται ἐπὶ τῶν
δωμάτων.
Λέγω δὲ ὑμῖν τοῖς φίλοις μου,
μὴ φοβηθῆτε ἀπὸ τῶν
ἀποκτεινόντων τὸ σῶμα καὶ
μετὰ ταῦτα μὴ ἐχόντων
περισσότερόν τι ποιῆσαι.
ὑποδείξω δὲ ὑμῖν τίνα φοβηθῆτε·
φοβήθητε τὸν μετὰ τὸ ἀποκτεῖναι
ἔχοντα ἐξουσίαν ἐμβαλεῖν εἰς
τὴν γέενναν. ναὶ λέγω ὑμῖν,
τοῦτον φοβήθητε. οὐχὶ πέντε
στρουθία πωλοῦνται ἀσσαρίων
δύο; καὶ ἓν ἐξ αὐτῶν οὐκ ἔστιν
ἐπιλελησμένον ἐνώπιον τοῦ θεοῦ.
ἀλλὰ καὶ αἱ τρίχες τῆς κεφαλῆς
ὑμῶν πᾶσαι ἠρίθμηνται. μὴ
φοβεῖσθε· πολλῶν στρουθίων
διαφέρετε.
Λέγω δὲ ὑμῖν, πᾶς ὃς ἂν
ὁμολογήσῃ ἐν ἐμοὶ ἔμπροσθεν
τῶν ἀνθρώπων, καὶ ὁ υἱὸς τοῦ
ἀνθρώπου ὁμολογήσει ἐν αὐτῷ
ἔμπροσθεν τῶν ἀγγέλων τοῦ
θεοῦ· ὁ δὲ ἀρνησάμενός με
ἐνώπιον τῶν ἀνθρώπων
ἀπαρνηθήσεται ἐνώπιον τῶν
ἀγγέλων τοῦ θεοῦ.

Μὴ νομίσητε ὅτι ἦλθον βαλεῖν εἰρήνην ἐπὶ τὴν γῆν· οὐκ ἦλθον βαλεῖν εἰρήνην ἀλλὰ μάχαιραν. ἦλθον γὰρ διχάσαι ἄνθρωπον κατὰ τοῦ πατρὸς αὐτοῦ καὶ θυγατέρα κατὰ τῆς μητρὸς αὐτῆς καὶ νύμφην κατὰ τῆς πενθερᾶς αὐτῆς, καὶ ἐχθροὶ τοῦ ἀνθρώπου οἱ οἰκιακοὶ αὐτοῦ.

Ὁ φιλῶν πατέρα ἢ μητέρα ὑπὲρ ἐμὲ οὐκ ἔστιν μου ἄξιος· καὶ ὁ φιλῶν υἱὸν ἢ θυγατέρα ὑπὲρ ἐμὲ οὐκ ἔστιν μου ἄξιος· καὶ ὃς οὐ λαμβάνει τὸν σταυρὸν αὐτοῦ καὶ ἀκολουθεῖ ὀπίσω μου, οὐκ ἔστιν μου ἄξιος. ὁ εὑρὼν τὴν ψυχὴν αὐτοῦ ἀπολέσει αὐτήν, καὶ ὁ ἀπολέσας τὴν ψυχὴν αὐτοῦ ἕνεκεν ἐμοῦ εὑρήσει αὐτήν.

Luke 12.51-53

δοκεῖτε ὅτι εἰρήνην παρεγενόμην δοῦναι ἐν τῇ γῇ; οὐχί, λέγω ὑμῖν, ἀλλ᾿ ἢ διαμερισμόν. ἔσονται γὰρ ἀπὸ τοῦ νῦν πέντε ἐν ἑνὶ οἴκῳ διαμεμερισμένοι, τρεῖς ἐπὶ δυσὶν καὶ δύο ἐπὶ τρισίν, διαμερισθήσονται πατὴρ ἐπὶ υἱῷ καὶ υἱὸς ἐπὶ πατρί, μήτηρ ἐπὶ τὴν θυγατέρα καὶ θυγάτηρ ἐπὶ τὴν μητέρα, πενθερὰ ἐπὶ τὴν νύμφην αὐτῆς καὶ νύμφη ἐπὶ τὴν πενθεράν.

Luke 14.26-27

εἴ τις ἔρχεται πρός με καὶ οὐ μισεῖ τὸν πατέρα ἑαυτοῦ καὶ τὴν μητέρα καὶ τὴν γυναῖκα καὶ τὰ τέκνα καὶ τοὺς ἀδελφοὺς καὶ τὰς ἀδελφὰς ἔτι τε καὶ τὴν ψυχὴν ἑαυτοῦ, οὐ δύναται εἶναί μου μαθητής. ὅστις οὐ βαστάζει τὸν σταυρὸν ἑαυτοῦ καὶ ἔρχεται ὀπίσω μου, οὐ δύναται εἶναί μου μαθητής.

Luke 17.33

ὃς ἐὰν ζητήσῃ τὴν ψυχὴν αὐτοῦ περιποιήσασθαι ἀπολέσει αὐτήν, ὃς δ᾿ ἂν ἀπολέσῃ ζῳογονήσει αὐτήν.

C. 24

Matt 10.40-42

Ὁ δεχόμενος ὑμᾶς ἐμὲ δέχεται, καὶ ὁ ἐμὲ δεχόμενος δέχεται τὸν ἀποστείλαντά με. ὁ δεχόμενος προφήτην εἰς ὄνομα προφήτου μισθὸν προφήτου λήμψεται, καὶ ὁ δεχόμενος δίκαιον εἰς ὄνομα δικαίου μισθὸν δικαίου λήμψεται. καὶ ὃς ἂν ποτίσῃ ἕνα τῶν μικρῶν τούτων ποτήριον ψυχροῦ μόνον εἰς ὄνομα μαθητοῦ, ἀμὴν λέγω ὑμῖν, οὐ μὴ ἀπολέσῃ τὸν μισθὸν αὐτοῦ.

Mark 9.37, 41

ὃς ἂν ἓν τῶν τοιούτων παιδίων δέξηται ἐπὶ τῷ ὀνόματί μου, ἐμὲ δέχεται· καὶ ὃς ἂν ἐμὲ δέχηται, οὐκ ἐμὲ δέχεται ἀλλὰ τὸν ἀποστείλαντά με.

Ὃς γὰρ ἂν ποτίσῃ ὑμᾶς ποτήριον ὕδατος ἐν ὀνόματι ὅτι Χριστοῦ ἐστε, ἀμὴν λέγω ὑμῖν ὅτι οὐ ἀπολέσῃ τὸν μισθὸν αὐτοῦ.

C. 25

Matt 23.1-12

Τότε ὁ ᾿Ιησοῦς ἐλάλησεν τοῖς ὄχλοις καὶ τοῖς μαθηταῖς αὐτοῦ λέγων· ἐπὶ τῆς Μωϋσέως καθέδρας ἐκάθισαν οἱ γραμματεῖς καὶ οἱ Φαρισαῖοι. πάντα οὖν ὅσα ἐὰν εἴπωσιν ὑμῖν ποιήσατε καὶ τηρεῖτε, κατὰ δὲ τὰ ἔργα αὐτῶν μὴ ποιεῖτε· λέγουσιν γὰρ καὶ οὐ ποιοῦσιν. δεσμεύουσιν δὲ φορτία βαρέα καὶ δυσβάστακτα καὶ ἐπιτιθέασιν ἐπὶ τοὺς ὤμους τῶν ἀνθρώπων, αὐτοὶ δὲ τῷ δακτύλῳ αὐτῶν οὐ θέλουσιν κινῆσαι αὐτά. πάντα δὲ τὰ ἔργα αὐτῶν ποιοῦσιν πρὸς τὸ θεαθῆναι τοῖς ἀνθρώποις· πλατύνουσιν γὰρ τὰ φυλακτήρια αὐτῶν καὶ μεγαλύνουσιν τὰ κράσπεδα, φιλοῦσιν δὲ τὴν πρωτοκλισίαν ἐν τοῖς δείπνοις

Luke 11.46

ὁ δὲ εἶπεν· καὶ ὑμῖν τοῖς νομικοῖς οὐαί, ὅτι φορτίζετε τοὺς ἀνθρώπους φορτία δυσβάστακτα, καὶ αὐτοὶ ἑνὶ τῶν δακτύλων ὑμῶν οὐ προσψαύετε τοῖς φορτίοις.

Mark 12.38-39

Καὶ ἐν τῇ διδαχῇ αὐτοῦ ἔλεγεν· βλέπετε ἀπὸ τῶν

. . .

καὶ τὰς πρωτοκαθεδρίας ἐν ταῖς
συναγωγαῖς. καὶ τοὺς ἀσπασμοὺς
ἐν ταῖς ἀγοραῖς καὶ καλεῖσθαι
ὑπὸ τῶν ἀνθρώπων ῥαββί.

γραμματέων τῶν θελόντων ἐν
στολαῖς περιπατεῖν καὶ
ἀσπασμοὺς ἐν ταῖς ἀγοραῖς καὶ
πρωτοκαθεδρίας ἐν ταῖς
συναγωγαῖς καὶ πρωτοκλισίας ἐν
τοῖς δείπνοις,

Luke 11.43

Οὐαὶ ὑμῖν τοῖς Φαρισαίοις, ὅτι
ἀγαπᾶτε τὴν πρωτοκαθεδρίαν ἐν
ταῖς συναγωγαῖς καὶ τοὺς
ἀσπασμοὺς ἐν ταῖς ἀγοραῖς.

Ὑμεῖς δὲ μὴ κληθῆτε ῥαββί·
εἷς γάρ ἐστιν ὑμῶν ὁ διδάσκαλος,
πάντες δὲ ὑμεῖς ἀδελφοί ἐστε.
καὶ πατέρα μὴ καλέσητε ὑμῶν
ἐπὶ τῆς γῆς, εἷς γάρ ἐστιν ὑμῶν ὁ
πατὴρ ὁ οὐράνιος. μηδὲ κληθῆτε
καθηγηταί, ὅτι καθηγητὴς ὑμῶν
ἐστιν εἷς ὁ Χριστός. ὁ δὲ μείζων
ὑμῶν ἔσται ὑμῶν διάκονος. ὅστις
δὲ ὑψώσει ἑαυτὸν ταπεινωθήσεται
καὶ ὅστις ταπεινώσει ἑαυτὸν
ὑψωθήσεται.

Mark 10.43

οὐχ οὕτως δέ ἐστιν ἐν ὑμῖν, ἀλλ᾽
ὃς ἂν θέλῃ μέγας γενέσθαι ἐν
ὑμῖν ἔσται ὑμῶν διάκονος,

Luke 14.11

ὅτι πᾶς ὁ ὑψῶν ἑαυτὸν
ταπεινωθήσεται, καὶ ὁ ταπεινῶν
ἑαυτὸν ὑψωθήσεται.

C. 26

3(a) πάντα οὖν ὅσα ἐὰν εἴπωσιν ὑμῖν ποιήσατε καὶ τηρεῖτε,
 (b) κατὰ δὲ τὰ ἔργα αὐτῶν μὴ ποιεῖτε· λέγουσιν γὰρ καὶ οὐ ποιοῦσιν.
5(a) πάντα δὲ τὰ ἔργα αὐτῶν ποιοῦσιν πρὸς τὸ θεαθῆναι τοῖς ἀνθρώποις·
 (b) πλατύνουσιν γὰρ τὰ φυλακτήρια αὐτῶν καὶ μεγαλύνουσιν τὰ
     κράσπεδα,

C. 27

Matt 23.8-10

(8) ὑμεῖς δὲ μὴ κληθῆτε ῥαββί· εἷς γάρ ἐστιν ὑμῶν ὁ διδάσκαλος, πάντες
    δὲ ὑμεῖς ἀδελφοί ἐστε.
(9) καὶ πατέρα μὴ καλέσητε ὑμῶν ἐπὶ τῆς γῆς, εἷς γάρ ἐστιν ὑμῶν ὁ
    πατὴρ ὁ οὐράνιος.
(10) μηδὲ κληθῆτε καθηγηταί, ὅτι καθηγητὴς ὑμῶν ἐστιν εἷς ὁ Χριστός.

A Hypothetical Reconstruction of the M Saying:

ὑμεῖς δὲ μὴ κληθῆτε ῥαββί· εἷς γάρ ἐστιν ὑμῶν ὁ διδάσκαλος. καὶ πατέρα
μὴ καλέσητε ὑμῶν, εἷς γάρ ἐστιν ὑμῶν ὁ πατήρ. μηδὲ κληθῆτε καθηγηταί,
εἷς γάρ ἐστιν ὑμῶν ὁ καθηγητής.

C. 28

Matt 23.13-33   Luke 11.52

Οὐαὶ δὲ ὑμῖν, γραμματεῖς καὶ   Οὐαὶ ὑμῖν τοῖς νομικοῖς, ὅτι ἤρατε
Φαρισαῖοι ὑποκριταί, ὅτι κλείετε   τὴν κλεῖδα τῆς γνήσεως· αὐτοὶ
τὴν βασιλείαν τῶν οὐρανῶν   οὐκ εἰσήλθατε καὶ τοὺς
ἔμπροσθεν τῶν ἀνθρώπων· ὑμεῖς   εἰσερχομένους ἐκωλύσατε.
γὰρ οὐκ εἰσέρχεσθε οὐδὲ τοὺς
εἰσερχομένους ἀφίετε εἰσελθεῖν.
Οὐαὶ ὑμῖν, γραμματεῖς καὶ
Φαρισαῖοι ὑποκριταί, ὅτι περιάγετε
τὴν θάλασσαν καὶ τὴν ξηρὰν
ποιῆσαι ἕνα προσήλυτον, καὶ
ὅταν γένηται ποιεῖτε αὐτὸν υἱὸν
γεέννης διπλότερον ὑμῶν.

Οὐαὶ ὑμῖν, ὁδηγοὶ τυφλοὶ οἱ
λέγοντες· ὃς ἂν ὀμόσῃ ἐν τῷ
ναῷ, οὐδέν ἐστιν· ὃς δ᾽ ἂν ὀμόσῃ
ἐν τῷ χρυσῷ τοῦ ναοῦ, ὀφείλει.
μωροὶ καὶ τυφλοί, τίς γὰρ μείζων
ἐστίν, ὁ χρυσὸς ἢ ὁ ναὸς ὁ
ἁγιάσας τὸν χρυσόν; καὶ ὃς ἂν
ὀμόσῃ ἐν τῷ θυσιαστηρίῳ, οὐδέν
ἐστιν· ὃς δ᾽ ἂν ὀμόσῃ ἐν τῷ
δώρῳ τῷ ἐπάνω αὐτοῦ, ὀφείλει.
τυφλοί, τί γὰρ μεῖζον τὸ δῶρον ἢ
τὸ θυσιαστήριον τὸ ἁγιάζον τὸ
δῶρον; ὁ οὖν ὀμόσας ἐν τῷ
θυσιαστηρίῳ ὀμνύει ἐν αὐτῷ καὶ
ἐν πᾶσι τοῖς ἐπάνω αὐτοῦ· καὶ ὁ
ὀμόσας ἐν τῷ ναῷ ὀμνύει ἐν
αὐτῷ καὶ ἐν τῷ κατοικοῦντι
αὐτόν, καὶ ὁ ὀμόσας ἐν τῷ
οὐρανῷ ὀμνύει ἐν τῷ θρόνῳ τοῦ
θεοῦ καὶ ἐν τῷ καθημένῳ ἐπάνω
αὐτοῦ.
Οὐαὶ ὑμῖν, γραμματεῖς καὶ
Φαρισαῖοι ὑποκριταί, ὅτι
ἀποδεκατοῦτε τὸ ἡδύοσμον καὶ
τὸ ἄνηθον καὶ τὸ κύμινον καὶ
ἀφήκατε τὰ βαρύτερα τοῦ νόμου,
τὴν κρίσιν καὶ τὸ ἔλεος καὶ τὴν
πίστιν· ταῦτα δὲ ἔδει ποιῆσαι
κἀκεῖνα μὴ ἀφιέναι. ὁδηγοὶ
τυφλοί, οἱ διϋλίζοντες τὸν
κώνοπα, τὴν δὲ κάμηλον
καταπίνοντες.
Οὐαὶ ὑμῖν, γραμματεῖς καὶ
Φαρισαῖοι ὑμοκριταί, ὅτι
καθαρίζετε τὸ ἔξωθεν τοῦ
ποτηρίου καὶ τῆς παροψίδος,
ἔσωθεν δὲ γέμουσιν ἐξ ἁρπαγῆς
καὶ ἀκρασίας. Φαρισαῖε τυφλέ,
καθάρισον πρῶτον τὸ ἐντὸς τοῦ
ποτηρίου, ἵνα γένηται καὶ τὸ

Luke 11.42

ἀλλὰ οὐαὶ ὑμῖν τοῖς Φαρισαίοις,
ὅτι ἀποδεκατοῦτε τὸ ἡδύοσμον
καὶ τὸ πήγανον καὶ πᾶν λάχανον
καὶ παρέρχεσθε τὴν κρίσιν καὶ
τὴν ἀγάπην τοῦ θεοῦ· ταῦτα δὲ
ἔδει ποιῆσαι κἀκεῖνα μὴ παρεῖναι.

Luke 11.39-41

εἶπεν δὲ ὁ κύριος πρὸς αὐτόν·
νῦν ὑμεῖς οἱ Φαρισαῖοι τὸ ἔξωθεν
τοῦ ποτηρίου καὶ τοῦ πίνακος
καθαρίζετε, τὸ δὲ ἔσωθεν ὑμῶν
γέμει ἁρπαγῆς καὶ πονηρίας.
ἄφρονες, οὐχ ὁ ποιήσας τὸ ἔξωθεν
καὶ τὸ ἔσωθεν ἐποίησεν; πλὴν τὰ
ἐνόντα δότε ἐλεημοσύνην, καὶ
ἰδοὺ πάντα καθαρὰ ὑμῖν ἐστιν.

ἐκτὸς αὐτοῦ καθαρόν.

Οὐαὶ ὑμῖν γραμματεῖς καὶ
Φαρισαῖοι ὑποκριταί, ὅτι
παρομοιάζετε τάφοις
κεκονιαμένοις, οἵτινες ἔξωθεν
μὲν φαίνονται ὡραῖοι, ἔσωθεν δὲ
γέμουσιν ὀστέων νεκρῶν καὶ
πάσης ἀκαθαρσίας. οὕτως καὶ
ὑμεῖς ἔξωθεν μὲν φαίνεσθε τοῖς
ἀνθρώποις δίκαιοι, ἔσωθεν δέ
ἐστε μεστοὶ ὑποκρίσεως καὶ
ἀνομίας.

Οὐαὶ ὑμῖν, γραμματεῖς καὶ
Φαρισαῖοι ὑποκριταί, ὅτι
οἰκοδομεῖτε τοὺς τάφους τῶν
προφητῶν καὶ κοσμεῖτε τὰ
μνημεῖα τῶν δικαίων, καὶ λέγετε·
εἰ ἤμεθα ἐν ταῖς ἡμέραις τῶν
πατέρων ἡμῶν, οὐκ ἂν ἤμεθα
αὐτῶν κοινωνοὶ ἐν τῷ αἵματι τῶν
προφητῶν. ὥστε μαρτυρεῖτε
ἑαυτοῖς ὅτι υἱοί ἐστε τῶν
φονευσάντων τοὺς προφήτας. καὶ
ὑμεῖς πληρώσατε τὸ μέτρον τῶν
πατέρων ὑμῶν. ὄφεις, γεννήματα
ἐχιδνῶν, πῶς φύγητε ἀπὸ τῆς
κρίσεως τῆς γεέννης;

Luke 11.44

Οὐαὶ ὑμῖν, ὅτι ἐστὲ ὡς τὰ μνημεῖα
τὰ ἄδηλα, καὶ οἱ ἄνθρωποι οἱ
περιπατοῦντες ἐπάνω οὐκ οἴδασιν.

Luke 11.47-48

Οὐαὶ ὑμῖν, ὅτι οἰκοδομεῖτε τὰ
μνημεῖα τῶν προφητῶν, οἱ δὲ
πατέρες ὑμῶν ἀπέκτειναν αὐτούς.
ἄρα μάρτυρές ἐστε καὶ
συνευδοκεῖτε τοῖς ἔργοις τῶν
πατέρων ὑμῶν, ὅτι αὐτοὶ μὲν
ἀπέκτειναν αὐτούς, ὑμεῖς δὲ
οἰκοδομεῖτε.

C. 29

A (16) οὐαὶ ὑμῖν, ὁδηγοὶ τυφλοὶ οἱ λέγοντες·
B   ὃς ἂν ὀμόσῃ ἐν τῷ ναῷ, οὐδέν ἐστιν·
            ὃς δ᾿ ἂν ὀμόσῃ ἐν τῷ χρυσῷ τοῦ ναοῦ, ὀφείλει.
C (17) μωροὶ καὶ τυφλοί,
D   τίς γὰρ μείζων, ὁ χρυσὸς ἢ ὁ ναὸς ὁ ἁγιάσας τὸν
            χρυσόν;
A′ (18) καί·
B′   ὃς ἂν ὀμόσῃ ἐν τῷ θυσιαστηρίῳ, οὐδέν ἐστιν·
            ὃς δ᾿ ἂν ὀμόσῃ ἐν τῷ δώρῳ τῷ ἐπάνω αὐτοῦ, ὀφείλει.
C′ (19) τυφλοί,
D′   τί γὰρ μεῖζον, τὸ δῶρον ἢ τὸ θυσιαστήριον τὸ ἁγιάζον
            τὸ δῶρον;

d′ (20) ὁ οὖν ὀμόσας ἐν τῷ θυσιαστηρίῳ ὀμνύει ἐν αὐτῷ
καὶ ἐν πᾶσι τοῖς ἐπάνω αὐτοῦ
d (21) καὶ ὁ ὀμόσας ἐν τῷ ναῷ ὀμνύει ἐν αὐτῷ
καὶ ἐν τῷ κατοικοῦντι αὐτόν,
e (22) καὶ ὁ ὀμόσας ἐν τῷ οὐρανῷ ὀμνύει ἐν τῷ θρόνῳ τοῦ θεοῦ
καὶ ἐν τῷ καθημένῳ ἐπάνω αὐτοῦ.

C. 30

Matt 23.34-39

Luke 11.49-51

Διὰ τοῦτο ἰδοὺ ἐγὼ
ἀποστέλλω πρὸς ὑμᾶς προφήτας
καὶ σοφοὺς καὶ γραμματεῖς· ἐξ
αὐτῶν ἀποκτενεῖτε καὶ
σταυρώσετε καὶ ἐξ αὐτῶν
μαστιγώσετε ἐν ταῖς συναγωγαῖς
ὑμῶν καὶ διώξετε ἀπὸ πόλεως εἰς
πόλιν· ὅπως ἔλθῃ ἐφ᾽ ὑμᾶς πᾶν
αἷμα δίκαιον ἐκχυννόμενον ἐπὶ
τῆς γῆς ἀπὸ τοῦ αἵματος Ἄβελ
τοῦ δικαίου ἕως τοῦ αἵματος
Ζαχαρίου υἱοῦ Βαραχίου, ὃν
ἐφονεύσατε μεταξὺ τοῦ ναοῦ καὶ
τοῦ θυσιαστηρίου. ἀμὴν λέγω
ὑμῖν, ἥξει ταῦτα πάντα ἐπὶ τὴν
γενεὰν ταύτην.

Ἰερουσαλὴμ Ἰερουσαλήμ, ἡ
ἀποκτείνουσα τοὺς προφήτας καὶ
λιθοβολοῦσα τοὺς ἀπεσταλμένους
πρὸς αὐτήν, ποσάκις ἠθέλησα
ἐπισυναγαγεῖν τὰ τέκνα σου, ὃν
τρόπον ὄρνις ἐπισυνάγει τὰ
νοσσία αὐτῆς ὑπὸ τὰς πτέρυγας,
καὶ οὐκ ἠθελήσατε. ἰδοὺ ἀφίεται
ὑμῖν ὁ οἶκος ὑμῶν ἔρημος. λέγω
γὰρ ὑμῖν, οὐ μή με ἴδητε ἀπ᾽ ἄρτι
ἕως ἂν εἴπητε·
εὐλογημένος ὁ ἐρχόμενος
ἐν ὀνόματι κυρίου.

διὰ τοῦτο καὶ ἡ σοφία τοῦ θεοῦ
εἶπεν· ἀποστελῶ εἰς αὐτοὺς
προφήτας καὶ ἀποστόλους, καὶ
ἐξ αὐτῶν ἀποκτενοῦσιν καὶ
διώξουσιν, ἵνα ἐκζητηθῇ τὸ αἷμα
πάντων τῶν προφητῶν τὸ
ἐκκεχυμένον ἀπὸ καταβολῆς
κόσμου ἀπὸ τῆς γενεᾶς ταύτης,
ἀπὸ αἵματος Ἄβελ ἕως αἵματος
Ζαχαρίου τοῦ ἀπολομένου
μεταξὺ τοῦ θυσιαστηρίου καὶ
τοῦ οἴκου· ναὶ λέγω ὑμῖν,
ἐκζητηθήσεται ἀπὸ τῆς γενεᾶς
ταύτης.

Luke 13.34-35

Ἰερουσαλὴμ Ἰερουσαλήμ, ἡ
ἀποκτείνουσα τοὺς προφήτας καὶ
λιθοβολοῦσα τοὺς ἀπεσταλμένους
πρὸς αὐτήν, ποσάκις ἠθέλησα
ἐπισυνάξαι τὰ τέκνα σου ὃν
τρόπον ὄρνις τὴν ἑαυτῆς
νοσσιὰν ὑπὸ τὰς πτέρυγας, καὶ
οὐκ ἠθελήσατε. ἰδοὺ ἀφίεται
ὑμῖν ὁ οἶκος ὑμῶν. λέγω δὲ ὑμῖν,
οὐ μὴ ἴδητε με ἕως ἥξει ὅτε
εἴπητε·
εὐλογημένος ὁ ἐρχόμενος
ἐν ὀνόματι κυρίου.

C. 31

Matt 11.28-30

A.   δεῦτε πρός με πάντες οἱ κοπιῶντες καὶ πεφορτισμένοι,
B.   κἀγὼ ἀναπαύσω ὑμᾶς.
A'.   ἄρατε τὸν ζυγόν μου ἐφ᾽ ὑμᾶς καὶ μάθετε ἀπ᾽ ἐμοῦ,
C.   ὅτι πραΰς εἰμι καὶ ταπεινὸς τῇ καρδίᾳ,
B'.   καὶ εὑρήσετε ἀνάπαυσιν ταῖς ψυχαῖς ὑμῶν·
C'.   ὁ γὰρ ζυγός μου χρηστὸς καὶ τὸ φορτίον μου ἐλαφρόν
       ἐστιν.

C. 32

Matt 18.18	Matt 16.19
Ἀμὴν λέγω ὑμῖν· ὅσα ἐὰν δήσητε ἐπὶ τῆς γῆς ἔσται δεδεμένα ἐν οὐρανῷ, καὶ ὅσα ἐὰν λύσητε ἐπὶ τῆς γῆς ἔσται λελυμένα ἐν οὐρανῷ.	δώσω σοι τὰς κλεῖδας τῆς βασιλείας τῶν οὐρανῶν, καὶ ὃ ἐὰν δήσῃς ἐπὶ τῆς γῆς ἔσται δεδεμένον ἐν τοῖς οὐρανοῖς, καὶ ὃ ἐὰν λύσῃς ἐπὶ τῆς γῆς ἔσται λελυμένον ἐν τοῖς οὐρανοῖς.

C. 33

A History of Traditions Represented in the M Sayings

I. *Sayings Representative of a Tradition Coming from a Christian Jewish Group*

     7. (Matt 6.1-6, 16-18) Beware that you do not perform your righteousness in front of people in order to be seen by them. But if you do not heed this, you do not have a reward from your father, the one who sees in secret. Therefore, when you give alms, do not sound a trumpet before you as the hypocrites do in the synagogues and roadways in order that they might receive glory from people. Amen, I say to you, they have their reward. But when you give alms do not let your left (hand) know what your right (hand) does; thus your alms may be in secret and your father who sees in secret will reward you.

     And when you pray, do not be like the hypocrites who love to pray while standing in the synagogues and on the street corners that they may be seen by people. Amen, I say to you, they have their reward. But when you pray, go into your inner room and when you have closed your door, pray to your father, the one who is in secret, and your father who sees in secret will reward you.

And when you fast, do not be downcast like the hypocrites, for they disfigure their faces so that they might be seen by people when they fast. Amen, I say to you, they have their reward. But when you fast, anoint your head and wash your face, so that you might not be seen by people while you are fasting, but rather that you might be seen by your father who is in secret and your father who sees in secret will reward you.

11.   (Matt 23.2-3, 5) (The scribes and the Pharisees) sit upon the chair of Moses. Therefore, do and keep whatever they say to you, but do not do according to their works; for they speak, yet they do not act. And they do all of their works in order to be seen by people; for they make their phylacteries broad and they lengthen their tassels.

9-10.   (Matt 10.5b-6, 23b) Do not go in the way of the Gentiles and do not enter the city of the Samaritans; but rather go out to the lost sheep of the nation of Israel. For amen, I say to you, you will not finish the cities of Israel before the Son of Man comes.

Sayings from an Interim Period

13.   (Matt 23.15) Woe to you, blind guides, because you travel around the sea and the land in order to make one proselyte, and when he becomes one you make him twice the son of Gehenna that you are yourselves.

14.   (Matt 23.16-22, 24, 33) Woe to you blind guides, the ones saying, 'Whoever swears by the temple, it is nothing; but whoever swears by the gold of the temple is obligated'. Fools and blind ones, because what is greater, the gold or the temple that makes the gold holy? And, 'whoever swears by the altar, it is nothing; but whoever swears by the gift on it, is obligated'. Blind ones, for what is greater, the gift or the altar that makes the gift holy? Therefore, the one who swears by the altar swears by it and by everything on it; and the one who swears by the temple swears by it and by the one who inhabits it; and the one who swears by the heaven swears by the throne of God and the one who sits upon it. Blind guides, those who strain out the gnat and gulp down a camel.

3(?).   (Matt 5.23-24) If, therefore, you are taking your gift up to the altar and if you remember that your brother has something against you leave your gift there before the altar and go, first be reconciled to your brother, and then when you have come offer your gift.

8. (Matt 6.7-8) But when you pray do not babble like the Gentiles, for they suppose that by their running off at the mouth that they will be listened to. Therefore, do not be like them, for your father knows the things of which you have need before you ask him.

15. (Matt 7.6) Do not give what is holy to dogs, neither cast your pearls before swine, lest they trample them with their feet and afterwards turn to attack you.

II. *Sayings Representative of a Tradition Coming from a Jewish Christian Community*

1. (Matt 5.19) Therefore, if anyone abolishes a single one of the least of these commandments and teaches others likewise then he will be called least in the Kingdom of Heaven. But if anyone should do one of the least of these commandments and teach others likewise he will be called great in the Kingdom of Heaven.

2. (Matt 5.21-22) You have heard that it was said to the ancients, 'Do not kill, whoever kills is liable to the judgment'. But I say to you that everyone who is angry with his brother is liable to the judgment; whoever says to his brother '*raka*', is liable to the court; whoever says '*fool*', is liable to the Gehenna of fire.

4. (Matt 5.27-28) You have heard that it was said, 'Do not commit adultery'. But, I say to you that anyone who looks at a woman for the purpose of desire already commits adultery with her in his heart.

5. (Matt 5.33-35, 37) You have heard that it was said to the ancients, 'You shall not break your oath, but offer your oath to the Lord'. But I say to you that you are not to swear at all; neither by the heaven, because it is the throne of God; nor by the earth, because it is a footstool for his feet; nor by Jerusalem, because it is the city of the great king. But let your word be yes, yes, no, no. (Beyond this is from the evil one.)

12. (Matt 23.8-10) But you, do not be called 'Rabbi'; for your teacher is one. And do not call someone among you 'Father'; for your father is one. Nor be called 'Instructors'; for your instructor is one.

16.   (Matt 12.36-37) And I say to you, in the day of judgment people will render account for every careless word which they have spoken. For out of your words, you will be judged, and out of your words, you will be condemned.

17.   (Matt 18.18) Whatever you bind upon the earth will be bound in heaven, and whatever you loose upon the earth wil be loosed in heaven.

18.   (Matt 18.19-20) I say to you that if two of you should agree about any matter upon the earth, which they should ask, it will be done for them by my father, the one who is in the heavens. For where two or three are gathered in my name, there I am in their midst.

19.   (Matt 19.12) For there are eunuchs such as those who are so begotten from the mother's womb, and those who are made eunuchs by men, and those who make themselves eunuchs because of the Kingdom of the Heavens.

Sayings Unaccounted for by the Tradition History

6.   (Matt 5.36) Nor may you swear by your head, because you are unable to make a single hair white or black.

BIBLIOGRAPHY

Abel, E. 'Who Wrote Matthew?', NTS 17 (1971) 138-52.

Albright, W., and Mann, C. *Matthew*, Garden City: Doubleday, 1971.

Allen, W.C. *A Critical and Exegetical Commentary on the Gospel According to S. Matthew*, 3rd edn; Edinburgh: T. & T. Clark, 1912.

Argyle, A. *The Gospel According to St. Matthew*, Cambridge: Cambridge University Press, 1964.

Bacon, B.W. 'Jesus and the Law', *JBL* 47 (1928) 203-31.

—*Studies in Matthew*, New York: Henry Holt, 1930.

Baltensweiler, H. 'Die Ehebruchsklausen bei Matthäus. Zu Matth. 5,32; 19,9', *TZ* (1959) 340-56.

—*Die Ehe im Neuen Testament*, Zürich: Zwingli, 1967.

Bamberger, B. *Proselytism in the Talmudic Period*, New York: KTAV, 1968 (1939).

Banks, R. *Jesus and the Law in the Synoptic Tradition* (SNTSMS, 28), Cambridge: Cambridge University Press, 1975.

—'Matthew's Understanding of the Law: Authenticity and Interpretation in Matthew 5.17-20', *JBL* 93 (1974) 226-42.

Barth, G. 'Matthew's Understanding of the Law', in G. Bornkamm, G. Barth, and H.J. Held, *Tradition and Interpretation in Matthew*, Philadelphia: Fortress, 1963, 58-164.

Bauer, W. *Orthodoxy and Heresy in Earliest Christianity*, G. Strecker and R. Kraft, eds.; Philadelphia: Fortress 1971.

Baumgarten, J. *Paulus und die Apokalyptik. Die Auslegung apokalyptischer Überlieferungen in den echten Paulusbriefen*. Neukirchen-Vluyn: Neukirchener Verlag, 1975.

Beare, F. 'The Sayings of Jesus in the Gospel According to St. Matthew', SE IV (TU 89; Berlin: Akademie, 1968) 146-57.

—'The Mission of the Disciples and the Mission Charge: Matthew 10 and Parallels', *JBL* 89 (1970) 1-13.

Bellinzoni, A.J. *The Sayings of Jesus in the Writings of Justin Martyr*, Leiden: Brill, 1967.

Benoit, P. *L'Evangile selon S. Mattieu*, Paris: Cerf, 1950.

Benoit, P., and Boismard, M.-E. *Synopse des quatre évangiles en français avec parallèles des apocryphes et des pères*, Paris: Cerf, 1966 (I), 1972 (II).

Berger, K. *Die Amen-Worte Jesu. Eine Untersuchung zum Problem der Legitimation in apokalyptischer Rede*, Berlin: Walter de Gruyter, 1970.

—*Die Gesetzauslegung Jesu. Teil I: Markus und Parallelen*, Neukirchen-Vluyn: Neukirchener Verlag, 1972.

—'Die sogenannten "Sätze heiligen Rechts" im Neuen Testament. Ihre Funktion und ihr Sitz im Leben', *ThZ* 28 (1972) 305-30.

—'Zu den sogennanten Sätzen heiligen Rechts', *NTS* 17 (1970-71) 10-40.

Betz, H.D. 'Eine judenchristliche Kult-Didache in Mt. 6.1-18', *Überlegungen und Fragen im Blick auf das Problem des historischen Jesus*, New Testament Festschrift for H. Conzelmann, G. Strecker, ed. (Tübingen: Mohr, 1975) 445-57.

—'The Sermon on the Mount: Its Literary Genre and Function', *JR* (1979) 285-97.

Blank, Sheldon H. 'The Death of Zechariah in Rabbinic Literature', *HUCA* 12-13 (1937-1938) 327-46.

Bonnard, P. *L'Evangile selon St. Mattieu* (CNT, 1), 2nd edn; Paris: Delachaux et Nestlé, 1970.

Boring, M. 'Christian Prophecy and Matthew 23.34-36: A Test Case', *SBL Seminar Papers 1977* (Missoula: Scholars, 1977) 117-26.

—*Sayings of the Risen Jesus. Christian Prophecy in the Synoptic Tradition* (SNTSMS, 46), Cambridge: Cambridge University Press, 1982.

Bornhäuser, K. *Die Bergpredigt*, Gütersloh: Bertelsmann, 1923.

Bornkamm, G. 'Der Aufbau der Bergpredigt', *NTS* 24 (1978) 419-32.

—'Die Binde- und Lösegewalt in der Kirche des Matthäus', *Geschichte und Glaube II* (Gesammelte Aufsätze, IV; München: Kaiser, 1971) 37-50. ET: 'The Authority to "Bind" and "Loose" in the Church in Matthew's Gospel', *Jesus and Man's Hope I*, edited by D. Buttrick (Pittsburgh: Pittsburgh Theological Seminary, 1970) 37-50.

—'Das Doppelgebot der Liebe', *Neutestamentliche Studien für R. Bultmann* (BZNW, 21; Berlin: Töpelmann, 1954) 85-93.

—'Ehescheidung und Wiederverheiratung im Neuen Testament', *Geschichte und Glaube I* (Gesammelte Aufsätze, III; München: Kaiser, 1968) 56-59.

—'Matthäus als Interpret der Herrenworte', *TLZ* 79 (1954) 341-46.

—'Wandlungen im alt- und neutestamentlichen Gesetzesverständnis', *Geschichte und Glaube II* (Gesammelte Aufsätze, IV; München: Kaiser, 1974) 73-119.

Bornkamm, G., Barth, G., and Held, H.J. *Tradition and Interpretation in Matthew*, Philadelphia: Westminster, 1963.

—*Überlieferung und Auslegung im Matthäusevangelium*, 5th edn; Neukirchen: Neukirchener Verlag, 1968.

Brandon, S. *The Fall of Jerusalem and the Christian Church*, 2nd edn; London: SPCK, 1957.

Branscomb, B. *Jesus and the Law of Moses*, New York: Smith, 1930.

Braude, W. *Jewish Proselytizing in the First Five Centuries of the Common Era: The Age of the Tannaim and the Amoraim*, Providence: Brown University, 1940.

Braun, H. 'Beobachtungen zur Tora-Verschärfung im häretischen Spätjudentum', *TLZ* 79 (1954) 347-52.

Broer, I. *Freiheit vom Gesetz und Radikalisierung des Gesetzes* (SBS, 98), Stuttgart: KBW, 1980.

Brown, J.P. 'The Form of "Q" Known to Matthew', *NTS* 8 (1961) 27-42.

Brown, R.E. *The Birth of the Messiah. A Commentary on the Infancy Narratives in Matthew and Luke*, Garden City: Doubleday, 1977.

—*The Community of the Beloved Disciple*, New York: Paulist, 1979.

—'Not Jewish Christianity and Gentile Christianity but Types of Jewish/Gentile Christianity', *CBQ* 45 (1983) 74-79.

Brown, R.E., Donfried, K., and Ruemann, J., eds. *Peter in the New Testament*, Minneapolis: Augsburg, 1973.

Brown, R.E., and Meier, J.P. *Antioch and Rome*, New York: Paulist, 1983.

Brown, S. 'The Two-Fold Representation of the Mission in Matthew's Gospel', *ST* 32 (1977) 21-32.

Bultmann, R. *Die Geschichte der synoptischen Tradition*, 3rd edn; Göttingen: Vandenhoeck & Ruprecht, 1957.

—*The History of the Synoptic Tradition*, trans., rev. edn; New York: Harper & Row, 1963.

Butler, B.C. *The Originality of St. Matthew*, Cambridge: Cambridge University Press, 1951.

Carlston, C.E. 'The Things that Defile (Mark VII. 14) and the Law in Matthew and

Mark', *NTS* 15 (1968-1969) 75-96.

Chapman, J. 'Zacharias, Slain Between the Temple and the Altar', *JTS* 13 (1912) 398-410.

Christ, F. *Jesus Sophia*, Zürich: Zwingli, 1970.

Clavier, H. 'Mattieu 5.39 et la non-résistance', *RHPR* 37 (1957) 44-57.

Colwell, E. *The Greek of the Fourth Gospel*, Chicago: University of Chicago, 1931.

Cope, O.L. *Matthew: A Scribe Trained for the Kingdom of Heaven* (CBQMS, 5), Washington: CBA, 1976.

Cox, G.E.P. *The Gospel According to Saint Matthew: A Commentary* (Torch Bible Commentaries), New York: Collier Books, 1962.

Crossan, J.D. *In Parables*, New York: Harper & Row, 1973.

Cullmann, O. *Peter, Disciple, Apostle, Martyr. A Historical and Theological Study*, 2nd edn; Philadelphia: Westminster, 1962.

Davies, W.D. 'Matthew 5.17-18', in *Mélanges bibliques redigés en l'honneur d' André Robert* (Travaux de l'Institut Catholique de Paris, 4; Paris: Bloud et Gay, 1957) 428-56.

—*The Setting of the Sermon on the Mount*, Cambridge: Cambridge University Press, 1964.

—'Torah and Dogma: A Comment', *HTR* 61 (1968) 87-105.

—*Torah in the Messianic Age and/or the Age to Come* (SBLMS, 7), Philadelphia: SBL, 1952.

Derwacter, F. *Preparing the Way for Paul. The Proselyte Movement in Later Judaism*, New York: Macmillan, 1930.

Dibelius, M. 'Die Bergpredigt, *Botschaft und Geschichte I*, Tübingen: Mohr, 1953.

—*Die Formgeschichte des Evangeliums*, 4th edn; Tübingen: Mohr, 1961.

—*From Tradition to Gospel*, 2nd edn; London: Ivor Nicholson, Watson, 1934.

—*James. A Commentary on the Epistle of James*, rev. by H. Greeven; Hermeneia: Fortress, 1976.

Dodd, C.H. *The Parables of the Kingdom*, rev. edn; New York: Scribner's 1961.

Donfried, K. 'The Allegory of the Ten Virgins (Matt 25.1-13) as a Summary of Matthean Theology', *JBL* 93 (1974) 415-28.

Dumbrell, W. 'The Logic of the Role of the Law in Matthew V 1-20', *NovT* 23 (1981) 1-21.

Dunn, J.D.G. 'Prophetic 'I'-Sayings and the Jesus Tradition: The Importance of Testing Prophetic Utterance within Early Christianity', *NTS* 24 (1978) 175-98.

Dupont, J. *Les Béatitudes*, 3 vols.; 2nd edn; Louvain: Nauwelauts, 1969-1973.

—'Le point de vue de Matthieu dans le chapitre des paraboles', in *L'Evangile selon Matthieu: Rédaction et Théologie*, M. Didier, ed. (Gembloux: Duculot, 1973) 221-59.

Edwards, R. *A Theology of Q*, Philadelphia: Fortress, 1976.

Eichholz, G. 'Die Aufgabe einer Auslegung der Bergpredigt', *Tradition und Interpretation. Studien zum Neuen Testament und zur Hermeneutik* (München: Kaiser, 1965) 35-56.

—*Auslegung der Bergpredigt*, Neukirchen: Neukirchener Verlag, 1965.

Ellis, P. *Matthew: His Mind and His Message*, Collegeville: The Liturgical Press, 1974.

Farmer, W.R. 'A Fresh Approach to Q', *SJLA* (1975) 39-50.

—*The Synoptic Problem: A Critical Analysis*, New York: Macmillan, 1964.

Fenton, J.C. 'Inclusio and Chiasmus in Matthew', *SE* I (TU 73; Berlin: Akademie, 1959) 174-79.

—*The Gospel of Saint Matthew* (The Pelican Gospel Commentary), Baltimore:

Penguin Books, 1963.

Fiebig, P. *Jesu Bergpredigt*, Göttingen: Vandenhoeck & Ruprecht, 1924.

Fiedler, M. 'Der Begriff DIKAIOSYNE im Matthäus-Evangelium, auf seine Grundlagen untersucht', Thesis, Halle, 1957. Reported in J. Rohde, *Rediscovering the Teaching of the Evangelists* (London: SCM, 1968), 90-91.

Filson, F. 'Broken Patterns in the Gospel of Matthew', *JBL* 75 (1956) 227-31.

—*A Commentary on the Gospel According to St. Matthew*, London: Black, 1960.

Finn, T. 'The God-Fearers Reconsidered', *CBQ* 47 (1985) 75-84.

Flusser, D. 'Two Anti-Jewish Montages in Mt 23, 1-36; 7, 21-23; 8, 11-12', *Immanuel* (1975) 37-45.

Fortna, R.T. *The Gospel of Signs. A Reconstruction of the Narrative Source Underlying the Fourth Gospel* (SNTSMS, 11), New York and Cambridge, 1970.

Foster, L. 'The "Q" Myth in Synoptic Studies', *Bulletin of the Evangelical Theological Society* 7 (1964) 111-19.

Frankemölle, H. 'Amtskritik im Matthäus Evangelium?' *Bib* 54 (1973) 247-62.

—*Jahwebund und Kirche Christi: Studien zur Form- und Traditionsgeschichte des Evangelium nach Matthäus*, Münster: Aschendorff, 1974.

Fuchs, E. 'Jesu Selbstzeugnis nach Matthäus 5', *ZTK* 51 (1954) 14-34.

—'Die vollkommene Gewissheit: Zur Auslegung von Matthäus 5, 48', *Zur Frage nach dem historischen Jesus*, 2nd edn; Tübingen: Mohr, 1965, 126-35.

Garland, D. *The Intention of Matthew 23* (NovTSupp, 52), Leiden: Brill, 1979.

Gärtner, B. 'The Habakkuk Commentary (DSH) and the Gospel of Matthew', *ST* 8 (1954) 1-24.

Gaston, L. *No Stone on Another: Studies in the Significance of the Fall of Jerusalem in the Synoptic Gospels* (NovTSupp, 23), Leiden: Brill, 1970.

Gerstenberger, E. 'The Woe-Oracles of the Prophets', *JBL* 81 (1962) 249-63.

Gibbs, J. 'The Son of God as the Torah Incarnate in Matthew', *SE* IV (TU 89; Berlin: Akademie, 1968) 38-46.

Gnilka, J. 'Die Kirche des Matthäus und die Gemeinde von Qumran', *BZ* 7 (1963) 43-63.

Ginsberg, L. *The Legends of the Jews*, 6 vols.; Philadelphia: The Jewish Publication Society, 1909.

Goulder, M. *Midrash and Lection in Matthew*, London: SPCK, 1974.

Green, H.B. *The Gospel According to Matthew*, Oxford: Oxford University Press, 1975.

Gundry, R.H. *Matthew, A Commentary on his Literary and Theological Art*, Grand Rapids: Eerdmans, 1982.

—*The Use of the Old Testament in St. Matthew's Gospel*, Leiden: Brill, 1967.

Haenchen, E. 'Matthäus 23', *ZTK* 48 (1951) 38-63.

Hamerton-Kelly, R. 'Attitudes to the Law in Matthew's Gospel: A Discussion of Matthew 5.18', *BR* 17 (1972) 19-32.

Hanson, P. *The Dawn of Apocalyptic*, rev. edn; Philadelphia: Fortress, 1979.

Hanssen, O. 'Zum Verständnis der Bergpredigt', in *Der Ruf Jesu und die Antwort der Gemeinde*, edited by E. Lohse (Göttingen: Vandenhoeck & Ruprecht, 1970), 94-111.

Hare, D. *The Theme of Jewish Persecution of Christians in the Gospel According to St. Matthew* (SNTSMS, 6), Cambridge: Cambridge University Press, 1967.

Harrington, D. 'The Reception of Walter Bauer's *Orthodoxy and Heresy in Earliest Christianity* During the Last Decade', *HTR* 73 (1980) 289-98.

Hawkins, J. 'Probabilities as to the So-Called Double Tradition of St. Matthew and St. Luke', in *Studies in the Synoptic Proplem by Members of the University of Oxford*, William Sanday, ed.; Oxford: Clarendon, 1911.

Held, H.J. 'Matthew as Interpreter of the Miracle Stories', in G. Bornkamm, G. Barth, and H.J. Held. *Tradition and Interpretation in Matthew* (Philadelphia: Westminster, 1963), 163-299.

Hill, D. *The Gospel of Matthew*, London: Oliphants, 1972.

Hoffmann, P. *Studien zur Theologie der Logienquelle* (NtAbh, 8), Münster: Aschendorff, 1972.

Honeymann, A. 'Matthew V. 18 and the Validity of the Law', *NTS* 1 (1954) 141-42.

Hooker, M. 'Uncomfortable Words X: The Prohibition of Foreign Mission', *ExpTim* 82 (1971) 361-65.

Hummel, R. *Die Auseinandersetzung zwischen Kirche und Judentum im Matthäusevangelium* (BEvt, 33), München: Kaiser, 1966.

Jeremias, J. *Abba*, Göttingen: Vandenhoeck & Ruprecht, 1966.

—*Die Bergpredigt*, Stuttgart: Calwer, 1959.

—*The Parables of Jesus*, 2nd edn; New York: Scribner's, 1972.

—'Zum nichtresponsorischen Amen', *ZNW* 64 (1973) 122-23.

Johnson, M. 'Reflections on a Wisdom Approach to Matthew's Christology', *CBQ* 36 (1974) 44-64.

Jones, F.P. 'The Sources of the Material Peculiar to Matthew', Th.D. dissertation, Union Theological Seminary, New York, 1938.

Käsemann, E. 'Sentences of Holy Law in the New Testament', *New Testament Questions of Today* (Philadelphia: Fortress, 1969), 66-81.

Kee, H.C. 'Review of H.-H. Stoldt, *Geschichte und Kritik der Markushypothese*', *JBL* 98 (1979) 140-43.

Keck, L. 'The Sermon on the Mount', in *Jesus and Man's Hope II*, edited by D. Hadidian (Pittsburgh: Pittsburgh Theological Seminary, 1971), 311-22.

Kelber, W. *The Oral and Written Gospel*, Philadelphia: Fortress, 1983.

—'Review of H.-H. Stoldt, *Geschichte und Kritik der Markushypothese*', *CBQ* 41 (1979) 499-501.

Kelly, M. 'The Woes Against the Scribes and Pharisees in Mt 23.13-23', Ph.D. dissertation, Bristol, 1971/72.

Kilpatrick, G.D. *The Origins of the Gospel Acording to St. Matthew*, Oxford: Oxford University Press, 1946.

Kingsbury, J. *Matthew* (Proclamation Commentaries), Philadelphia: Fortress, 1977.

—*Matthew: Structure, Christology, Kingdom*, Philadelphia: Fortress, 1975.

—*The Parables of Jesus in Matthew 13*, Richmond: John Knox, 1969.

—'The Structure of Matthew's Gospel and his Concept of Salvation History', *CBQ* 35 (1973) 451-74.

Kittel, G. 'Die Bergpredigt und die Ethik des Judentums', *ZST* 2 (1925) 555-94.

Klein, G. 'Rein und unrein Mt 23, 25. Lc 11, 27, 42', *ZNW* 7 (1906) 252-53.

Kline, L.L. *The Sayings of Jesus in the Pseudo-Clementine Homilies* (SBLDS, 14), Missoula: Scholars, 1975.

Kloppenburg, J. 'Tradition and Redaction in the Synoptic Sayings Source', *CBQ* 46 (1984) 34-62.

Klostermann, E. *Das Matthäusevangelium* (HNT, 4), Tübingen: J.C.B. Mohr, 1927.

Koester, H. *Introduction to the New Testament*, 2 vols.; Philadelphia: Fortress, 1982.

—*Synoptische Überlieferung bei den Apostolischen Vätern* (TU, 65), Berlin: Akademie, 1957.

Koester, H; and Lambdin, T., trans. 'Gospel of Thomas', in *The Nag Hammadi Library in English*, edited by James M. Robinson; New York: Harper & Row, 1977.

Robinson, J.M.; and Koester, H. *Trajectories through Early Christianity*, Philadelphia: Fortress, 1971.

Kümmel, W.G. *Introduction to the New Testament*, 17th edn; Nashville: Abingdon, 1973.

Künzi, M. *Das Naherwartungslogion Matthäus 10,23, Geschichte seiner Auslegung* (BGBE, 9); Tübingen: Mohr, 1970.

Kysar, R. *The Fourth Evangelist and His Gospel. An Examination of Contemporary Scholarship*, Minneapolis: Augsburg, 1975.

Lachs, S.T. 'On Matthew 23.27-28', *HTR* 68 (1975) 385-88.

Lange, J. *Das Erscheinen des Auferstandenen im Evangelium nach Matthäus*, Würzburg: Echter Verlag, 1973.

Lagrange, M. *Evangile selon S. Matthieu*, 5th edn; Paris: Gabalda, 1948.

Lasor, W.S. *The Dead Sea Scrolls and the New Testament*, Grand Rapids: Eerdmans, 1972.

Lerle, E. *Proselytenwerbung und Urchristentum*, Berlin: Evangelische Verlagsanstalt, 1960.

Ljungmann, H. *Das Gesetz erfüllen, Matthäus 5,17ff und 3,15 untersucht*, Lund: Gleerup, 1954.

Lohmeyer, E. *Das Evangelium des Matthäus*, 4th edn; edited by W. Schmauch; Meyer K. Sonderband; Göttingen: Vandenhoeck & Ruprecht, 1967.

Lohr, C.H. 'Oral Techniques in the Gospel of Matthew', *CBQ* 23 (1961) 403-35.

Longstaff, T.R.W. *Evidence of Conflation in Mark? A Study in the Synoptic Problem* (SBLDS, 28), Missoula: Scholars, 1977.

Lührmann, D. *Die Redaktion der Logienquelle* (WMANT, 33), Neukirchen-Vluyn: Neukirchener Verlag, 1969.

Luz, U. 'Die Erfüllung des Gesetzes bei Matthäus', *ZTK* 75 (1978) 398-435.

Mann, J. 'Oaths and Vows in the Synoptic Gospels', *AJT* 21 (1917) 260-74.

Manson, T.W. *The Sayings of Jesus*, London: SCM, 1949.

—*The Teachings of Jesus*, 2nd edn; Cambridge: Cambridge University Press, 1935.

Mantel, H. *Studies in the History of the Sanhedrin* (HSM, 17), Cambridge, MA: Harvard University Press, 1961.

Martyn, J. Louis. 'Glimpses into the History of the Johannine Community', in *L'Evangile de Jean, Sources, rédaction, théologie*, edited by M. de Jonge (BETL, 44), Leuven: Leuven University Press 1977.

—*The Gospel of John in Christian History*, New York: Paulist, 1978.

—*History and Theology in the Fourth Gospel*, 2nd edn; Nashville: Abingdon, 1979.

McDermott, J.M. 'Mt 10.23 in Context', *BZ* 28 (1984) 230-40.

McKenzie, J. 'Matthew', *JBC*, II; Englewood Cliffs: Prentice-Hall, 1968, 62-114.

McNeile, A.H. *The Gospel According to St. Matthew. The Greek Text with Introduction, Notes, and Indices*, New York: Macmillan, 1915; reprint edn, Grand Rapids: Baker, 1980.

Meier, J.P. *Law and History in Matthew's Gospel. A Redactional Study of Mt 5.17-48* (AnBib, 71), Rome: Biblical Institute Press, 1976.

—'Salvation-History in Matthew: In Search of a Starting Point', *CBQ* 37 (1975) 203-15.

—*The Vision of Matthew. Christ, Church and Morality in the First Gospel*, New York: Paulist, 1979.

Metzger, B.M. *A Textual Commentary on the Greek New Testament*, London: United Bible Societies, 1971.

Michel, O. 'Der Abschluss des Matthäus-Evangeliums', *EvT* 10 (1950) 16-26.

Minear, P. 'The Disciples and the Crowds in the Gospel of Matthew', *ATRSup* 3 (1974) 28-44.

—'False Prophecy and Hypocrisy in the Gospel of Matthew', in *Neues Testament und Kirche*, edited by J. Gnilka (Frieburg: Herder, 1974), 76-93.

—'"Yes or No": The Demand for Honesty in the Early Church', *NovT* 13 (1971) 1-13.

Moore, G. *Judaism in the First Centuries of the Christian Era*, 2 vols.; New York: Schocken, 1971 (1927, 1930).

Morosco, R.E. 'Redaction Criticism and the Evangelical: Matthew 10 a Test Case', *Journal of the Evangelical Theological Society* 22 (1979) 323-31.

Moulton, J.H. *A Grammar of the Greek New Testament*, 4 vols.; Edinburgh: T. & T. Clark, 1908, 1929, 1963, 1967. Vol. IV: *Style*, by N. Turner.

Müller, D.H. *Die Bergpredigt im Licht der Strophentheorie*, Vienna: Holder, 1908.

Müller, G. *Zur Synopse. Untersuchungen über die Arbeitsweise des Lukas und Matthäus und ihrer Quellen* (FRLANT, 11), Göttingen: Vandenhoeck & Ruprecht, 1908.

Neirynck, F. 'La rédaction matthéenne et la structure du premier évangile', *ETL* 43 (1967) 41-73.

Nepper-Christensen, P. *Das Matthäusevangelium. Ein judenchristliches Evangelium?*, Aarhus: Universitetsforlaget, 1958.

Nickelsburg, G.W.E. *Jewish Literature Between the Bible and the Mishnah. A Historical and Literary Introduction*, Philadelphia: Fortress, 1981.

Orchard, B. *Matthew, Luke and Mark. The Griesbach Solution to the Synoptic Question*, Manchester: Koinonia Press, 1976.

Pesch, W. 'Theologische Aussagen der Redaktion von Matthäus 23', in *Orientierung an Jesus*, edited by P. Hoffmann (Freiburg: Herder, 1973), 286-99.

Plummer, A. *An Exegetical Commentary on the Gospel According to S. Matthew*, London: Stock, 1909.

Pokorny, P. *Der Kern der Bergpredigt*, Hamburg: Evangelischer Verlag, 1969.

Polag, A. *Die Christologie der Logienquelle* (WMANT, 45), Neukirchen: Neukirchener Verlag, 1977.

—*Fragmenta Q. Textheft zur Logienquelle*, Neukirchen: Neukirchener Verlag, 1979.

Przybylski, B. *Righteousness in Matthew and his World of Thought* (SNTSMS, 41), Cambridge: Cambridge University Press, 1980.

Quesnell, Q. '"Made Themselves Eunuchs for the Kingdom of Heaven", (Mt 19, 12)', *CBQ* 30 (1968) 335-58.

Rabinowitz, J. 'The Sermon on the Mount and the School of Shammai', *HTR* 49 (1956) 79.

Rausch, J. 'The Principle of Nonresistance and Love of Enemy in Mt 5.38-48', *CBQ* 28 (1966) 31-41.

Riddle, D.W. 'Die Verfolgungslogien in formgeschichtlicher und soziologischer Beleuchtung', *ZNW* 33 (1934) 271-89.

Robertson, A.T. *A Grammar of the Greek New Testament in Light of Historical Research*, Nashville: Broadman, 1934.

—*Word Pictures in the New Testament*, 6 vols.; Nashville: Broadman, 1930.

Robinson, J.M.; and Koester, H. *Trajectories through Early Christianity*, Philadelphia: Fortress, 1971.

Robinson, T. *The Gospel of Matthew*, London: Hodder and Stoughton, 1928.

Rothfuchs, W. *Die Erfüllungszitate des Matthäus-Evangeliums*, Stuttgart: Kohlhammer, 1969.

—'Die sogenannten Antithesen des Matthäusevangeliums und ihr Gesetzesverständnis untersucht im Zusammenhang Mt 5, 17-28', *Lutherischer Rundblick* 16 (1968) 95-109.

Sand, A. *Das Gesetz und die Propheten. Untersuchungen zur Theologie des Evangeliums nach Matthäus*, Regensburg: Friedrich Pustet, 1974.

—*Reich Gottes und Eheverzicht im Evangelium nach Matthäus* (SBS, 109), Stuttgart: Katholisches Bibelwerk, 1983.

Sanders, E.P. *The Tendencies of the Synoptic Tradition*, Cambridge: Cambridge University Press, 1969.

Schlatter, A. *Der Evangelist Matthäus*, 3rd edn; Stuttgart: Calwer, 1948.

Schmid, J. *Das Evangelium nach Matthäus*, 5th edn (RNT, 1), Regensburg: Pustet, 1965.

Schmitt, J. 'Contribution à l'étude de la discipline pénitentielle dans l'Eglise primitive à la lumière des textes de Qumran', *Les Manuscrits de la Mer Morte*, Colloque de Strasbourg, 25-27 Mai, 1955; Paris, 1957.

Schnackenburg, R. 'Bergpredigt' (*LTK*, II; Freiburg: Herder, 1958) 225-26.

Schniewind, J. *Das Evangelium nach Matthäus*, 12th edn; Göttingen: Vandenhoeck & Ruprecht, 1968.

Schoeps, H.J. *Die jüdischen Prophetenmorde* (Symbolae Biblicae Upsalienses, 2), Uppsala: Wretmans Boktryckeri A.-B., 1943.

—*Theologie und Geschichte des Judenchristentums*, Tübingen: Mohr, 1949.

Schulz, S. *Q die Spruchquelle der Evangelisten. Griechisch-deutsche Synopse der Q-Überlieferungen*, Zürich: Theologischer Verlag, 1972.

Schürmann, H. *Traditionsgeschichtliche Untersuchungen zu den synoptischen Evangelien*, I, Düsseldorf: Patmos, 1968.

Schweizer, E. *The Good News According to Matthew*, Atlanta: John Knox, 1975.

—*Matthäus und seine Gemeinde*, Stuttgart: KBW, 1974.

—'Mt 5.17-20—Anmerkungen zum Gesetzverständnis des Matthäus', *TL* 77 (1952) 479-84.

—'Observance of the Law and Charismatic Activity in Matthew', *NTS* 16 (1969-70) 213-30.

Seitz, O. 'Love your Enemies', *NTS* 16 (1969-70) 39-54.

Senior, D. *Invitation to Matthew*, Garden City, NY: Doubleday, 1977.

Smith, M. 'Jesus' Attitude Towards the Law', *Fourth World Congress of Jewish Studies, I* (World Union of Jewish Studies, 1967) 241-44.

—'Mt 5.43 "Hate thine Enemy"', *HTR* 45 (1952) 71-73.

—*Tannaitic Parallels to the Gospels*, Philadelphia: SBL, 1951.

Smyth, H.W. *Greek Grammar*, Cambridge, MA: Harvard University Press, 1920; rev. edn, 1956.

Soulen, R. *Handbook of Biblical Criticism*, Atlanta: John Knox, 1976.

Staab, K. *Das Evangelium nach Matthäus*, Würzburg: Echter Verlag, 1951.

Stagg, F. 'Matthew' (*The Broadman Bible Commentary*, Vol. VIII; Nashville: Broadman Press, 1969) 61-253.

Stendahl, K. 'Matthew', *PCB* (London: Nelson, 1962) 769-98.

—*The School of St. Matthew*, 2nd edn; Philadelphia: Fortress, 1968.

Stoldt, H.H. *Geschichte und Kritik der Markushypothese*, Göttingen: Vandenhoeck & Ruprecht, 1977; ET: *History and Criticism of the Markan Hypothesis*, Macon, GA: Mercer University, 1980.

Strassny, J. 'Jesus accomplit la promesse. Essai d'interprétation de Mt 5, 17-19', *BVC* 59 (1964) 30-37.

Strecker, G. 'Die Antithesen der Bergpredigt (Mt 5.21-48 par)', *ZNW* 69 (1978) 36-72.

—'Das Geschichtsverständnis des Matthäus', *EvT* 26 (1966) 57-74; abbreviated trans.: 'The Concept of Salvation-History in Matthew', *JAAR* 35 (1967) 219-230.

—*Das Judenchristentum in den Pseudoklementinen* (TU 70), 2nd edn; Berlin: Akademie, 1981.

—*Der Weg der Gerechtigkeit. Untersuchung zur Theologie des Matthäus* (FRLANT, 82), Göttingen: Vandenhoeck & Ruprecht, 1962.

Streeter, B.H. *The Four Gospels. A Study of Origins.* London: Macmillan, 1927.

Suggs, M.J. 'The Antitheses as Redactional Products', in *Überlegungen und Fragen im Blick auf das Problem des historischen Jesus*, New Testament Festschrift for H. Conzelmann, edited by G. Strecker (Tübingen: Mohr, 1975), 433-44.

—*Wisdom, Christology and Law in Matthew's Gospel*, Cambridge, MA: Harvard University Press, 1970.

Tannehill, R. 'The "Focal Instance" as a Form of New Testament Speech: A Study of Matthew 5.39b-42', *JR* 50 (1970) 372-85.

Taylor, V. *New Testament Essays*, Grand Rapids: Eerdmans, 1968.

Thompson, W. 'An Historical Perspective in the Gospel of Matthew', *JBL* 93 (1974) 243-63.

—*Matthew's Advice to a Divided Community. Mt. 17,22-18, 35* (AnBib, 44), Rome: Biblical Institute Press, 1970.

Thompson, W. and LaVerdiere, E. 'New Testament Communities in Transition: A Study of Matthew and Luke', *TS* 37 (1976) 567-97.

Tödt, H.E. *The Son of Man in the Synoptic Tradition*, Philadelphia: Westminster, 1965.

Trilling, W. *The Gospel According to St. Matthew*, 2 vols. London: Burns and Oates, 1969.

—*Das Wahre Israel: Studien zur Theologie des Matthäus-Evangelium* (Erfurter Theologische Studien, 7), Leipzig: St. Benno-Verlag, 1959.

Turner, H.E.W. *The Pattern of Christian Truth: A Study in the Relations between Orthodoxy and Heresy in the Early Church*, London: Mowbray, 1954.

Vaillant, A. *Le Livre des Secrets d'Hénoch*, Paris: Institut d'Etudes Slaves, 1952.

Vassiliadis, P. 'The Nature and Extent of the Q Document', *NovT* 20 (1978) 49-73.

Weiss, B. *Die Quellen des Lukasevangeliums*, Stuttgart: Cotta, 1907.

Wellhausen, J. *Das Evangelium Matthaei*, 2nd edn; Berlin: Reimar, 1914.

Windisch, H. *Der Sinn der Bergpredigt*, 2nd edn; Leipzig: Hinrichs, 1937.

Worden, R.D. 'Redaction Criticism of Q', *JBL* 94 (1975) 532-46.

Wrege, H. *Die Überlieferungsgeschichte der Bergpredigt* (WUNT, 9), Tübingen: Mohr, 1968.

Zahn, T. *Das Evangelium des Matthäus*, Leipzig: Deichert, 1903.

INDEXES

INDEX OF BIBLICAL REFERENCES

INDEX OF AUTHORS

JOURNAL FOR THE STUDY OF THE NEW TESTAMENT
Supplement Series